DATE DUE

AP 3 03			

DEMCO 38-296

An Illustrated History of
EIGHTEENTH-CENTURY
BRITAIN, 1688–1793

An Illustrated History of EIGHTEENTH-CENTURY BRITAIN, 1688–1793

JEREMY BLACK

Manchester University Press

Manchester and New York

distributed exclusively in the USA
by St. Martin's Press

Published by Manchester University Press
Oxford Road, Manchester M13 9NR, UK
and Room 400, 175 Fifth Avenue,
New York, NY 10010, USA

Distributed exclusively in the USA
by St. Martin's Press, Inc.,
175 Fifth Avenue, New York, NY 10010, USA

British Library Cataloguing-in-Publication Data
A catalogue record for this book is available from the British Library

Library of Congress Cataloging-in-Publication Data
Black, Jeremy.
An illustrated history of eighteenth-century Britain, 1688–1793 /
Jeremy Black.
    p.   cm.
  ISBN 0–7190–4267–4.
    1. Great Britain—History—18th century—Pictorial works.
I. Title.
DA480.B557   1996
941.07—dc20   96–15120
                                                              CIP

ISBN 0 7190 4267 4 **hardback**

First published in 1996
00 99 98 97 96   10 9 8 7 6 5 4 3 2 1

Printed in Great Britain
by Redwood Books, Trowbridge

This book is dedicated to my father, Cyril Black, whose love for the past and zest for reading played a major role in awakening and sustaining my interest in history.

CONTENTS

ILLUSTRATIONS

Acknowledgements

I am most grateful to Nigel Aston, John Derry, Grayson Ditchfield, David Eastwood, Bill Gibson, Bob Harris, Colin Haydon, Jo Innes, Murray Pittock and Shearer West, for commenting on earlier drafts of sections of this book, and to Wendy Duery for coping with my handwriting. I would like to thank the copy-editor, Richard Wilson, for his valuable assistance.

1 HOSTILE ENVIRONMENT

Life in eighteenth-century Britain was grim. It was of course grim by modern standards: accounts, for example, of the extraction of teeth using pliers might strike some as amusing, but pain and discomfort were frequent, if not continual. Life was also grim to contemporaries: sudden and painful death an ever-present reality. The poses adopted in portraits, whether heroic or familiar, provide no hint of the suffering, often tragedy, of individual lives, of Dr Johnson, for example, lancing his own swollen testicle, or Queen Anne finding her numerous pregnancies to no lasting avail.

Disease and injury were aspects of what was a hostile environment. Many of the problems still exist today, but modern familiarity with and understanding of such problems as disease or adverse weather conditions should not lead us to neglect their significance. They affected the attitudes and the actions of individuals.

DEMOGRAPHY, DISEASE AND DEATH

In the century between 1650–1750 Britain's population did not rise greatly, and in England it probably fell between 1660 and 1690 and in Ireland and Scotland in the 1690s. Declining fertility was probably the crucial factor in explaining the relative stagnation that followed the population growth of 1500–1650, certainly in 1671–91. For example, in Micheldever in rural Hampshire the number of baptisms in 1711–24 was lower than in 1611–24 despite the intervening population growth, and by 1711–24 the surplus of baptisms over burials was slight. In Britain as a whole death-rates were of greater importance from 1691 until 1751: most growth was wiped out by episodes of crisis such as 1696–99, 1727–30 and 1741–42.

The first official census was not until 1801, 1821 for Ireland, and compulsory registration of vital statistics did not begin until 1855. Current estimates

Publiſh'd as the Accidents June 1773
Published by John Heywood Sc Excelsior Works Manchester.

Tim. Boh. inv. Pinx. et del.

The Extraction of Teeth, 1773. The extraction of teeth by pliers was a painful process, requiring considerable force. Though frequently lessened by alcohol and laudanum, the pain was great.

of population size for England and Wales are, in millions, 5.18 (1695), 5.51 (1711), 5.59 (1731), 6.20 (1751), 6.97 (1771), 8.21 (1791) and 8.66 (1801), with the growth-rate being highest in 1781–91 at 0.83 per cent per annum. Whereas population growth in the first half of the century was lower than the rate of growth in agricultural output, so that grain prices fell and England became an important grain exporter, especially in the 1730s, the situation changed from mid-century and became more difficult. Despite emigration to North America, the Scottish population rose from about 1.3 million in 1755 to 1.6 million in 1801, the Irish from about 1.8–2.1 million in 1700 and 2.2–2.6 million in 1753 to 4.4 in 1791 and 5.5 by 1800, with Ulster as the most densely populated province. The rate of growth, less emigration, in 1755–1801 was 0.6 per cent per annum in Scotland, about twice that percentage in England and nearly three times that percentage in Ireland, thus ensuring that real wages were under least pressure in Scotland. On the Isle of Man the population rose from 14,426 in 1726 to 19,144 (1757), 24,924 (1784) and 27,913 (1792).

From the mid-eighteenth century the British population rose. It is easy to discuss this as a uniquely British phenomenon, and to consider it as a cause or response to agricultural or industrial development in the British Isles. But population growth was general throughout Europe. Detailed variations in population movements, both in Europe and within the British Isles, provide some clues to the reasons for change, at the same time as they make a general thesis more difficult to devise. In the century 1640–1740 the British demographic pattern had been one of generally late marriages. As illegitimacy rates were low, very low by modern standards, this ensured that childbearing was postponed until an average of over ten years past puberty for women at the end of the seventeenth century. The eighteenth-century rise of the British population has been attributed not so much to a declining death-rate, although that was certainly important, not least among under-10s in Scotland, as to a fall in the age of marriage and to more fertile marriages, so that the birth-rate rose. This ensured that the percentage of children in the population rose.

At the end of the seventeenth century English men married at about 28 and women at about 27. In addition many men and women never married: about 23 per cent of people aged 40–44 stayed unmarried in England. By the start of the nineteenth century the average age of marriage in England was 25.5 for men and 23.7 for women and less than 9 per cent of people remained unmarried. The illegitimacy rate in England had risen to 5 per cent of known births from 1.8 per cent in the late seventeenth century. The rise in the birth-rate may be linked to greater economic opportunities, in for example Yorkshire or the Lancastrian coal-mining village of Whiston where in 1725–49 the age at first marriage for both sexes was about three years less than in nearby marshland townships. The population of industrial and mining townships in both Lancashire and the Vale of Trent rose at a greater rate than that in agricultural townships. The relationship between economic opportunity and demographic circumstances, however, is less clear in other areas. Furthermore, real wages started to rise in the second half of the seventeenth century, but the age of marriage only in the second quarter of the eighteenth. It is far from clear precisely why population rose. Both birth- and death-rates would have been affected by the absence of civil conflict from the late 1740s on and by the degree to which the British army was small and wars were in part waged using foreign subsidised and hired troops. More effective poor relief and better storage and distribution of food may also have been important.

The demographic (population) history of the period is generally presented in aggregate national terms, but it is possible that there should be a greater emphasis on spatial variations in the trajectory of population growth. It was certainly the case that migration played a major role, with the major cities, such as London, Liverpool and Portsmouth, gaining numerous migrants both from surrounding rural areas and from further afield: both London and Portsmouth had large Irish populations. London's growth from about 400,000 in 1650 to about 675,000 in 1750 was such that it could have absorbed about half the surplus of births over deaths from the rest of England. Between the 1660s and the 1750s the population of south-west Lancashire, an area of mining and industry, trebled, largely due to migration. There was particularly strong demographic growth in the eighteenth century in other areas of mining and industrial development, such as the Staffordshire potteries, the coalfields of north-east England and Cumbria, and the tin- and copper-mining districts of west Cornwall. In Cumbria, Whitehaven's population quadrupled between 1715 and 1785. More generally, much more of the population was much more mobile as the century progressed. This greater mobility had crucial economic and cultural consequences.

Although the population rose, serious disease continued to affect it.

Disease was a significant killer both as a constant presence and through dramatic epidemics. Barriers against disease were flimsy, reactions to it clumsy and erratic due to prevailing attitudes and the limited nature of medical knowledge. In contrast to the modern assumption that there should be a cure for everything, little could be done about most diseases. Even the most sophisticated experts were ignorant of the true cause of infection.

There was, however, one major improvement: after 300 years of periodic attack, the plague was no longer a problem – it last hit Scotland in 1649 and England in 1665 (except for a minor outbreak in Suffolk in 1906–19 and another in Glasgow) – but this owed little to human action. Mutations in the rat and flea populations were probably more important in preventing a recurrence of plague than clumsy and erratic public health measures and alterations in human habitat thanks to construction with brick, stone and tile, for example the move away from earthen floors, although these remained common in the dwellings of the poor.

There were still, nevertheless, other major killers, including a whole host of illnesses and accidents that can generally be tackled successfully in modern Europe, although it is impossible to be precise about the seriousness of individual diseases. The quantification of disease patterns is hindered by the imprecision of many contemporary medical terms. About 45 out of a total population of about 100 in Ashton-under-Hill in the West Midlands died quickly in 1728 of 'swellings in the throat and other distempers'. 'Decline', 'consumption' and 'palsy' were really conventional terms for symptoms preceding death, while 'ague', 'gout' and 'flux' were very imprecise labels, diagnosed with an unknown extent of variability. As the cause of puerperal fever, the major killer of babies, was not understood until the following century, it is not surprising that medical provision appears to have had little effect on infant mortality.

One of the most serious diseases was smallpox, which proved difficult to conquer, although from the early eighteenth century it was largely confined to children. Of the children born in Penrith in 1650–1700, 38 per cent died before reaching the age of 6. The majority of Scottish deaths from smallpox were of children under 2 years old. Smallpox epidemics there were superimposed on the pre-existing cycles of mortality which were linked to movements in grain prices. This led to corresponding fluctuations in susceptibility to smallpox, thereby exacerbating the oscillations in child mortality. Smallpox affected the Scottish island of Bute every sixth or seventh year, and Alva and Tranent every fourth year.

Inoculation was of only limited value against smallpox, not least because those inoculated, when not isolated, were a source of infection. Inoculation was first used in Scotland in 1726, but many rejected it as tempting divine providence. It was introduced into the Orkneys in 1758 and the Hebrides in 1763. In Chichester inoculation helped to overcome an outbreak of smallpox in 1739, but twenty years later it proved fatal to some and was therefore discontinued for many for the summer, with fatal consequences. In order to educate the public, *Lloyd's Evening Post* of 6 February 1761 reported that whereas 1 in 4 of Chichester's sufferers who had not been inoculated had died during the summer, only 1 in 37 of those inoculated had perished, and that when in the autumn inoculation was again practised more generally it had had beneficial results. The publication of statistical information reflected an increasing common interest in discussing issues by such means and a greater confidence in empirical rather than theoretical approaches. Inoculation became safer after the Suttonian method of inserting only the smallest possible amount of infectious matter was widely adopted from about 1768. Vaccination was even safer than inoculation and it played a major role in defeating smallpox, but was not first performed until 1796.

Typhus, typhoid and relapsing fever were endemic and could become epidemic: there was a typhus epidemic in 1782–85. Influenza was a serious problem, as were dysentery, chicken-pox, measles and syphilis. From the 1730s epidemics of 'putrid sore throat' – scarlet fever or diphtheria – occurred for the rest of the century. The year could be divided by the prevalence of different diseases. Apart from fatal diseases there were others that were debilitating and for which there were few or no cures, including rheumatism, scurvy and jaundice.

The virulence of diseases was a product not only of their history but also of the circumstances of the age. The absence of antibiotics and the limited use of condoms ensured that venereal disease was a constant concern of the period. Poorly-drained marshy areas were prone to malarial attacks. The crowded housing conditions of the bulk of the population, in particular the habit of sharing beds, were conducive to a high incidence of respiratory infections. In the North Riding of Yorkshire, labourers' cottages were generally small and low, commonly only one room, damp and unwholesome. Population growth was generally accommodated by infilling rather than by the extension of built-up areas, and this increased density and crowding. Much of the new housing was of relatively poor quality. The growth of more than 10 per cent in Nottingham's population in 1780–1801 was met by back-to-back housing in courts with access to streets via narrow tunnels through houses on the street frontages. The rise in Lancaster's population, from 4–5,000 in the 1700s to 9,030 in 1801 led to a major increase in population density as back gardens were turned into houses, with access through doors and arches on main roads, but without water supplies, sewerage or lighting.

Sanitary practices and standards of personal cleanliness were important, particularly in communities with a high density of population. The habit of washing in clean water was limited, and most dwellings had no baths. Louse infestation was related to crowding, inadequate bathing facilities and the continual wearing of the same clothes. An eyewitness report in Macclesfield when the Jacobite army was there in 1745 described the main street as soiled from end to end. 'Gardy-loo', the shout whereby warning was given of the imminent emptying of slops from upper windows, was not limited to Edinburgh. More generally, the proximity of animals and dunghills to humans was unhelpful for health. Manure stored near buildings was hazardous and could contaminate the water supply. Effluent from undrained privies and animal pens flowed into houses and across streets. Northallerton in Yorkshire was typical in having a very unsanitary system. Privies with open soil pits lay directly alongside dwellings and under bedrooms, and excrement flowed on and beneath the surface into generally porous walls. Typhus was one result; the disease was partly responsible for a rise in winter mortality in London in the first half of the century. Clean drinking water was particularly lacking in large towns, coastal regions and lowland areas without large wells. River water in London was often muddy while pump-water there was affected by sewage. Relatively clean piped water only began to become available in Edinburgh from the 1720s and that city, like most others, still had mounds of dung on its thoroughfares. Glasgow had no public sewers until 1790 and the situation thereafter remained inadequate for decades. The privies developed by Alexander Cummings (patented in 1775), Joseph Bramah (patented in 1778) and others, were used by few.

Poor and inadequate nutrition also contributed to the spread of infectious diseases, by lowering resistance. Furthermore, malnutrition limited sexual desire and activity, hindered successful pregnancy, and, if chronic, delayed sexual maturity and produced sterility in women. Fruit and vegetables were expensive and played only a minor role in the diet of the urban poor, who were also generally ill-clad. Only the wealthy had baths with hot and cold running water. Only the well-off regularly ate meat on the Isle of Man. Thus health and wealth were related in Britain, although the prominent and affluent also suffered greatly from the impact of disease. The Society for Bettering the Condition of the Poor noted in 1805

> that many of the inhabitants of the more crowded parts of the Metropolis [London] suffer very severely under infectious fever . . . that in many parts the habitations of the poor are never free from the febrile infection; there being not only courts and alleys, but some public buildings, in which it has continued for upwards of 30 years past; – and that, by means of the constant and unavoidable communication which exists between the different classes of the inhabitants of the Metropolis, and between the Metropolis and other parts of the kingdom, this dreadful disease has frequently been communicated from the London poor to country places, and to some of the more opulent families in the Metropolis.[1]

Henry Pelham, later First Lord of the Treasury, lost his two sons, Thomas (1729–39) and Henry (1736–39) of 'an epidemical sore throat' within a day of each other. Two months later his daughters Lucy (c. 1729–40) and Dorothy, an infant, both died; though his other four daughters survived him. Pelham's cousin, another Henry Pelham, MP (c. 1694–1725), died of consumption. When Sir John Rushout died in 1697 he left only five of his nine children alive. His heir, James, and James's wife both died in 1705, aged 29 and 25 respectively. They left two young children, one of whom soon died. The dangers of childbirth were not lessened by social status and neither rich nor poor had access to effective contraceptives. There were no chemical contraceptives and sheaths (condoms) were primitive and used rather to avoid venereal disease than to prevent conception. *Coitus interruptus* seems to have been practised very widely. There was also no safe method of abortion.

Wealth and fecundity were linked, probably the result of many of the rich putting out their infants to wet nurses rather than breast-feeding themselves, which would have delayed the return of fertility. Thus, in Aberdeen in 1695–96 rich couples listed in the poll book had a ratio of babies baptised twice that of the other couples. Problems of food shortage and cost ensured that the bulk of the population lacked a balanced diet even when they had enough food. The poor ate different food: less meat and, outside southern England, less wheat and more oats. If the food supply broke down there could be shortages or even famine, as in Ireland in 1727–29 and 1740–41. The former led to thousands of deaths, the latter to hundreds of thousands. There were also Irish harvest crises in 1718–19, the mid–1730s, 1745–46, and 1755–57. The severity of the Scottish famine of 1696–99 was such that the population of Aberdeenshire, and indeed much of eastern Scotland, did not regain the 1695 level for more than half a century after it had ended, while many Scots emigrated to Ulster. There were other harvest failures and severe crises of food supply in the Highlands in 1741, 1753, 1763, 1772, 1782–84 and 1796, although none had the impact of the 1696–99 famine. Bad harvests led to higher death-rates, as in Worcestershire in 1708–12. In London high grain prices tended to increase the incidence of epidemic diseases and deaths among middle and older age groups. Climatic factors were also of great significance, particularly in weakening resistance. Most dwellings were neither warm nor dry and savage climatic conditions were exacerbated by shortages of firewood.

In Britain the situation from mid-century both became more favourable and remained fragile. Even Ireland was able to absorb population pressure, due to increased reliance on the potato, subdivision of holdings, greater employment in textile production and the growth of jobs in Dublin, but population increase served to push up the numbers and percentage of the poor, exacerbating a long-term social problem.

Alongside a rapid rise in the British population, there were also crises, mortality peaks reflecting problems with subsistence and/or disease. Thus, the general rise in population did not free communities from anxiety. It is not surprising that food featured prominently in popular fantasies. Concern over its distribution could also lead to mass popular violence, as in the English riots of 1740, 1766 and 1773 and those in Irish towns in 1778, and to political anxiety, as in 1789. Attacks on mills led to an extension of the Riot Act in 1769 to make attacks on mills a felony and a capital offence. Wagons and boats in ports were also attacked. Food was the largest single item of expenditure for the bulk of the population and when prices rose demand for other goods and services was restricted. The bleakness of the situation should not be overlooked. The London printer Edward Owen noted in 1757 'Bread is getting so excessive dear . . . which makes it go very hard with the poor, even in the City'.[2] Fears about the consequences of subsistence crises ensured that even those who were never short of food had to consider its supply.

Rising population encouraged emigration. The British Atlantic had 'shrank' between 1675 and 1740 as a result of significant improvements such as the invention of the helm wheel, which dramatically increased rudder control on large ships. The number of transatlantic voyages increased greatly, as did the number of ships that extended or ignored the optimum shipping season on several major routes. Many of these ships carried emigrants, especially from the 1760s when the nature of migration altered, so that it occurred in good as well as bad years, affected skilled individuals and originated from districts not hitherto noted for emigration. Total numbers were considerable: possibly 75,000 Scottish emigrants to North America during the century out of a nation whose total population in mid-century was only about 1.3 million.

The general rise in population had many consequences. It led to increased pressure on the socio-economic system as more sought land, employment, food and relief. The pressure on the land was a serious problem because the state of agricultural techniques and technology ensured that the area under cultivation could not be greatly increased. Thanks to private initiative, areas of 'waste' land not hitherto cultivated were farmed and a third of the Enclosure Acts brought 'waste' land into cultivation, while efforts were made to raise the general intensity of agricultural land use, but land hunger became a major factor, spurring emigration. In the second half of the century, the population of the Scottish Highlands showed a dramatic increase, raising pressure on a small and finite amount of arable land.

Monument to Joseph Gascoigne Nightingale and his wife, Lady Elizabeth Nightingale. Joseph (1695–1752), the eldest son of the vicar of Enfield, succeeded in 1722 to a great inheritance worth nearly £300,000 left by his first cousin Sir Robert Nightingale, and then adopted the additional name of Nightingale. In 1725 he married Lady Elizabeth Shirley, daughter of the 2nd Earl Ferrers of Chartley, near Stafford, and in 1727 was elected MP for Stafford. Lady Elizabeth died in childbirth, having previously been frightened by lightning. The monument shows her husband trying to protect her from the fleshless and shrouded figure of Death. It was erected under the will of their second son Washington in Westminster Abbey and was the last major work of Louis Roubiliac, a French sculptor who made his career in England. The monument was completed in 1761.

The rise in population disrupted local economies, affected employment opportunities and living standards, and put pressure on limited systems of social welfare. It thus became part of a more hostile environment. Human action also helped to make the environment more unattractive, if not hazardous, by polluting it. By modern standards the damage was limited, but it was particularly acute in cities. Thus in 1772 John Evelyn's *Fumifugium: or the Inconvenience of the Aer* [sic]*, and Smoake of London Dissipated* (1661) was republished. Evelyn complained of 'the Hellish and dismall Cloud of Sea-Coal' which perpetually enveloped London, and proposed to banish trades such as brewers, dyers, soap- and salt-boilers, and lime-burners to a distance of several miles from London. The flame-lit glory of industrial activity and energy that fascinated some commentators, such as the painters of Coalbrookdale, oppressed others.

Human vulnerability was not only displayed in the face of demographic pressures. The full range of calamities that could affect individuals and communities in this period revealed the fragility of personal circumstances and the weakness of communal responses. Non-epidemic illnesses could be a crushing blow to sufferers and there was little that could be done either to cure the illnesses or alleviate the pain. Opium and alcohol were the only painkillers or dullers and cheap laudanum was a universal panacea. There was

little to ease the pain of dying, except opiates. Childbirth was often a killer, disrupting families. English maternal mortality rates rose in the second half of the seventeenth century, but in the following century an increasing number of mothers survived childbirth, the rate by the second half of the century being less than half that of a hundred years earlier.

Agricultural labour was arduous, generally daylight to dusk in winter and 6 a.m. to 6 p.m. in summer. Fishing was dangerous, as were such extractive activities as collecting seabirds and eggs on the cliffs of St Kilda. Industrial employment was also arduous – up to sixteen hours a day in the Yorkshire alum houses – and was frequently dangerous. Millers worked in dusty and noisy circumstances, frequently suffered from lice and often developed asthma, hernias and chronic back problems. Disorders could result from the strain of unusual physical demands or postures, such as those required of tailors and weavers. Many places of work were damp, poorly ventilated and/or badly lit. Many occupations involved exposure to dangerous substances, such as lead and mercury. Construction work was very dangerous. The presence of explosive gas in mines made the use of candles there very dangerous. In about 1730 Carlisle Spedding invented the steel mill, a turning steel wheel that when struck by a flint gave off a series of sparks to provide

Keelmen Heaving in Coals by Moonlight by J. M. W. Turner. The expansion in coal production was fundamental to the economic growth of the period and to the development of a number of regional economies. A bulky product, coal was generally moved by water: by sea and, increasingly, by canal. London obtained its coal by sea from Newcastle. Heaving coal was arduous labour.

light. The sparks, however, could ignite gas; Spedding himself was killed by an explosion of firedamp in 1755, and the situation did not improve until the Davy safety lamp came into use after 1815. Apart from numerous accidents, mining also led to respiratory diseases due to dust and gas. Miners were affected by pneumoconiosis, mystagmus, rheumatism and premature ageing and had a short life expectancy. The increased demand for coal after 1750 led to the growing employment of women and children in mining jobs formerly done by men, for example working underground to tend the roads and the horses. In 1802 124 women aged 9 to 81, over a quarter of the work-force, were on the payroll of Howgill colliery in Cumbria. The notions of health and safety at work were barely understood.

Medical care was of limited assistance in dealing with these problems, as medical knowledge was often deficient and skilled practitioners were few, generally concentrated in the towns and expensive, although a degree of such care was increasingly provided in most parishes. Medical training could be very good, especially at Cambridge and Edinburgh; the latter's medical school developed greatly. Nevertheless, there was no effective treatment available for typhus, typhoid and dysentery. Medical treatments such as blistering or mercury were often painful, dangerous or enervating and some patients refused treatment. Surgery was primitive and performed without anaesthetics.

Medicine was scarcely more efficacious in the case of animal diseases, such as the severe cattle plague of the mid-century, which had serious economic consequences. The primitive nature of veterinary science ensured that the response to disease could not be preventive. Instead, as with cattle in 1749–50, animals had to be slaughtered, their movement prohibited. The situation at the level of the individual proprietor was of a hostile and unpredictable environment, of forces that could not be understood, prevented or propitiated, of the effort of years swept away in an instant. The line between independence and calamity, between being poor and falling into pauperdom, could be crossed easily and fast.

The climate presented a similar challenge. In general, the climate may have become more favourable, with warmer and drier summers improving crop yields. The 'little ice age' of the seventeenth century came to an end. In the first quarter of the eighteenth century average August temperatures were a full degree centigrade higher than in the last quarter of the seventeenth. This may in part have been responsible for a marked decline in deaths due to 'griping in the guts': bacillary dysentery. However, at the level of the individual the capriciousness of the climate could be a major problem, and the limited capacity of communal action could be all too apparent. An obvious example was flooding, both coastal and riverine. Most rivers were not canalised and their flow was unregulated by any system of dams or reservoirs. Coastal defences were often inadequate or non-existent. Flooding could interfere with transport, along and across rivers, and fishing, disrupt the activities of industries, such as milling, that were dependent on water power, and damage the most fertile agricultural areas. Much of lowland Somerset was flooded after a bad storm in February 1750. Water-power was also vulnerable to the ice of winter, which prevented mills from operating, causing unemployment and flour shortages. An alternative source of energy was wind, but windmills were affected by storms. Coastal areas were also affected by blowing sand, which did great damage in the Hebrides in 1697 and 1749. An Act of the Edinburgh Parliament of 1695 forbade pulling up plants by the

William Hunter (1718–83) by Sir Joshua Reynolds. Intended for the Church, Hunter was greatly influenced by William Cullen and became a surgeon. Educated at Glasgow and Edinburgh, he went to London in 1741 and became a noted anatomical lecturer. He became Physician Extraordinary to Queen Charlotte in 1764 and in 1768 the first Professor of Anatomy to the Royal Academy. He created a medical museum. His brother John (1728–93) rose to be head of the surgical profession in London and considerably advanced the theory and practice of the subject.

roots because much 'land, meadows and pasturages lying on the sea coasts have been ruined and overspread in many places . . . by sand driven over from adjacent sandhills'. Fires could devastate towns, for example Northampton in 1675, Kelso in 1684 and Warwick in 1694.

Agriculture was naturally vulnerable to the weather. There were few improved crop strains, and rainy winters produced diseased and swollen crops, while late frosts attacked wheat.

Agriculture was also vulnerable to another aspect of the hostile environment, the confrontation between man and other beasts. The absence of pesticides and difficulties in protecting crops and stored food exacerbated the situation. Mice and rats destroyed a lot of food and crops, predators attacked farm animals. Humans had few defences against a whole range of the natural world from lice, bed-bugs and fleas to tapeworms. Ministering to the poor,

The Thames during the Great Frost of 1739–40 by John Griffier, the younger son of the Amsterdam painter Jan Griffier who settled in London in the 1660s and painted many Thamesside scenes. The younger Griffier practised in London in his father's style and died there; his elder brother Robert also painted London scenes. The family's careers reflected the close links between England and the United Provinces, particularly London and Amsterdam, and the openness of English culture to foreign influences. Until the Thames was deepened and embanked in the nineteenth century it froze over in severe winters and became the setting for fairs.

John Wesley frequently suffered from fleas and lice. Straw-thatched buildings provided attractive environments for numerous pests and were also fire hazards, not least because they often lacked chimneys. In 1714 the 2nd Earl of Cromartie had to use arsenic to deal with rats that were eating his books.

The threat from real animals was joined by the anxieties aroused by imaginary creatures. In addition, fear of witches, although much lessened, persisted. So also did traditional astrological beliefs and practices, particularly in rural areas. An Edinburgh report in the *Newcastle Courant* of 4 February 1744 noted, 'We learn that a great many people, who have little sense and a great deal of superstition, are in a prodigious panic, on consulting their almanacs, when they find Easter Sunday happens on Lady-day, grounding their fear on the prophecy: "When our Lord falls in our Lady's lap, England beware of a great mishap."' Although the last recorded witch trial in England occurred in 1717 and the Witchcraft Act of 1736 banned accusations of witchcraft and sorcery, while the last legal execution in Scotland was in 1706, popular views proved more intractable. There was an execution at Dornoch in 1727 following an illegal local trial. The *Reading Mercury, and Oxford Gazette* of 15 March 1773 reported:

The ridiculous notion of witches and witchcraft still prevails amongst the lower sort of people, as the following account will sufficiently evince: A few days ago at the village of Seend, in Wiltshire, a report prevailed, that a woman who was dangerously ill of a putrid fever was bewitched, and this report excited the curiosity of numbers of her neighbours to go and see her. The fever attending the dying person was so high, as to render her delirious, and in that state she often cried out, 'She is pinching me to death'. This left it beyond doubt to the credulous vulgar, that an old woman who had long unfortunately been considered by them to be a witch, was the cause of her torment; and near a hundred of these *wise* people went instantly to the supposed witch's house, procured a rope, tied it about her middle, and carried her to a mill pond, where they cruelly gave the accustomed discipline of ducking. On throwing her twice or three times headlong into the water, and being unable on account of her cloaths to keep her under, they were perfectly convinced of her power of witchcraft, and supposing this discipline might deter her from exercising any further cruelties to the poor woman, they suffered her to go home. The woman's fever, however, increasing they went again the next day to the supposed witch's house, determining to give her another ducking; but were happily prevented by a Magistrate, who was accidentally informed of their intentions; by whose means it is probable, the poor old woman escaped falling a sacrifice to their resentment.

Popular beliefs had also been thwarted at Wilton in Wiltshire, where *Lloyd's Evening Post* of 2 January 1761 reported:

A few days ago, one Sarah Jellicoat escaped undergoing the whole discipline usually inflicted by the unmerciful and unthinking vulgar on witches (under pretence, that she had bewitched a farmer's servant maid, and a tallow-chandler's soap, which failed in the operation) only by the favourable interposition of some humane gentlemen, and the vigilance of a discreet magistrate, who stopped the proceedings before the violence thereof had gone to a great pitch, by binding over the aggressors by recognizance to appear at the next assizes, there to justify the parts they severally acted in the execution of their pretended witch law.

It was an animistic world and one inhabited by spirits, with death no necessary barrier to activity, experience and intervention. The Reverend Robert Kirk, Episcopal minister in Aberfoyle, Perthshire, published in 1691 his *The Secret Commonwealth; or an Essay on the Nature and Actions of the Subterranean (and for the most part) Invisible People heretofoir going under the name of Faunes and Fairies, or the lyke, among the Low Country Scots, as they are described by those who have the second sight.* For revealing this knowledge he was allegedly abducted by the 'little people' in 1692. There was widespread belief in such fairies, 'the gentle folk', in Ireland. They were seen as having a capacity for good or ill and it was necessary to propitiate them, for example by offering food and drink. The world outside people's dwellings, especially after dark, seemed more hostile and mysterious than is comprehensible to the people of the late twentieth century who are used to using electricity for illumination and clarification. In the absence of the moon, the night was pitch dark, especially in rural areas. Within houses it was shadowy when the candles were lit and dark when they were snuffed.

Popular religious beliefs, however removed from the teachings of the churches, did not amount to an alternative religion. Pagan practices were not the same as paganism. Instead, such beliefs and practices coexisted or were intertwined with Christian counterparts with little sense of any incompatibility, especially among ordinary lay folk in rural areas. The devil continued to play a major role in Christian consciousness, and could also be understood in terms of 'folk' religion. At the popular level, hostile external forces were blamed for intractable illness. Many Catholics continued to seek healing at shrines and holy wells such as St Patrick's Well in Galloon, county Monaghan. St Winiboid's well in Flintshire was famous for helping Queen Mary to conceive 'James III'. Articles of clothing from unwell persons were left at 'clooty' burns and wells in Scotland and healing supposedly followed. Superstitions continued to be very important, for example the belief that there were lucky and unlucky days. Herbs gathered before sunrise or on certain days only were believed in Ireland to cure men or cattle. Many pre-Christian customs continued with little or no veneer of Christianity. Edward Wakefield's *Account of Ireland* (1812) recorded many, including the swinging of children over, and driving of cattle through, fires lit on St John's Eve, in order to ensure health and fortune. New developments could be accommodated in the world of superstition. Thus, in Cornwall legends developed describing how Wesley met ghosts and devils. Wesley's *Arminian Magazine* contained many accounts of the occult, including ghost riders in the sky, apparitions, portents and miraculous healings. Wesley believed in guidance by dreams, and spiritual healing.

As old superstitions persisted, it could be suggested that the cultural gap between popular and elite beliefs had grown wider than in the previous century, that views and activities hitherto general, such as belief in astrology, had been driven down the social scale. Most of the wealthy and well-educated appear to have lost their faith in magical healing, prophecy and witchcraft.

This argument has to be advanced with care. Clearly fashion played an important role in elite culture, increasingly so as the growth in the quantity of printed works spread knowledge of what was judged desirable. It is difficult to assess the significance of the changes in fashion, but the popularity, for example, of suspect medical cures and the vogue in the 1780s for the theory of animal magnetism, suggest that it is dangerous to regard the culture of the elite as clearly better-informed. Rather, their superstitions were faddish.

At all levels of society there was a wish to understand the hostile environment and to cope with the fears that it inspired. There was a search for stability in an essentially unstable world, an attempt to reconcile divine justice with human suffering, and to order experience in a way that reflected the hard and arbitrary nature of life. The religious world-view provided the most effective explanatory model, the best psychological defences and the essential note of continuity. Faced with calamities, communities and individuals maintained their belief in religion. William Grasing, a Gloucestershire farmer who died in 1798, recorded in his much-thumbed notebook charms to be sung to bring health. That to stop bleeding was a statement of faith beginning 'I believe Jesus Christ to be the son of god . . . This charm must be repeated five times.' However, advancing unorthodox providential views in public could lead to difficulties. Richard Brothers (1757–1824), a religious enthusiast, wrote to George III, the government and the Speaker in 1792 informing them that God had commanded him to go to the House of Commons and announce the coming of the apocalypse. Further prophecies led to his being treated as a criminal lunatic from 1795.

The hostile environment was understood in terms of retribution with the possibility of gaining remission by good actions, either in terms of religious services or by satisfying the demands of the occult and spirit world. There was, it is true, an increasing questioning of the notion of divine intervention, for example growing scepticism that earthquakes reflected divine displeasure. Yet this was not a secular society and the contemporary notion of progress was not inherently sceptical. It rested in part on a diluted millenarianism, as well as on the traditional conviction that God provided means to cure all ills if only they could be discovered.

There was also much criticism of new ideas. For example, inoculation was condemned by those who championed the doctrine of providential affliction, the notion that God was responsible and that His reasons should not be questioned or defied. In 1755 Richard Tucker, sometime Mayor of Weymouth, wrote to his son Edward, then at university, about the Lisbon earthquake, 'A dreadful sudden call has lately happened to thousands in a neighbouring kingdom, and the same fate may attend others when the Great Governor of the world pleases.'[3] Thus, for most people, every disease and accident had a cause arising from the travails of the soul and the temptations of sin. Moral behaviour would be rewarded with health and thus restraint in personal conduct was prudent as well as virtuous. This combination underlay criticism of, for example, drunkenness, and influenced medical theory. In his lectures in the 1750s and 1760s the leading Scottish medical academic William Cullen related health and virtue in arguing that health was to be preserved by preventing disease through a rational lifestyle.

The search for divine support did not necessarily lead to worldly passivity. If the environment was understood as hostile, there was, nevertheless, much activity aimed at surmounting the challenge or coping with the consequences. Infirmaries were built in many large towns from the early eighteenth century, and the practice spread. In 1720–80 four voluntary hospitals opened in London, twenty-three elsewhere in England and three in Scotland. Jonathan Labray's Hospital for decayed framework knitters opened in Nottingham in 1726, followed in 1782 by a public infirmary or general hospital provided by public subscription. An infirmary in Bristol was erected by public subscription in 1737, and at least seven more almshouses were built in the city. The first medical hospital in Worcestershire, the Royal Infirmary, was established in 1745. Addenbrooke's General Hospital was built in Cambridge in 1763–66. The Lock Hospital was founded to help sufferers from venereal disease. In Birmingham the workhouse gained an infirmary wing in 1766 and a general hospital, with 40 beds, opened in 1779, its construction funded by philanthropy and by charity concerts in 1768 and 1778. The Royal Infirmary in Edinburgh opened in 1729. By 1776 there were 22 county infirmaries helping with the sick poor in Ireland. The level of provision in the British Isles was inadequate, especially outside the towns, but a letter from County Down sent in 1769 by Edward Southwell, MP, to George, Viscount Townshend, the Lord Lieutenant in Ireland, was symptomatic of a shift in priorities: 'The Gentlemen of this county about three years ago entered into a subscription for an infirmary. The experiment, though on so small a scale, as to contain only ten patients, has succeeded so well, that they are now inclined to enlarge their plan, if they could procure a building large enough for their purpose.' Southwell sought the use of a barracks, 'out of repair, not having been made any use of, for 20 years'.[4]

Dispensaries, institutions that provided out-patient care, were founded in numbers from 1770: by 1793 there were nineteen in the English provinces and annual admissions were probably in the tens of thousands. The purposes of medical and other charitable foundations revealed the poor state of social welfare, the failure of family networks to care for all the destitute and the grim nature of much of life. Thus in London, charitable donors sought to provide adequate care for lying-in women and their babies, to rescue the all-too-numerous orphaned and abandoned children and to rehabilitate those driven into prostitution by poverty. The mentally ill and those with disabilities suffered especially. The first institutions seeking to provide employment for the blind were not founded until 1791 (Liverpool) and 1793 (Edinburgh). Furthermore, the care that was provided to the indigent was provided to the 'deserving poor'. In both England and Scotland the 'undeserving poor' were treated harshly, a situation that reflected not only the disposition of power, but also the ability of those with authority to define and thus control others.

As so often with historical judgements, the question of whether to place the emphasis on change or continuity is subjective. In some areas progress was definitely made. For most people in England by the second half of the century, the environment was palpably less hostile than in, say, Poland, Naples or the Massif Central of France. Some allowance needs to be made for Britain's relative position, but the situation in Ireland was considerably less happy than in England and the average standard of living in the Thirteen Colonies, the future USA, was higher than in England. There were attempts to ameliorate conditions in Britain, from friendly societies to increasingly generous poor relief and advances in medical science. Moreover, eighteenth-century science was beginning to transform the relationship between man and the environment: buildings were better constructed, lightning was tamed by lightning conductors, some illnesses were mitigated, and nature was seen in more benign terms.

Yet the constraints and catastrophes that affected individuals and communities continued to be grievous. In his first *Essay on the Principle of Population* (1798) Thomas Malthus, then living in Surrey, wrote 'the sons of labourers are very apt to be stunted in their growth and are a long while arriving at maturity. Boys that you would guess to be fourteen or fifteen are . . . frequently found to be eighteen or nineteen . . . a want either of proper or sufficient nourishment'. Malthus advocated celibacy and delayed marriage as the means to cope with over-population. Suicide was known as the 'English disease', a practice that was regarded as far more common there than elsewhere in Europe. It was seen as the culmination of the melancholia that was regarded as characteristic of the nation.

The limited progress that was made in improving the circumstances of life is understandable in light of the restricted technology of the age and the scanty resources of government. It also reflected contemporary attitudes. Alongside the confidence of some in the possibility of human progress through communal action, much of the population lived in a precarious fashion, fearful of the future and possessing only limited aspirations. This popular conservatism was to play a major part in affecting plans for change.

2 ECONOMIC FRAMEWORK

In 1688 Britain was an important economic force, but by 1793 it had become the most important developing economy in the world. This change reflected shifts in agriculture, industry and commerce and the nature, causes, interaction and consequences of these shifts have been the subject of considerable debate, not least because they focus on the issue of the identity and causation of the Industrial Revolution. At the popular level there is little doubt that there was such a revolution, and it is commonly dated to the years after 1760 and associated with technological change. In scholarly circles there has been more debate over the chronology and description of industrial change. In general, the emphasis has been on the limited and mostly gradual nature of change in the late eighteenth century and the persistence of traditional manufacturing methods far into the following century. Again, the question is one of emphasis, not only of change or continuity, but also on the extent to which the British economy was becoming distinctive. Furthermore, as in other spheres, there is the question of how far national trends can be discerned and whether it is more appropriate to think in terms of regional economies. As, however, with the generally close relationships between landowners and merchants, there was also a relative degree of intra-regional harmony: certainly there were no domestic trade barriers other than those affecting Ireland, nor were there powerful bodies able to advance rival regional economic interests.

AGRICULTURE
The majority of the population lived in the countryside. Agriculture was the principal source of employment and wealth, the most significant sector of the economy, the basis of the taxation, governmental, ecclesiastic (tithes) and proprietorial (rents), that funded most other activities. Land and its products

Peasant Ploughing with Two Horses by Thomas Gainsborough. Working the soil took up much of the time of men in rural society. Ploughing and then weeding were crucial preparations for sowing; though ploughs improved in the period, the absence of mechanised means for breaking the soil ensured that much ploughing was arduous, especially on the clay soils of the English Midlands.

provided the structure of the social system and the bulk of the wealth that kept it in being.

The links between agriculture, industry and trade were close. The limited advances in the state of technological and scientific knowledge ensured that manufacturing was based on natural products. The age of synthesised goods had not yet arrived. Much manufacturing involved the processing of agricultural goods, particularly if forestry is included. It was a continuum that included the recipes of the household economy for food preservation: curing, bottling and making vinegars. The staple industrial activities were concerned with the production of consumer goods: food, drink, clothes, shoes and furniture. Though some processing involved agricultural products produced outside Europe, such as cotton, sugar-cane and tobacco, the source of most goods was British. Thus much industrial activity, whether urban or rural, was closely involved with the agricultural hinterland.

As the bulk of the population lived in rural areas and engaged in agricultural activities, it is not surprising that these activities played a significant role

in determining the level of purchasing power. Rural wealth created a market both for industrial goods and for expensive agricultural products, such as meat; conversely poverty limited both. Any rise in the cost of agricultural products, particularly grain, affected the urban population, reducing purchasing power and restricting the market for manufactured goods. The general fall in grain prices between 1670 and 1750 freed income for the purchase of manufactured goods, but put pressure on the rural economy, leading to heavy rent arrears and requests for rent abatements. For example, on the estates of the Duke of Kingston, which spread over six counties, rent arrears rose in the 1730s and 1740s. The low wheat prices of 1730–33 were accompanied by an upswing of arrears. On the Monson estates in Lincolnshire and Rutland, the Duke of Devonshire's properties at Bolton Abbey, Yorkshire, the Bouverie and Stapleton estates in Kent and the Duke of Ancaster's estates in Lincolnshire, rents also fell and arrears rose in the 1730s and early 1740s. Wheat, barley and oats prices all reached their lowest levels in the period in 1743–47, falling by more than 15 per cent relative to the prices of the 1720s,

The Harvest Wagon, by Thomas Gainsborough, 1767. The agrarian economy was dependent on a network of local transport links, most of which changed little during the century. Though often seen as an urban culture, Hanoverian Britain had also a rusticity and pastoralism seen in such aspects as the parks of stately homes, songs, most famously 'He Shall Feed His Flock' from Handel's *Messiah*, and poetry such as James Thomson's *The Seasons* (1726–30), Thomas Gray's *Elegy in a Country Churchyard* (1751) and John Dyer's *The Fleece* (1757).

19

though there were great regional variations in the nature and impact of the agricultural depression of the second quarter of the century. There were few problems in the Coke estates in Norfolk, the Leveson–Gower estates in Shropshire and Staffordshire and the Beaumont estates in West Yorkshire, but the open-field farmers on the heavy Midlands soils of Warwickshire, Leicestershire and Northamptonshire did badly. The rising relative profitability of animal-rearing encouraged the latter to switch to it, a process that involved enclosure and that led to a rise in the production of meat and dairy products. Throughout the period, the rural economy was affected by alterations in the prices of agricultural products, due to harvest variations and seasonal factors, though, at the same time, English agricultural wages remained below fifteenth- and early sixteenth-century levels in real terms throughout the eighteenth century, and that eased the position of farmers employing labour.

Britain was self-sufficient in food until the 1760s, from when grain price rose sharply and imports from elsewhere in Europe began. Demographic growth from the mid-century thus led to greater demand on the rural economy, which maintained its prosperity, thus in turn increasing the demand for manufactured goods. Greater demand affected both Britain and Ireland. From the 1760s English demand for Irish grain, beef and dairy products helped in the commercialisation of Irish agriculture, thus encouraging agrarian discontent. Food sources in North America, Argentina and Australasia did not develop until refrigeration, tins and the steam-powered iron ship changed the situation in the late nineteenth century.

Prior to that the need for food in an agricultural regime characterised by uncertain production and, by modern standards, low productivity, obliged all regions, however unfavourable they might be for food production, to devote attention to agriculture. For the bulk of the population, the harvest was the key factor in individual and communal fortunes, the only other developments of comparable importance – epidemic disease and warfare – being episodic.

There are many signs during the period, especially from the mid-century, of an improvement in agricultural output and productivity, the dissemination of new ideas and techniques and a greater role for specialisation, commerce and the cash economy. Farming was, however, diverse, and there were also signs of continuing conservative practices.

Increases in British production owed something to an extension of the cultivated area, for example in the mountain valleys and along the lough shores of Ulster, in the peat mosses of Scotland and north-west England, and in the Lincolnshire Fens, although most of what could be readily farmed was so already. There were also important qualitative advances. The increased use of lime as fertiliser helped to raise agricultural productivity: the limekilns were fired by coal. The spread of fodder crops, such as clover, sainfoin, trefoil, coleseed and turnips, helped to eliminate fallow and to increase the capacity of the rural economy to rear more animals, sources both of crucial manure and of valuable capital, for animals were the most significant 'cash crop' in the economy, providing both the 'roast beef of old England' and woollen cloth. Charles, 2nd Viscount Townshend, a leading Norfolk landowner, popularised the idea of incorporating turnips in his crop rotations in the 1730s. Known as 'Turnip Townshend', he carried out experiments on his estate at Rainham. The spread of convertible or 'up and down' husbandry, in which land alternated between pasture and arable after a number of years, was also of importance, resulting in increased yields when the land was cultivated, and improved grass at other times. In Thanet in Kent, for example, the widespread cultivation of sainfoin, rotations and the intensive stocking of barley lands with sheep controlled by folds, boosted agricultural productivity in the first half of the century. Mixed farming reduced the impact of bad harvests or animal diseases. Jethro Tull, a Berkshire landowner, invented a seed drill and horse-hoe in about 1701 and 1714 respectively and published his *Horse-Hoeing Husbandry* in 1733.

The Leicestershire grazier Robert Bakewell (1725–95) concentrated on improving his stock, producing the Dishley cattle, the Leicestershire breed of sheep and a breed of black horses for farm work. Bakewell reflected the inventiveness, entrepreneurship, sociability and politeness of the century. He used double floors in his stalls in order to collect dung, which he turned into liquid manure. He collected skeletons and carcases in order to further his studies of animal breeds, established the trade of ram-hiring on a large scale, founded the Dishley Society to maintain the purity of the breed and insisted on treating his animals well.

Changes were aided by the practice of enclosing land. Consolidated, compact and enclosed holdings were not an innovation of the period, but their presence increased, especially in the English Midlands. During the century about 21 per cent of England was affected by enclosure acts. They were especially common during the 1760s and 1770s when the heavy clay soils of the Midlands were enclosed, and there was widespread conversion from arable to pasture. Enclosure entailed either the reorganisation of fragmented holdings in open fields or the subdivision of former common pastures and wastes; it was often accompanied by revision in tenure and by a series of expensive changes including improved land drainage, farm buildings and roads, and new agricultural methods. Enclosure, however, did not necessarily increase efficiency, and there are examples of unenclosed areas that witnessed agricultural improvement, the introduction of new crops and techniques and better strains of livestock. Those who farmed the land were more interested in such improvements than those who owned it. Enclosure appears, nevertheless, to have made it easier to control the land, through leases and hence higher rents, and was often accompanied by a redistribution of agricultural income from the tenant farmer to his landlord as rents rose more than output. There was an increasing gulf between the landowner and the tenant in terms of disposable income; *rentier* landowners can therefore be seen as less 'progressive' than yeoman farmers. Enclosing landowners alarmed much of the rural population and created wide disruption of traditional rights and expectations, common lands and routes. However, being labour- rather than capital-intensive, processes like enclosure entailed much employment on tasks such as hedging and ditching, and hedges became even more characteristic of lowland Britain.

In Scotland enclosure was less of a factor, but the rotation of crops also helped to raise agricultural productivity. Scottish improvers, such as William Cullen, Sir Archibald Grant of Monymusk and Alexander Murray, advocated sowing grass seeds to improve grazing and growing root crops and criticised overstocking, poor ploughing, insufficient manuring and run-rig farming with its interspersed stripes of land. Grant was planting leguminous crops by 1719 and turnips by 1726 and was active in reafforestation, draining and enclosing. The 1st Earl of Cromartie recruited Dutch experts to reclaim low-lying land

and in the 1690s was interested in turnip cultivation and enriching rotations. In the 1730s the 3rd Earl introduced new rotations on his estate. In 1695 the Scottish Parliament passed two Acts relating to the division of commonties and lands lying run-rig, that aided the processes of consolidation of holdings and enclosure. In Galloway, however, the enclosure of pasture land for cattle-grazing led in 1724 to the Levellers Revolt in which the local peasantry knocked down the dry-stone dykes. Troops were used to suppress the revolt. On the Cromartie estates in 1766 the small tenants attacked the tacksmen's sheep and broke down dykes in order to pasture their own cattle illegally. In Ireland, the hougher outbreak in Connacht in 1711–12 was a movement of agrarian protest that led to attacks on livestock. The Whiteboys resisted enclosure of Irish commons and the payment of tithes during 1761–65 in counties Cork, Kilkenny, Limerick and Waterford by attacking agents and destroying fences, hedges and walls, and maiming cattle. The Whiteboys re-emerged in 1769–76, affecting Tipperary, Kilkenny, Carlow, Kildare, Wexford and Queen's county, while in Antrim, Armagh, Derry, Down and Tyrone opposition to increased rents led to the Hearts of Steel agitation in 1769–72.

Britain was prominent in the field of agricultural literature. Works such as Timothy Nourse's *Campania Foelix, or a Discourse of the Benefits and Improvements of Husbandry* (London, 1700), and John Houghton's periodical *A Collection for the Improvement of Husbandry and Trade* (1692–1703) offered practical suggestions. Henry Home, Lord Kames (1696–1782), a prominent Scottish jurist and intellectual, was also a great agricultural improver, who improved part of the moss of Kincardine and in 1776 published *The Gentleman Farmer; being an attempt to Improve Agriculture by subjecting it to the test of Rational Principles* (Edinburgh), a popular work, the fourth edition of which appeared in 1798. The practical nature of much agricultural literature and its basis in long experience were indicated by works such as *A Treatise on Watering Meadows* (1779) by the Dorset farmer, George Boswell, and *Observations on Livestock* (1786) by the Northumberland farmer George Culley, an improver who bred the new Border Leicester or Culley sheep, drained marshy land and introduced new crops and rotations.

Numerous agricultural societies were founded. British agricultural methods were advanced by European standards. However, the nature of regional and social differences and the role of emulation were indicated by a notice from the Glamorgan Society for the Encouragement of Agriculture published by the *Gloucester Journal* on 10 April 1780:

> This Society has been already very successful in introducing the culture of turnips and cabbages, in the field way, which undoubtedly are very beneficial to the farmers, as well as an improvement to the soil, and consequently advantageous to the landlord by supporting a much larger stock . . . [hope to spread benefits] even to the hills . . . The form and situation of this county, as well as the illiterateness of the generality of small farmers make us near half a century behind some parts of England in the art of agriculture, which renders an Association of this kind particularly necessary here . . . The gentlemen of this county, from their observations in travelling, and from books, and their own experience, discover many improvements as to mode of tillage, different kinds of manure, succession of crops, artificial grasses, implements, etc. which they cannot prevail upon the farmers to adopt so speedily, any other way as by pecuniary rewards . . . The utility and importance of provincial societies for the encouragement of agriculture are now universally acknowledged, they diffuse a spirit of emulation and industry among farmers of

every rank, and they promote the study and knowledge of agriculture, by corresponding with each other, and by directing and rewarding a course of regular experiments, and publishing the effects thereof.

That year the Society awarded prizes (among others) for the best crops of cabbages, red clover seed, rye grass seed, potatoes, sainfoin and turnip seed, for reclaiming rough lands, draining land and being an active Highway Surveyor. The Brecknockshire Society, founded in 1755, sought to achieve similar goals. Belts of trees were planted as windbreaks and new strains of livestock, such as New Leicester sheep, introduced. The Royal Dublin Society was founded in 1731 to improve 'Husbandry, Manufactures and other Useful Arts'.

Arthur Young, the great publicist of agricultural improvement whose many works included the foundation and part-authorship of the monthly *Annals of Agriculture* (1784–1809), in 1771 praised Charles Turner, who on his Cleveland estate at Kirkleatham had created compact farms, constructed new farm buildings and introduced cabbages, clover and improved breeds of cattle. However, most Cleveland farmers did not use clover and Young criticised the failure to reclaim much of the moorland. Agricultural improvement was also limited in north-east Scotland until after 1790: there was only a limited use of fallow and nitrogenous crops, and of the light but effective ploughs that could be pulled by two horses rather than a larger team, usually of oxen. Clover was introduced on the Isle of Man in 1770 and turnips in 1772, while threshing mills had arrived by 1793 and rotations by 1800. However, much agricultural practice on the island remained conservative, not least in the farm implements used. Most British small farmers lacked the necessary capital and willingness to accept risk for a programme of agricultural improvement. Illiteracy also limited receptiveness to agricultural innovations.

A major factor encouraging change was the continued growth and integration of the market economy as transport links improved and the growth in population fostered demand. This was intense near major centres, for example in Essex, but could also affect distant areas. Thus in Cleveland enclosure of both open field arable and commons owed much to the increase in pastoral farming for the London market. Cleveland produced good quality wheat and after 1769, when the Tees was bridged at Stockton, large quantities were shipped thence to London. Good quality butter was also moved to London by sea: from Malton via Scarborough, Whitby and Hull, while cows were driven south from Yorkshire. Scottish linen and cattle exports to England rose after the Union of 1707: cattle from about 30,000 yearly to perhaps 80,000 a year in the 1750s. Welsh cattle were driven to Kent to be fattened for the London market. Manufacturing areas, such as east Ulster, provided growing markets, in this case for the barley and oatmeal of nearby counties such as Monaghan and for the young stock reared in nearby uplands.

Agricultural development owed little to positive action on the part of government. Indeed Young told the Count de la Bourdonaye in 1788, 'he knew very little of our government, if he supposed they would give a shilling to any agricultural project or projector; that whether the ministers were whig or tory made no difference, the party of the plough never yet had one on its side . . . our husbandry flourished . . . by the protection which civil liberty gives to property'. This was indeed true. Continuity among the farming population through regularly renewed leases was crucial in assisting the development of the land's potential.

However, there was far less continuity at more humble levels. In the Scottish Lowlands, for example, the cottars or subtenants with smallholdings, the majority of the population before 1750, had been partly eliminated by 1820, in order to increase the size and efficiency of farms. Agricultural improvement between 1755 and the 1790s was responsible for a fall in the population of most Scottish rural parishes, a process helped by the brevity of tenancies: from four to nineteen years. In England yeoman farmers – small-scale owner-occupiers – were in part displaced to make more room for land-lords and tenant farmers. Enclosure was helped by the extent to which, unlike on much of the Continent, peasant ownership of the land was limited. The system of tenure in Britain helped to perpetuate landlord control. The social context of enclosure did, however, vary. In some areas, such as Hampshire and Sussex, enclosure was by private agreement and caused less tension than in others, such as Northamptonshire, where landlords secured parliamentary Acts to further their interests. Enclosure produced much hardship for those who had relied on access to common land and helped to encourage migration. Prior to enclosure, a large number of families in areas with common fields lived, in part, off the income from working or letting very small amounts of land; at least a third of the population of the open-field Midlands did so. The more extensive common 'waste' of upland regions supported others. Whether landholders or not, English peasants enjoyed common rights. The right to use common pasture land was particularly valuable to many small occupiers. Combined with rents generally lower than those in enclosed villages, and with comparatively ready access to land, common rights offered a degree of insula-tion against general movements of prices and wages, contributed to the vital-ity of a peasantry that relied on shared land use, and thus ensured that enclosure could be very detrimental to small farmers.

Thus in Northamptonshire an alliance of small occupiers and landless commoners resisted parliamentary enclosure with petitions, threats, attacks on gates, posts, rails and other crimes. This was not a rural society of defer-ence and order, but one in which aristocratic hegemony was seen as selfish and disruptive. The reorganisation of agriculture drove labour from the land and increased the amount available for industry. The precondition of eco-nomic growth was the ability to maintain agricultural development whilst shedding labour from agriculture to secondary production. By European standards British agriculture was efficient.

Enclosure, and the opportunities and discontent it could create, were not new: there had been much unrest about agricultural change in the sixteenth century. Indeed, any notion of an 'agricultural revolution' in the eighteenth century has to take note of the importance of long-term changes. This was true of regions at the forefront of new techniques, such as Norfolk, where some of the changes commonly associated with the eighteenth century, such as fodder crops, had in fact been introduced in the Middle Ages. On the other hand, the proportion of Norfolk and Suffolk farmers growing turnips or clover rose dramatically from the 1660s to the 1720s: probate inventories suggest 1.6 per cent to 52.7 per cent of farmers growing turnips. The Norfolk four-course rotation (of wheat, turnips, barley and clover) was established on many farms by the mid-century. Continuity in change can also be emphasised for less 'developed' regions, such as Aberdeenshire where many of the mea-sures taken by the agricultural improvers in the mid-eighteenth century had already been tried in the seventeenth, for example attempts to persuade tenants to plant trees and sow legumes. Similarly, organisational changes, such as the reduction of multiple tenancies and the commutation of rents in kind, had begun in the seventeenth century and accelerated in the eighteenth.

This stress on long-term change suggests that care is necessary before concluding that an agricultural revolution encouraged the onset of an industrial counterpart. Agricultural shifts can be seen in part as responses to climatic changes and also to market opportunities, such as the expansion of population from the mid-century. Portsmouth, for example, acted as a growing market for the grain and livestock of West Sussex and Hampshire. Irish dairy and livestock production developed in response to external demands, for example with substantial exports of beef and butter to England and salted pork to colonies such as Newfoundland. This suggests that, rather than seeing agriculture as an external force, provoking and making possible other changes, it should be seen as a part of a more complex interactive system.

INDUSTRY

The phenomena commonly understood by the term 'Industrial Revolution', such as steam-driven power and specialised factories, and associated social changes such as widespread urbanisation, were not typical in this period. Nevertheless, there was a substantial shift in the occupational profile of the population and it is foolish to present the century in terms of a failure to achieve an Industrial Revolution.

Manufacturing was affected by factors of demand and supply. Demand was principally affected by domestic population, purchasing power and consumer attitudes, although an increasing quantity of manufactured goods was exported, particularly to Britain's North American colonies. Most industrial production was able to serve existing and developing demands profitably without seeking to alter its supply-side capability. However, supply-side factors were of importance and there were significant changes. These included the quality of entrepreneurship, the supply of skilled labour, technological developments and changes in industrial organisation and location that permitted the cutting of costs.

The last is commonly associated with 'proto-industrialisation', the development of rural regions in which a significant portion of the population became dependent on income from the industrial production of goods for interregional or international markets. This has been seen as the consequence of the expansion of traditional rural domestic craft production without any technological advance. Labour was more flexible and cheaper than in the towns. In rural areas a lower wage economy stemmed from the absence of alternative non-agricultural employment and of a tradition of organised labour, and the presence both of grinding poverty and of income from farming. Energy costs may also have been significant. Water-power was easier to utilise in areas of rapid flow, and wood supplies were more plentiful in the countryside, as was coal in coal-mining regions. Demand was an important element in rural industrialisation, for, despite the general availability of cheap rural labour, most rural areas, for example most of Ireland, did not become important centres of industry. Demand reflected the presence of markets, and entrepreneurial activity was crucial in producing a symbiotic relationship between rural activity and urban funds, markets and, frequently, stages in manufacture. Entrepreneurial activity was necessary to enable rural industry to move from the stage of direct sale by domestic craftsmen to that of sale to

A View of Wallbridge, artist unknown, *c.* 1785. Wallbridge was a textile-manufacturing town on the Stroudwater canal. The Cotswolds were an important textile-manufacturing region, but one that was in relative decline, especially in face of major growth in the West Riding of Yorkshire.

distant markets. The merchant-hosiers, who controlled the knitting of worsted stockings in rural Aberdeenshire, provided the wool and collected the stockings. In Wales drovers acted as bankers. The capital and skill of Dublin merchants was crucial to the development of Ulster's linen industry.

Textile production lent itself readily to rural industrialisation. Power could be supplied by rivers, traditions of rural domestic textile manufacture were strong, wheels and looms could be found in the countryside, and textiles could be transported without much risk of damage. The rural and urban aspects of textile manufacturing were intimately linked. Finishing processes were usually concentrated in towns. They were also financed by the merchants who organised the system of outwork and then marketing of the final product. West Yorkshire was an important site of the rural manufacture of woollen cloth and Ulster became one for linen. By 1770 the bleacher and linen manufacturer John Flounders had four sites for collecting linen in Cleveland and sixteen receiving agencies between Newcastle and York.

The development of rural industry should not necessarily be seen as a stage on the path to 'full' industrialisation. 'Proto-industrialisation' is a term that is often used with the implications of development and growth, yet in many senses rural industrialisation was a stabilising factor. It made it possible to deal with the demands of a rising consumer population without increasing costs excessively and thus squeezing demand. It also brought more prosperity to rural zones, limiting emigration and supporting marriage at an early age. Individual households in Aberdeenshire were the units of production. Most of the knitting was done by women. In cloth production there women and children prepared and spun the wool which the men wove. Most rural industry was not mechanised to any significant extent; often products were for a local market only, techniques were limited and the capacity for innovation low. Only larger markets and the more substantial capital of major entrepreneurs could lead to experimentation in, for example, dyeing and new technology.

For the ordinary small man making a livelihood with perhaps a small-holding and his weaving, the local product made in the traditional way was all that he had time to produce. Areas characterised by such industry, for example Devon, Somerset, Dorset, Wiltshire, Essex, Norfolk, Suffolk, Worcestershire and rural Aberdeenshire, did not advance in the way that the more specialised and faster-growing regions did. The important hand-knitting of stockings, gloves and caps that provided much employment for women and girls in the western dales of North Yorkshire lacked capital and fuel for steam power and lost ground to mechanised industry elsewhere at the end of the century. However, large-scale concentration in factories did not really begin until the 1790s, and prior to that rural textile production grew. It was also widespread. In Scotland, for example, the spinning of linen yarn spread to remote districts such as Highland Perthshire, the Moray Firth, Ross and Orkney. Putting-out systems developed considerably in scale during the century. In Norwich the manufacture of worsted stuffs remained important and its output rose until the 1780s, but the industry remained essentially domestic and quasi-domestic, no factories of any size were built, and competition from the West Riding of Yorkshire had passed it by the mid-century. Partly as a consequence, popula-tion growth in the city was limited: from nearly 30,000 people in the 1690s to 36,000 in 1752 and 41,000 in 1786 and then a fall to 37,000 in 1801. The great growth in textile production in Yorkshire and Lancashire was achieved in part at the expense of traditional manufacturing towns, such as Colchester, Worcester and Exeter. Labour was cheaper in Yorkshire and Lancashire, and the textile industry less restricted by corporatist traditions than it was in tradi-tional centres such as Norwich. Population growth reflected and sustained this relationship. In contrast to Norwich's stagnation and an annual average increase for England and Wales in 1750–70 of 0.75 per cent, the percentage for the West Riding of Yorkshire was 1.7. The Suffolk yarn industry had col-lapsed by 1800, unable to compete with the uniform quality and lower prices of machine-spun yarns from the West Riding.

For rapid industrial growth, the essentials were capital, transport, markets and coal. Coal, a readily transportable and controllable fuel, was useful even in the preparatory stages of traditional manufacturing methods, such as soap-boiling, let alone in factories. Wood, with its greater bulk for calorific value and less readily controllable heat, was a poor basis for many industrial pro-cesses, as well as for the development of large new industrial populations, with attendant demand for bricks, pottery and all the other fuel-consuming ancillaries of towns.

Coal had to be mined and transported, and both these requirements acted as spurs for innovation and activity, particularly the construction of canals and of railways, along which horse-drawn wagons moved large quantities of coal, for example to the banks of the river Tyne, where it was used in manu-facturing or shipped to London. In the 1730s the first railway bridge in the world, Causey Arch, was built for the movement of Durham coal towards the Tyne. It had the largest span of any bridge built in Britain since Roman times, and the architect had to work from Roman models. Without transport, coal was of scant value, but coal with transport could serve as the basis for the creation of buoyant mixed-industrial regions with large pools of labour and demand, and specialist services.

Yet the technological level of most industries was fairly low, and innovations often spread only very slowly. Much industrial plant was primitive, prone to climatic disruption, a particular problem with mills, and dependent on an often poorly-educated labour force. The provision of fuel was often erratic, fuel economy limited and mechanical working parts prone to break down. Poor communications affected industrial efficiency. Industrial units were generally very small, with little specialisation either in machinery or labour. Most mines had a very small labour force. There was a general disinclination to innovate, understandably so in a culture where training was largely acquired on the job and where tradition determined most industrial practices; the apprenticeship system did not encourage new methods. Artisanal mentality included a sense of the importance of traditional values and communal stability. However, there were also changes. Entrepreneurs brought innovation and there was an openness to new technology in crucial sectors; there was also much skill amongst a wide cross-section of the work-force. Skills were being extended and intensified because of the increasing specialisation of labour functions in many sectors of the economy.

The limited and precarious financial resources of most enterprises discouraged innovation. Most contracts were short-term, hindering the develop-

The Royal Canal in Dublin. The canal was built between 1789 and 1817 to link Dublin and the Irish midlands. Although the canal network was far less extensive in Ireland than in England, canals nevertheless played an important role in the Irish economy.

ment of a relative security that might encourage often expensive investment in new plant. This ensured that investors with substantial disposable funds were of great importance: major landowners, for example, played a crucial role in the expensive business of developing coal-mines and attendant transport facilities, as in Ayrshire, Cumbria, Lancashire and north-east England. James Lister of Shibden Hall in Yorkshire wrote to his brother in 1772, 'We are very busy laying out our money at Mytham, but not so forward yet as to have a pit sunk, neither do we expect to have one this year . . . likely to cost a thousand pounds or upwards . . . the reason of its costing so much money, is that we make wheels and preparations for a corn mill, in case there should be water sufficient to pump the water from the coal, and turn a corn-mill'.[1] Earl Gower, the 1st Marquis of Stafford (1721–1803), was actively involved in coal, lime and iron stone extraction and the development of canals and mineral railroads. Scottish landowners also played a prominent role in harbour construction, salt-boiling, the production of coal-tar, glass and lime, and canal and turnpike development.

Most industrial plant was fairly simple and there was rarely an opportunity or need for the costly retooling that might have encouraged innovation. In most spheres technological developments were limited, and industrial activity was characterised by many problems and often poor products. Skilled labour was frequently in short supply. Skills were often not readily transmissible, except by acquiring the men who had them; books or blueprints would not suffice. By the end of the century steam power was still only used for paper-making in very few places.

The factors inhibiting developments made the changes that occurred more impressive. In some spheres, such as mine drainage, technology offered the possibility of extending activities in hitherto closed directions, for example by sinking deeper pits; in other spheres, such as textiles, technological developments permitted the production of goods more rapidly or in greater quantities. Although most power generation at the end of the century was still by traditional methods, the introduction, for mining and manufacturing purposes, of the steam engine at the beginning of the century in England offered an alternative source of power. Steam engines were expensive and not free from problems and were best suited to enterprises such as large mines, where substantial quantities of energy were required for a long period. They were particularly useful for pumping water out of mines. The first Newcomen steam engine in the Cumbrian coalfield was completed in 1717 and the use of another made possible the sinking of the important Saltom Pit there in 1730. Although their introduction was slower, the coal-mining county of Ayrshire contained at least five steam engines by 1750. Steam engines were also used for winding and, by the end of the century, for driving machinery. The Newcomen engine was improved as the casting and boring of cylinders developed, particularly thanks to the new boring machines developed by Wilkinson in 1774 and 1781. This allowed the steam engine to become more efficient in its fuel use and more regular in its operation. The use of steam engines in Europe was concentrated in Britain, where in 1769 the Scot James Watt, the first to perfect the separate condenser for the steam engines, patented an improved machine that was more energy-efficient and therefore less expensive to run, although more expensive to buy. In 1779 James Pickard, a Birmingham button-manufacturer, fitted a crank and flywheel to his Newcomen engine in order to use its steam power to drive a mill that could

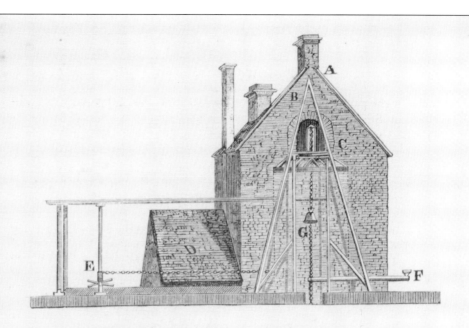

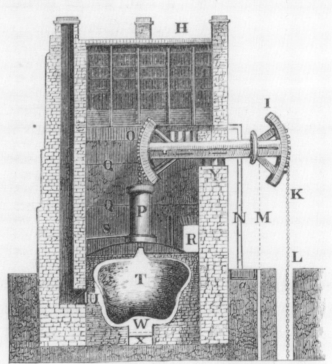

NEWCOMEN ATMOSPHERIC ENGINE, POOL MINE, 1746.

A, south front of fire-engine house ; B, triangle for tending the engine-pumps ; C, arch for main bob to play in ; D, coal-house and fire-place ; E, capstan and cable for the triangle ; F, balance-bob to assist the draught ; G, the bell.

H, section from the west ; I, south end of the main bob ; K, main chain, to draw up the water from the bottom ; L, end of balance-bob, marked F in Fig. 1 ; M, a small chain, drawing from the adit to a cistern ; N, force-pump to supply the cistern for the boiler T, &c. ; O, north end of the main bob ; P, the cylinder ; R, the eastern door ; S, pipes to let out the air and steam from the cylinder ; T, the boiler which supplies the steam ; U, the damper to moderate the fire ; W, the fire-place ; X, the ash-pit ; Y, the axis of the main bob.

grind metals. This innovation greatly enlarged the market for steam engines which was exploited by the partnership of Watt and the Birmingham industrialist, Matthew Boulton. Steam power freed industries from having to locate near riverine sites where water power could be obtained.

Significant technological innovation, in which Britain led the way, also occurred in metallurgy where the smelting of iron and steel using coke, rather than charcoal, freed an important industry from dependence on wood supplies: mineral replaced organic sources of power. This innovation by Abraham Darby (1709) was not widely applied initially because of cost and quality factors, but from the 1750s charcoal costs rose and the process spread rapidly. Henry Cort's method of puddling and rolling, invented in 1784 but not adopted until the 1790s, produced malleable iron with coal more cheaply than the charcoal forge and refinery. Combined with the application of steam power to coal mining, blast furnaces and the new rolling and slitting mills, this led to a concentration of the iron industry on or near the coalfields, for example in South Wales. The development of the South Staffordshire coalfield owed much to the construction of ironworks, the first, outside Dudley, in 1772, and fourteen in all by 1794. The greater production of iron served as a stimulus for the metalworking industries of the West Midlands, for example the manufacture of nails and needles in north Worcestershire. Copper smelting also came to be located on the coalfields, for example in south and northeast Wales.

The production of iron rose from an annual average of about 27,000 tons in 1720–24 and 1745–49 to 80,000 in 1789. Iron spurred the demand for coal, so that the expansion of coalmining was both the product and the cause of economic development. In 1700 the production of about 3 million tons had been largely for domestic heating, and the north-east of England had been the most important coalfield. Output rose by just over 1 per cent per year to 5.2 million tons by 1750, and then by over 2 per cent per year for the rest of the century: to 8.8 million tons by 1775 and 15 million by 1800. There was particularly important expansion after 1750 in Lancashire and south Wales. Mining benefited from a number of innovations including the introduction of explosives, better methods of lining shafts and supporting roofs, improved underground transport, especially with the adoption of rails, longwall mining and the use of the steam engine for pumping and winding. Coalmining was affected not only by the application of steam power, but also by improvements in the transportation of bulk goods by water and, to a lesser extent, road, that ensured a fall in the price of coal. The first coal barge arrived in Birmingham on the new Birmingham canal in 1772.

Textiles was another sphere that witnessed technological development in which Britain led the way. John Kay's flying shuttle of 1733 increased the productivity of handloom weavers by making it possible both to weave double-width cloths and to weave more speedily, although it was not in general use in Yorkshire until the 1780s and was only slowly spreading elsewhere in England twenty years later. The early machinery of woollen textile manufacturing, such as James Hargreaves's hand-powered spinning jenny (1764) and scribbling and carding machines, dramatically raised the productivity of labour. The spinners saw the new technology as a threat to their livelihood, and Hargreaves's machines were destroyed by rioters in Blackburn in 1768–69. The 1760s–1780s saw a series of developments that produced machine-spun cotton yarn strong enough to produce an all-cotton cloth, particularly Richard

Facing page: Thomas Newcomen's Steam Engine. The first steam engine was developed by Thomas Savery in 1695 and was improved by Thomas Newcomen with his Atmospheric Engine of 1712. In the latter the injection of water condensed steam in the cylinder, causing the piston to descend under the weight of the atmosphere. The piston was then returned to the top of the stroke by the weight of the beam; the beam transmitted power by moving a chain attached to the pump rod, but on the down stroke only. Newcomen's steam engine was used for pumping, first in the important Cornish tin industry and later in coal-mines. It was progressively improved during the century, not least with better cylinders and valves, which increased its energy efficiency, but was eventually superseded by James Watt's steam engine with its separate condenser. Watt also developed an engine that could transmit power on both strokes.

James Watt (1736–1819) by Sir Henry Raeburn, 1815. The Scottish engineer considerably advanced the utilisation of steam power. He invented the separate condenser which greatly increased the fuel efficiency of steam engines; his first steam engine was installed in 1776. In 1782 he patented fresh innovations that gave a comparative uniformity of rotary motion, and this increased the capacity of steam engines to drive industrial machinery. Settled in Birmingham, Watt was active in scientific life there, meeting Priestley, Wedgwood and others in the Lunar Society, which met monthly. He made substantial sums and purchased estates in Radnorshire and Warwickshire.

Arkwright's water frame (1768), which applied the principle of spinning by rollers, and Samuel Crompton's mule (1779) with its spindle carriage.

The yarn produced by Arkwright's water frame was of a firmer texture than that spun by the jenny, and the smoothness and evenness of the yarn ensured that stockings woven from it were much better than those woven from hand-spun cotton; unlike the jenny, the process was continuous. In 1773 Arkwright produced a cloth solely of cotton, an innovation in England; in 1775 he brought out a patent for a series of changes allowing the entire process of yarn manufacture to be performed on one machine. Arkwright and his partners built a number of water-powered cotton mills in Lancashire and the Midlands, the first in Derbyshire in 1771, that displayed the characteristics of the factory system, including the precise division of labour and the continual co-operation of workers in the different manufacturing processes. In 1772 his mill in Nottingham employed over 300 people, some children from the parish workhouses.

In 1776 Arkwright's new factory at Birkacre near Chorley in Lancashire was burnt down by rioters angered by the offer of work at lower rates. Over 100 machines were destroyed in the Lancashire riots of that year. Nevertheless, in 1780 Parliament responded to a petition by the cotton-spinners by supporting the use of machines. In 1790 Arkwright erected a Boulton and Watt steam engine in his Nottingham mill.

The new technology encouraged the move of spinning from home to factory production. The first worsted spinning mill was erected in 1784, and by 1794 at least five more were in operation. All depended on water power. However, weaving continued to be managed by the putting-out system. Effective power looms were not produced until the following century. Cotton production grew by nearly 13 per cent in the 1780s, a very high rate of growth for eighteenth-century industry and one that reflected the boom of 1783–92 following the War of American Independence and the reopening of the crucial export trade to America, and technological development.

Though technological innovations were particularly associated with the fields of steam power, metallurgy and textiles, they were not restricted to it. Developments in ceramic technology led to hard, high-fired and commercially successful British china. Josiah Wedgwood turned a craft into an industrial process, creating a major export industry in the process. The Staffordshire pottery industry needed cheap transport, for clay and for finished products. The spread of mining led to greater interest in railroads. Sophisticated engineering was developed by the innovations of men such as Matthew Boulton. The first rolling mill in Birmingham was opened in 1740. From the first half of the century the rolling mill was applied to tin-plate,

Thomas Rothwell's view of the Forest Copper works, Morriston 1791. Jabez Fisher, a visiting American Quaker, commented in 1776 that the works `vomit out vast columns of thick smoak, which curling as they rise, mount up to the clouds'. The copper works in the lower Swansea Valley depended on sea-borne supplies and used Cornish, Irish and Welsh copper. The valley dominated the non-ferrous smelting industry in Britain.

Old and New Wales. The ruins of Neath Abbey with, in the foreground, a horse-gin and a train of trams leaving a colliery, from *Descriptive Excursions through South Wales and Monmouthshire* by Edward Donovan, who travelled there extensively in the summers from 1800 and in 1805 published his account illustrated with coloured engravings from his own sketches. Donovan was a naturalist who had already published an *Essay on the Minute Parts of Plants* (1793). Neath had twelve lead and two copper furnaces in 1708, but Swansea became a more important centre of smelting.

giving the English tin-plate industry a major competitive advantage. Although developments with steam-powered machinery were more dramatic, there was also important progress with hand tools and small machinery, particularly in the metal trade, which benefited from improvements in drilling equipment, innovations in button making, and from two patents of 1790, one for manufacturing nails by machine, the other for producing lead pipes by drawing them through rollers. Metalworking was crucial to what was termed 'toymaking', the manufacture of small metal objects such as buckles, buttons and snuffboxes, the great expansion of which was part of the world of goods in this period.

Once again, it is unclear where to place the emphasis. Technological innovation and a large percentage of the national income coming from non-agricultural activities, especially overseas trade, were distinguishing and advanced features of the British economy. The active culture of print, especially newspapers and magazines, helped to sustain and disseminate fashions in a society in which fashion and social emulation played a growing role in creating a consumer market attuned to new developments. This was essentially the market of the 'middling orders', greatly concerned about social status and aspiration, who by 1725 had seen an appreciable increase in the scale of their material possessions, such as pottery and furniture. The enhanced purchasing power of the bulk of the population in the first half of the century also helped industrial developments, with, for example, the rise of gin distilling, a new industry, albeit a highly controversial one. Yet over much of the British

Isles industry was still far less important than agriculture as a source of wealth and employment at the end of the century. If poverty and communication costs and problems restricted markets, a lack of capital and the limited pool of skilled labour were also significant constraints. Psychological rigidities were also important: technological possibilities were not grasped in many sectors.

Industrialisation was a highly regional process. Contemporaries were certainly aware of the pace of change in the regions concerned. However, as yet technological transformation was selective and change slow, firm size was small and organisation personal, labour markets local, outwork common and factories rare. Ayrshire, though a major coal-mining county, was typical at the end of the period in having most of its manufacturing carried on in small hand-, horse- and water-powered units. Similarly, most of the tasks in the important British linen industry were performed by hand. Flax-spinning and linen-weaving were cottage-based. Larger factory-type units serving wider areas were created only for the finishing processes of bleaching and bettling. The important Warrington file-making concern of Peter Stubs relied mostly on outworkers at the end of the century.

By the 1790s industrial change had a clear regional pattern that was reflected in indicators such as expenditure on poor relief per head of

The Fellow Prentices at their Looms by William Hogarth. Hogarth's exemplary engraving of 1747 illustrated the extent to which the working parts of machines were large and still dependent on human energy. Power-driven looms came to play a greater role during the century. In Hogarth's sequence the idle apprentice was eventually hanged.

35

population. In 1801 the average figure for England and Wales was 9s 1d (45p), but in the industrial counties it was far lower – 4s 4d in Lancashire and 6s 7d in the West Riding of Yorkshire – while counties with hardly any industry, such as Sussex, or with declining industries, such as Essex, Norfolk and Suffolk, had to pay far more than the average.

Apart from Ulster, where linen-weaving developed strongly by mid-century in much of the east and south, Ireland had comparatively little industrial growth, although the linen economy also affected other regions including Roscommon, Mayo and Cork. Scotland, with a more self-sufficient and mixed agricultural sector, coal, and more favourable political, financial and social circumstances than Ireland, developed considerably from mid-century on, especially in industry and banking in the central Lowlands. Prior to that, the Scottish economy had been relatively backward with limited long-distance trade and an economy dependent on England, to which cattle and linen were exported and from which manufactured goods were imported. The Act of Union admitted Scotland to a free-trade area that comprised Great Britain and the colonies. Complementary and competitive Scottish industries, such as linen, benefited greatly, as did the west of Scotland, which could now trade freely with the West Indies and North America. Less competitive industries, such as fine woollens, collapsed.

From mid-century the availability of capital clearly interacted with the investment opportunities provided by new technology. Although the extensive sugar and tobacco trades based on Glasgow were enclave activities that had little direct effect on the rest of the economy, the profits gained from them acted as stimuli for other sectors of the economy, as did the industrial opportunities created by war. A certain amount of mercantile capital was spent on the purchase of landed estates, but there was no wholesale transfer of funds from industry and trade. The investment of profits from the tobacco trade substantially funded the development of the chemical industry in west–central Scotland. Similarly the liquidity of banks such as the Edinburgh-based Royal Bank was increased by the profits of the tobacco merchants. The early 1760s witnessed the appearance of provincial banks in Aberdeen, Ayr, Dundee, Glasgow and Perth. Several industries saw considerable growth. Whereas only seven Newcomen steam engines appear to have been in operation in Scotland in 1759, increasing numbers were used in coal-mining thereafter, and the industry grew in the 1760s. From the early 1750s there was a build-up of forge and foundry establishments, particularly around Glasgow. By 1761 the Carron Company at Falkirk, a leading metallurgical enterprise founded in 1759 that concentrated on ironmaking, had 615 employees and was an example of the increased amount of capital being invested in industry and the consequent larger size of industrial concerns. Scotland's biggest manufacturing industry, linen, experienced rapid growth in 1740–80 with output more than doubling, while cotton manufacture developed in Lanarkshire. The Scottish chemical industry developed using coal in the mid-century, with sugar-boiling in Dundee and a vitriol (sulphuric acid) works opened at Prestonpans in 1749. Four new paper-mills were established in 1750–56, while the printed linen industry grew from 1753. Agricultural improvements were actively pursued, the potato being introduced as a field crop in 1743. There was also a growth in scientific, intellectual and material inquiry; the Honourable Society of Improvers, the Board of Trustees for Fisheries and Manufactures, and the Select Society, founded in 1723, 1727 and 1754 respectively, being prominent Scottish professional clubs and institutions promoting advances and improvement. The Royal Medical Society was founded in 1737, the Scottish Society of Antiquaries in 1780 and the Royal Society of Edinburgh in 1783.

There were naturally still major difficulties, and Scotland remained much poorer than England. Agricultural prices remained dangerously susceptible to variable harvests with consequent problems for other areas of the economy. There were also difficulties with credit; in 1761 the Scottish credit system was revealed to have an inadequate cash basis. Nevertheless, the growth in the economy of central Scotland showed both what was possible in this period and what could be mirrored elsewhere.

In England industry was becoming particularly important in the North and the Midlands, especially in and near coalfields. Lancashire, Yorkshire and the West Midlands were the principal centres of industrialisation. In addition, urban manufacturing was very important: towns such as Derby, Newcastle and Nottingham became major centres of activity. The relationship between urbanisation and industrialisation became closer with the growing cities closely associated with manufacturing or with related commerce and services. Nottingham had a major pottery industry: the production of salt-glaze stone-ware started between 1688 and 1693. Framework knitting was also of great importance. The stocking industry moved from London to the Midlands, especially Nottingham, and in 1750 there were said to be 1,200 frames in the city. The manufacture of glass was also of consequence there. Building on the pioneering efforts of Thomas Cotchett, Thomas Lombe, who introduced Italian silk-throwing machinery into England and patented it in 1718, erected a large water-driven factory on the river Derwent at Derby in 1719. The first silk-throwing mill in north-west England was opened at Stockport in 1732. Yet such factories were still atypical.

The processing of goods imported from across the oceans was also of great importance. Bristol had a tobacco industry, for example milling snuff, as well as sugar-refining, with a peak of sixteen refineries, and in 1731 chocolate and cocoa-making began there. In the second half of the century there were at least three cotton mills in Bristol, while the city benefited from coal from the nearby Forest of Dean in the development of industries such as zinc and copper smelting, iron founding, lead works, gunshot making, salt refining and soap making. The first English brass-making foundry was established there.

Agricultural improvement, the construction of canals and better roads, and the development of industry and trade, led to a growth in national wealth and a gradually emerging new economy. The percentage of the male labour force employed in industry rose from 19 (1700) to 30 (1800), while, although agricultural productivity increased, that in agriculture fell from 60 to 40. The British economy developed powerful comparative advantages in trade and manufacturing and greatly impressed informed foreign visitors. A sense of economic change and the possibilities of progress was widely experienced amongst many people in the later eighteenth century and can be glimpsed in depictions of industrial scenes, for example Coalbrookedale. In the Frog Service that Wedgwood designed for Catherine the Great each piece of china was painted with a different British scene; these included not only landscapes such as Stowe, but also the Prescot glass works on Merseyside. From the 1730s and 1740s the majority of British commentators argued that modern achievements were superior to those of former times, especially the ancient world. A culture of improvement lay at the heart of much innovation and the diffusion of new techniques and machinery.

Progress took many different forms. There was a marked increase in the number of patents issued from 1759. Industrial development led to more specialisation, division of labour and the growth of capital. Gross National Product per head is very difficult to assess in this period, but it was probably considerably higher than in France. There were important changes in the experience and intensity of work, the organisation of labour and in material conditions. There was a greater emphasis on the need for constant and regular labour: new working practices and technology required a more disciplined work-force. The Derby clock- and instrument-maker John Whitehurst (1713–88) designed the first factory time-clocks, and Boulton manufactured and sold them. Although by the end of the century fewer than 2,000 steam engines had been produced, they each represented a decision for change. The cumulative impact of often slow and uneven progress was impressive by the end of the century, and, by then, the rate of industrial growth had risen markedly.

3 THE MEANS OF COMMERCE

COMMUNICATIONS

Agricultural and industrial development depended on a number of factors, but one of the most significant was the nature of the infrastructure. Without effective transport systems, regions could not benefit from improvements or the cultural changes that influenced demand. Economic activities had different requirements, and improvements in infrastructure did not necessarily benefit all, particularly if the two-way flow of improved communications led to competition from better or cheaper products. However, problems with communications and credit were of general importance.

Communications were a serious problem, whether in terms of the movement of people or of goods, of transport with speed or in bulk. Poor communications magnified the effects of distance and imposed high costs on economic exchange. Without modelled roads or mechanised transportation, land communications were generally slow. The quality of the roads reflected the local terrain, in particular drainage and soil type, and the ability and determination of local communities to keep the road in good repair. The resistance of the road surface, generally loose and rough, to bad weather or heavy use was limited, but frequent repair was expensive in terms of money and manpower. As a result of the Statute for Mending of Highways of 1555, each parish in England and Wales was responsible for the upkeep of roads in it, but the duty was generally not adequately carried out, certainly not to the standards required by heavy through traffic. Narrow wheels chewed the roads into ruts. As a result, from the 1750s planners advocated broader wheels for carriages and wagons. In the 1770s James Sharp advocated rollers sixteen inches wide rather than wheels, claiming that they would consolidate the road surface. There was parliamentary support for such rollers, but they were cumbersome and expensive, and there was no significant improvement until the Scots McAdam and Telford improved the road surfaces with new construction techniques.

Poor roads led to long and unpredictable journeys that strained individuals, damaged goods and tied up scarce capital in goods in transit. A wagon drawn by four horses pulling 4,000 lbs could rarely cover more than 20 miles daily. Poorly constructed roads often enforced the use of light carts with only two horses, increasing the number of carts necessary to move a given load and the consequent cost in manpower and forage. Still more often, burdens were limited to 2.5 cwt (280 lbs) or so, which could be carried in panniers on a horse or mule, against the 10 cwt (1,120 lbs) which could be drawn by a single horse over good roads. Pack-horses were still very common in Britain's advancing areas even in the 1800s, and the construction of good roads could therefore offer a fourfold increase in loads. Droving was the principal method of transporting livestock; East Anglian turkeys and Scottish cattle were thus moved to London. Stockbridge in Hampshire still has eighteenth-century grafitti from drovers who met there before approaching London. Scottish cattle were fattened near Norwich.

Wagons and carts often provided merchandise only inadequate shelter, and the methods of packing and of moving heavy goods on to carts were primitive. Draught animals were affected by the weather and the availability of forage. These problems faced road transport even over favourable terrain; in difficult terrain there were additional hazards. Road construction and maintenance techniques were of limited effectiveness in marshy regions or areas with a high water table, such as the heavy clays of the English Midlands, and mountainous terrain increased the need for draught animals and limited the speed of transport. Significant road improvements were made, especially, but not only, in England. A sizeable network of 'turnpikes' was created, radiating from London by 1750 and from the major provincial centres by about 1770; the main impetus for this came from trade and the desire of local merchants and manufacturers for growth. Unlike elsewhere in Europe, the government played only a small role, although in the Scottish Highlands it used the army in the 1720s and 1730s to build roads to aid a rapid response to any rebellion.

Some improvements were made to the major roads in Ireland, and these could be of considerable importance in affecting the relative position of towns. Thus when the road from Naas to Maryborough was turnpiked in 1731, Kildare found itself on the new main route between Dublin and the south-west, and benefited accordingly. Turnpike trusts constructed a number of new arterial routes in the 1730s–1750s. The first coach service between Limerick and Dublin was established in the 1750s, although as a summer service only. Local landlords sponsored a widespread turnpike system in the linen region of Ulster. A Road Act of 1765 allowed county grand juries to levy a charge per acre on all farming households for roads and bridges. It replaced the earlier requirement on every landholding to supply six days of free labour to mend roads in the parish, an unpopular demand that helped to lead to the formation of the Hearts of Oak, a movement of rural agitation, in mid- and south Ulster in 1763. The Act unlocked the resources of an increasingly prosperous society and led to a major expansion and improvement of the Irish rural road network. Further Acts followed in 1771–72, allowing Ulster parishes to raise an extra tax for roads, and permitting grand juries to raise funds to construct roads through unimproved regions. The Irish road system was, however, worse than that in Britain.

Turnpike roads were constructed by turnpike trusts authorised by Parliament to raise capital for such purposes and to charge travellers on the roads. Thus the road system came in part to reflect the degree of dynamism of individual trusts and the ability of particular routes to produce revenue, a consequence essentially of the strength of the regional economy and the role of the route in intra-regional communications. Parliament oversaw the system through renewal and amendment acts that reflected the strength of local interests.

The first Turnpike Trust was passed in 1663 and by 1770 there were 519 trusts covering 14,965 miles of road. The first section of the London–Norwich road was turnpiked under an act of 1696. Early trusts dealt largely with repairs rather than the construction of new roads. Many trusts, such as the Bath trust, founded in 1707, had considerable success in improving the situation. The Act of 1727 granting permission for the turnpiking of the Cirencester–Lechdale road, a crucial route by which cloth from Stroud moved towards London, noted that the road 'by reason of many heavy carriages frequently passing . . . [has] become very ruinous and deep, and in the winter season many parts thereof are so bad, that passengers cannot pass and repass without great danger'. The turnpike brought considerable improvement on that route, as, in 1785, did the Stroudwater canal. Although trusts reflected local initiatives, a national turnpike system was created. By 1750, for example, London and north-west England were well linked with the road to Chester and both roads to Manchester turnpiked for most of their length. By then three routes from Yorkshire to Manchester were also turnpiked, as were the routes from London to Bath, Canterbury and Portsmouth.

The 1750s and 1760s were decades of particular activity following two decades of limited progress. The first turnpike from Chichester was begun in 1749 and by 1779 the city was the junction of four turnpiked roads. The first Devon trust, the Exeter Trust, was established in 1753, and was rapidly followed by many others, leading to major improvements. Most roads between Norwich and rural Norfolk were turnpiked between 1760 and 1800. By 1770, when there were 24,000 kilometres (15,000 miles) of turnpike road in England, most of the country was within 20 kilometres (12.5 miles) of one. Even in remote Montgomeryshire in Wales, a turnpike trust was authorised in 1769 and the first turnpike was in use from the early 1770s, although the first trust in north-east Scotland was not formed until 1795. Toll gates, at which travellers paid, became a standard feature. Turnpikes were not just commercial ventures; the trusts were dominated by noblemen and the squirearchy and the turnpikes were seen as a form of social improvement.

Stone bridges were built, replacing wooden ones or ferries. Thus, in Cambridge the Great Bridge was rebuilt in stone in 1754. The Old Bath Bridge was rebuilt in 1754 and Pulteney Bridge added in the city between 1769 and 1774. A wide new three-arched bridge over the Avon was opened at Bristol in 1768. A stone bridge was built at Stockton between 1764 and 1768 replacing ferries and fording points and supplanting Yarm Bridge as the lowest bridging point on the Tees. In 1774 a new crossing was built over the Exe, replacing the ferry from Exmouth to Starcross and providing a bridge downstream of Exeter. The New Bridge, the second bridge across the Clyde in Glasgow, was built in the 1760s, a new bridge at Worcester in 1780 and the Skerton Bridge at Lancaster in 1788.

Better road links were used to transport both people and goods. It became easier to move between major centres. Travel was made faster by the cross-breeding of fast Arab horses, while further improvement came from the replacement of leather straps by steel coach springs and the introduction of elliptical springs. There were very important improvements in carrying services using the roads; the first regular Norwich–London coach service taking less than a day started in 1761 and by 1783 there were 25 departures a week from Norwich to London, as well as 2 departures of stage wagons. The same year about 150 places within 30 miles were visited at least once weekly by a carrier from Norwich. Birmingham similarly benefited from the convergence on it of improved communications: the Bromsgrove (1726), Hagley (1753) and Dudley (1760) turnpikes. Sheffield was very isolated before river and road improvements, especially the Don navigation scheme, completed in 1751, revolutionised access to existing and new markets. This was crucial to the development of new methods of steelmaking in Sheffield. By 1788 the Pickford family was sending a wagon from Manchester to London every day bar Sunday. Driving fast was a craze of the 1780s and 1790s.

Despite improvements, the road system still had many deficiencies. Jeremy Lister wrote from Gainsborough in December 1782, 'the roads are exceeding bad, the road towards Lincoln being the only one that is anything tolerable, and that in general is through very deep sand'.[1] It was not until the 1780s that John McAdam began experiments on improving road surfaces, by consolidating a layer of small, broken hard stone to form a very hard surface with a camber for drainage. McAdam did not publish his major works on the subject until 1819–20. Road accidents were frequent, particularly the overturning of coaches; many roads that were not turnpiked, for example those on the Isle of Man, remained inadequate.

The difficulties and cost of road transport helped to ensure that much was moved by sea or river. Water was particularly favourable for the movement of heavy or bulky goods for which road transport was inadequate and expensive. Thus cloth at the beginning of the century was generally taken from Stroud to London by Thames barge from Lechdale. It cost 33s 4d (£1.67 in modern currency) a ton to move goods by road from London to Reading in 1792, but only 10s [50p] by water.

However, the river system was not always helpful: many rivers were not navigable, transport was often only easy downstream, rivers did not always supply the necessary links, and many were obstructed by mills and weirs. Thus, the navigable rivers in the North Riding of Yorkshire, the Tees, Ouse and Derwent, were all on its boundaries, while the Swale, Esk and Rye were too swift, shallow or liable to flood for navigation. As a result lead from the western dales had to be moved overland to the Tees ports, an expensive process.

The canalisation of rivers and the construction of canals was the response to problems with the river system. It represented a determined human attempt to alter the environment and make it operate for the benefit of man. As with the turnpikes and again unlike elsewhere in Europe, private enterprise and finance were crucial. If the development of such a costly and inflexible transport system reflected the difficulties of moving bulky goods cheaply by road transport, it also increased the comparative economic advantage of particular regions or interests within them and was therefore actively supported.

Reasons for making the River Avon Navigable from Bristol to Bath, an undated flysheet, stated:

Bristol and Bath are situate in a rich soil, but surrounded by a mountainous country; so that land carriage is very chargeable and difficult, and therefore not only weighty, but light and bulky things are there carried on horseback, or on men's shoulders . . . the neighbouring counties of Gloucester, Wiltshire etc. find it more easy to bring goods fourscore miles from London, than twenty from Bristol. Whereas if this river be made navigable, it will open such a prospect for trade in all the adjacent counties . . . silence those who take advantage from their being locked in, and enclosed by rocks and mountains, for enhancing the prices of all necessaries.[2]

Thus geography was to be defied and a national market created. The River Avon Navigation was fully opened by 1727. Landlocked counties found their relative position transformed, particularly by canal building which was especially active in the 1770s and 1790s. In 1765 Wedgwood turned to James Brindley to link the Trent and the Mersey, and Brindley did this with the 'Grand Trunk' canal. The building of the Staffordshire and Worcestershire canal between 1766 and 1770 added a link to the Severn, so that Staffordshire's coal, iron and pottery could be readily transported to the major English cities. The first canal town, Stourport, was founded where the canal joined the Severn. Brindley had made his reputation planning the canal, completed in 1763, by which the Duke of Bridgewater could move coal from his Worsley mines to nearby Manchester. The Sankey Brook Navigation, completed in 1757, carried coal from St Helens to Liverpool and stimulated the development of coal-consuming industries on Merseyside and the expansion of Cheshire's salt industry, which depended on coal-fired salt pans. The Coventry Canal brought coal to Coventry from the 1780s; similarly the opening of the Monkland Canal in 1793 stimulated the development of the Lanarkshire coal market to serve the rapidly growing Glasgow market. In 1790 the Oxford Canal reached Oxford, creating the final link in a network joining the rivers Trent, Mersey and Thames. The first section of the canal designed to link the Leeds–Liverpool canal to Lancaster opened in 1797.

This sort of building feat was more impressive than the canalisation of rivers because it created completely new links. Canal construction also employed formidably large numbers. Canals were dug by hand by workers known as 'navigators'. Nevertheless, the improvement of rivers was important, especially until the 1750s, when canal construction really began. There were peaks of activity in the late 1690s and in 1719–21; the Aire and Calder navigation to Leeds and Halifax in 1699–1700 was a major step. Between the late seventeenth and the mid-eighteenth century the Yare was improved so as to be navigable for quite large ships between Yarmouth and Norwich, assisting Norfolk's grain exports and the movement of coal to Norwich. Work on the Mersey to improve navigation to Manchester began in 1724 and by 1734 sailing boats could make the journey. The River Douglas between Wigan and the sea was opened to navigation in 1742. The improvement of the Weaver navigation helped Cheshire's economic growth. In the 1750s a programme of works on the Shannon included the cutting of a canal that bypassed the obstacles to navigation in the main channel at Athlone. Through traffic was therefore made possible for the first time.

Canals were expensive and faced problems, not least preventing leaks and securing an adequate water supply. Due to financial problems the 38-mile Forth–Clyde canal, which had 39 locks, was begun in 1768 but not finished until 1790. The scheme to make the Swale navigable to Northallerton, with branches to Bedale and Thirsk, approved by Parliament in 1767, was never completed. Most goods and people in the British Isles continued to move by road. The canal network was sparse, somewhat fragmented and especially limited in Scotland, Wales and Ireland. Nevertheless, in the last, the Newry Navigation, linking Lough Neagh with the sea at Newry (1734–42), opened up links between mid-Ulster and Dublin, though it did not provide the hoped-for cheap Irish coal. In Ulster the Lagan Navigation, the Tyrone Navigation and the Strabane Canal were all completed by 1796, while the Grand (1756–1805) and Royal (1789–1817) canals linked Dublin to the Irish midlands.

Coastal trade was more important for these areas. Thus, Bristol received copper for smelting from Anglesey and Cornwall, China clay from Cornwall, and iron, coal and naval timber from the Forest of Dean. Port Penrhyn was developed by Richard Pennant, 1st Lord Penrhyn, who developed the systematic working of Snowdonia's slate after 1765. Slate was also dispatched via the ports of Bangor and Caernarvon, nearly 250 cargoes from the latter in 1793. The widespread improvement in docks and harbour facilities benefited domestic as well as international trade. An Act of Parliament of 1749 enabled the new Port Commission of Lancaster to develop St George's Quay (1750–55), and this was followed by a Custom House (1764) and the New Quay (1767). Mineral owners developed ports in order to ship Cumbrian coal: the Curwens at Workington and Harrington, the Senhouses at Maryport (founded 1749) and the Lowthers at Whitehaven. Milford Haven was developed to serve Pembrokeshire.

There was scant improvement in the condition of marine transport. It still remained heavily dependent on the weather. The seasonal variation of insurance rates reflected the vulnerability of wind-powered wooden ships, which had not yet reached their mid-nineteenth-century levels of design efficiency. Sea travel was very slow compared with what it was to become in the following century. However, it was the cheapest method for the movement of goods, and the sea brought together regions such as south-western Scotland and eastern Ireland, whose road links to their own hinterlands were poor. Inland towns might be most accessible via their nearest ports rather than by long-distance overland routes. The east coast, where Captain Cook acquired his nautical skills, was an important route, especially for the shipment of coal from Newcastle to London and intermediate ports. The Irish Sea also formed an economic zone held together by marine links based on major ports, such as Liverpool, Whitehaven, Lancaster, Milford Haven, Belfast, Dublin and Bristol, as well as now-forgotten or tiny ports, such as Parkgate in Wirral. Ireland's fuel shortage was met by coal from Cumbria and, to a lesser extent, Ayrshire.

Changes in transport were limited during the period, certainly compared to the following century. Exciting technical developments, such as railroads and the hot-air balloons of the 1780s, had scant immediate impact. Road construction usually followed existing routes and the balance between land and sea transport did not alter significantly. Turnpikes and canals were clearly of considerable importance in shrinking distance and developing intra-regional links. New and improved transport links required large amounts of capital and led to increased employment. Transport costs were reduced, thus helping to increase and extend consumption and markets. The increased speed and frequency of deliveries also improved the integration of production and consumption and furthered the development of the market; it became easier to dispatch salesmen, samples, catalogues, orders and replacements.

The British iron, pottery and textile industries benefited from cheaper transport costs and more reliable links than their French counterparts. Regional specialisation increased, because regions that could produce goods cheaply were now better able to compete in areas with higher-cost local production. This was crucial to economic development because division of labour was only effective with a high volume of production, and thus with a large market. Whereas Newcomen steam engines had been constructed on the site where they were to be used, Watt engines were built at a central site.

The improvement in the road system extended London's influence. The canals, though, did not centre on London. Instead, they particularly strengthened links between Lancashire, Yorkshire and the Midlands, thus, for example, encouraging the industries of the West Midlands to use Liverpool as a port rather than Bristol. Canals therefore both improved links between particular regions and sections of the economy and created or emphasised differences in access. In the British Isles as a whole, however, although Arthur Young's works suggest that even local roads were improving from the 1770s, much of the dense network of local routes changed little during the century, in quality, direction or use. Only levels of use increased.

Transport improvements were a cause of contention, the nature of which reflected the public and participatory nature of the British state. Thus Parliament had hearings over the merits of the Aire and Calder navigation scheme in 1698, petitions were presented and *Reasons* printed on both sides. In 1785 a committee was founded in Worcester to resist any parliamentary bill for tolls on the Severn. In 1789–90 the proposal for a bridge over the Ouse near Selby led to a general meeting at York, which feared it would affect its navigation, and to a request to the Duke of Leeds to oppose the measure.[3] The respective merits of schemes were widely canvassed in the press, public meetings and Parliament.

MONEY AND CREDIT

By European standards, the British Isles both constituted a relatively uniform economic system, especially as links between the English and Scottish economies developed, and had sophisticated capital markets. Scottish law differed from that in England and Wales, but within each country there were neither significant legal variations nor internal tariffs. The principal difference from most of Europe was the calendar. New Style dating, used by the bulk of Europe, was ten, and from 1700 eleven, days ahead of Old Style, and Britain switched only in 1752. Within Britain there were variations in standards: each region had its own variants of such customary measures as tons, chaldrons and bushels.

The Act of Union decreed that English standards of weights and measures were to be used throughout Britain, but Scottish weights and measures were in fact retained, and two bills introduced in 1765 to establish uniform weights and measures were not enacted. Within Scotland the old Scottish Trone weights, abolished in 1617 when Scottish Troy weights were made standard, were, nevertheless, still used. In parts of Scotland, such as the Hebrides, the standard weights and measures were not used. The Linlithgow boll, a unit for the dry measure of grain, abolished in 1696, remained the general measure but was variously defined. Within England there were different measures for stones, bushels and acres.

The Act of Union also provided for a uniform coinage, though Scottish currency remained in circulation until the nineteenth century. The British coinage was based on specie, although complications were created by a general shortage of specie which led to the circulation of coins from foreign countries. Portuguese gold and Spanish silver coins circulated in England. Spanish dollars, overstruck as worth 4s 9d, were common in Scotland in the second half of the century. There was a particular shortage of small copper coin, which encouraged the use of tokens.

The availability of bullion was reduced because of the need to finance negative trade balances, particularly with China and India. Bullion was also reduced through use in non-monetary forms and through the continuous loss of metal from coins due to processes such as wear, reminting and fraudulent clipping.

These shortages encouraged the use of paper money, and the eighteenth century witnessed the spread both of banking and of banknotes. However, the precarious nature of most banking firms and the vulnerability and short-term nature of most credit created difficulties. There was an exchange crisis between England and Scotland in the 1760s. The nature of trans-oceanic trade required long credit in precarious circumstances and this created many problems. Yet, by European standards, the British banking system was reasonably stable. The Bank of England, founded in 1694, operated successfully as a source of government credit and this helped to bring relative stability and growth to the banking system. As today, however, banks were prone to influence by political crisis. In 1745, during the Jacobite rising, the Bank of England only prevented a run on the pound by ordering clerks to work slowly. The French Revolutionary War led to a run on the banks in 1797. Progress in development in the provision and means of credit was not, however, bought without a cost in terms of periodic crises and instability. The dependence of the economy and confidence on credit helps to explain the severity of laws against fraud. The Bank of Scotland was founded in 1695, although, unlike the Bank of England, it did not lend money to the government. The Royal Bank of Scotland followed in 1727, as a second Scottish public bank. By mid-century there was a third public bank, the British Linen Bank, again Edinburgh-based, which began issuing notes in 1750 and specialised in credit for the linen industry, as well as nearly twenty important private banks in Edinburgh. Although there was in effect a British banking system for foreign exchange and general credit, the Scottish banking system was in general largely independent of that of England.

A variety of informal lending and notarial activities developed into a banking system with the emergence of distinct banking functions. Banking houses, single-unit partnerships with unlimited liability for their losses, developed in London and the provinces, especially in the second half of the century. The first bank in Norwich was opened in 1756, in Chichester in 1779 and in Lancaster in 1794. By the end of the century there were several hundred provincial banks, highly local in their operation, helping to keep the money supply buoyant and circulating, and to spread credit. An inter-regional credit structure based on London developed ensuring that local economies were very much linked to national financial developments and also thus to each other at the national level. The establishment of a bank clearing house in Lombard Street in London in 1775 led to a great improvement; banks were allowed to balance credits and withdrawals by a ticket system. The first Scottish provincial banking companies were established in Aberdeen (1747), Glasgow (1749, four founded by the mid-1760s), Dundee (1763), Ayr (1763),

Perth (1766) and Dumfries (1766). Banking also developed in Ireland. Banks were a part of increasingly complex commercial mechanisms, including growing insurance and stock markets. The 1690s saw a major expansion in the establishment of joint-stock companies, and the emergence of the stockjobber as a figure for criticism. This was taken further when the South Sea Bubble, a great speculation in trading opportunities, government finance and speculation itself, burst in 1720. The crash led to the Bubble Act, which limited the flotation of small joint-stock enterprises. In 1773 a group of brokers subscribed towards the acquisition of a building which became known as the Stock Exchange. London was emerging as the powerful financial centre of the world's leading commercial empire.

TRADE

The volume of British trade rose significantly. Britain became the major trans-oceanic trading nation, dominating the North Atlantic trade as well as becoming the leading trader to India and China. Average annual exports rose from £4.1 million in the 1660s to £6.9 (1720), £12.7 (1750), £14.3 (1770) and £18.9 (1790), during a period of only modest inflation. Imports rose from £6 million (1700) to £6.1 (1720), £7.8 (1750), £12.2 (1770) and £17.4 (1790). Trade helped to ensure that the British economy benefited from comparative advantages: thanks to imports, British industry was able to benefit from Baltic and North American timber, hemp and iron. More important than the numerical change was the diversification of markets and products. The relative importance both of woollen exports and of trade with nearby areas of Europe declined, while that of oceanic trade increased. Average annual exports to North America rose from £0.27 million in 1701–05 to over £2 million in 1786–90. Thanks in large part to the protective system created by the Navigation Acts, British-owned shipping tonnage grew appreciably: English shipping tonnage rose from 340,000 in 1686 to 421,000 (1751), 523,000 (1764), 608,000 (1775) and 752,000 (1786). The number of Glasgow's ships rose from 30 in the late 1680s to 70 by the 1730s. Lancaster's shipping tonnage rose from 1,000 tons in 1709 to 10,700 in 1792, with more regular foreign trading voyages from the 1730s. Britain's maritime and colonial triumphs over France and Spain, especially in the Seven Years War (1756–63) were seen to benefit the economy and led to a marked increase in national self-confidence. Britain was seen as an imperial trading power. The *Monitor* of 21 August 1762 sought to refute claims that Britain lacked the wealth to continue fighting: 'Great Britain only can boast of her own intrinsic wealth. She has never had so many ships at sea, nor greater quantities of merchandise in her warehouses. With these rises the value of her receipts of customs and of her manufactures. She sits in the midst of a mighty affluence of all the necessaries and conveniences of life. If our silver and gold diminish, our public credit continues unimpaired.' Trade encouraged industry, leading to the integration of numerous areas into a global economy. In his *Tour in Scotland, 1769* (1771), Thomas Pennant recorded of Kendal,

> The number of inhabitants is about seven thousand; chiefly engaged in manufactures of linsies, worsted stockings woven and knit, and a coarse sort of woollen cloth called cottons sent to Glasgow, and from thence to Virginia for the use of the Negroes. The carding and the frizing mills, the rasping and cutting of logwood by different machines are well worth seeing . . . the manufactures employ great quantities of wool from Scotland and Durham.

Ideas of free trade had little currency until the end of the century, Adam Smith's *Inquiry into the Nature and Causes of the Wealth of Nations* only appearing in 1776. Economic regulation promised government protectionism and this was further encouraged by the notion that the volume of trade was essentially constant, so that an increase in that of one power would necessarily lead to a reduction elsewhere, and by the weakness of currency mechanisms which led to a stress on bullion and therefore on a favourable balance of trade that would maintain bullion inflows. The government sought to create a protected home market and to encourage a positive balance of trade in manufactured products. The export of raw materials such as raw wool and thus sheep, was prohibited, as was that of textile machinery and the emigration of artisans. Manufactured imports were restricted or prohibited, for example silks and printed calicoes in 1700 and all manufactured silks and velvets in 1766, a great advantage to the British silk industry. The 1721 ban on the wearing of imported printed fabrics, passed in order to protect native manufactures of wool and silk stuffs from the competition of Indian calicoes imported by the East India Company, instead stimulated the growth of a British cotton industry.

The Irish and colonial economies were regulated and restricted in order to make them assist, not rival, that of Britain. The Cattle Acts of 1666–67 hit Irish exports, until suspended in 1758–59, giving the Scots a relative advantage in English markets. Irish trade was dominated by the British market, which absorbed about 75 per cent of Irish exports by late century, but the terms of this trade were set in London, leading to pressure for free trade, as in 1779. Irish exports of wool or woollen textiles to foreign and colonial markets were banned in 1699, although the percentage of Irish exports going to the New World colonies, as a percentage of total Irish exports, rose from about 6 per cent in 1698 to nearly 20 per cent in 1784. Nevertheless, most of this trade depended on English intermediaries and Irish expatriates, especially in London. Irish exports rose from £1.25 million in 1770 to £4.8 million in 1790. The *Bristol Journal* of 27 January 1750 reported, 'We are assured, that the Master and Company of Soap Makers in this city, have received a very favourable answer from . . . [the] Governor of Jamaica, to a remonstrance which the said company sent over to his Excellency, complaining of the illicit trade of exporting soap and candles from Ireland to the said island'. Irish manufacturing was increasingly affected by British exports as its largely domestic and quasi-domestic structure was unable to compete with cheaper and better-finished goods produced by new methods. The Irish silk industry collapsed between 1775 and 1783.

Trade also entailed competition with foreign powers. For example the history of the Hudson's Bay Company, founded in 1670 and granted monopoly rights to fur-trading in northern Canada, illustrates the influence of war. Sporadic hostilities with the French between 1683 and 1713 led to no dividend being paid between 1690 and 1718. Awarded to Britain at the Peace of Utrecht (1713), the Company's bases competed with those of French Canada. Until about 1730 competition was noticeable only at the bottom of the bay, but in the 1730s and 1740s the French established a line of posts across the river routes to the bay. In response to this and to domestic criticism, the British company adopted a more energetic attitude to exploration and expansion after 1750 and began constructing posts away from the bay.

The Hudson's Bay Company also provided an example of the primarily

commercial interests of a privileged company concerned to maintain and develop its privileges and profits. This led to criticism of its effectiveness in upholding national interests in the face of French competition and of its lack of interest in expanding into the interior, criticism that led to a parliamentary enquiry in 1749 and to an unsuccessful attempt by London merchants in 1752 to obtain trading privileges in Labrador. Other privileged companies, such as the Royal Africa Company, faced similar criticism. Their monopolies aroused anger in those excluded from their benefits, principally the merchants of secondary ports. Some critics argued that these companies were too concerned with their profits to risk them by expansion, either by increasing the volume of trade and thus lowering prices, or by adding to their overseas territorial interests and thus increasing costs. However, most British trade was not controlled by such companies.

The rising importance of trade entailed the greater significance of merchants and mercantile lobbies. It led to a new geography of Britain, one in which proximity to the Atlantic was most important. Initially, this benefited Bristol, especially after some of the regulatory framework that had maintained London's control over certain trades was dismantled. The freeing of the African trade from the control of the Royal Africa Company in 1698 legalised the position of interlopers. This helped Bristol merchants develop the triangular trade in which they took goods to West Africa and used them to purchase slaves who were then taken to the West Indies and North America. In 1725 Bristol ships carried about 17,000 slaves and between 1727 and 1769 thirty-nine slavers were built there. Bristol's mercantile standing and prosperity were reflected in the New Exchange of 1743 designed by the great architect of elegant gentility in Bath, John Wood the Elder. By 1750 it had replaced Norwich as the second most populous city in England.

However, although the volume of Bristol's shipping rose, its importance declined. The city's trade was hit by the War of American Independence, especially as it was more exposed to French privateers than its principal rivals, Liverpool and Glasgow. Glasgow's outport, Newport, later named Port Glasgow, developed from 1668. Glasgow increasingly dominated the import of tobacco and Liverpool the slave, American and Newfoundland trades. By 1752 Liverpool had 88 slavers, with a combined capacity of over 25,000 slaves. Liverpool also had better port facilities, especially a wet dock, the only one outside London. The Old Dock was followed by the Salthouse Dock (1753), George's (1771), Duke's (1773) and King's (1788). Bristol suffered from congestion in the city docks, an absence of industry in the hinterland,

The Properties of Benjamin Lester and Company, Trinity, Newfoundland, artist unknown, *c.* 1800. Benjamin Lester was a Trinity firm that from its warehouses, stores and wharves controlled much of the Newfoundland fish trade. Much of the fish was dried on flakes (drying platforms). Trinity had been developed by merchants from Poole in England between 1713 and 1760, and in 1801 most of those of English origin living there were from Dorset or nearby. The firms in Trinity collected cod from the outharbours for shipment overseas and distributed food, clothing and fishing equipment and provided credit in return.

entrepreneurial failure in the tobacco and slave trades and an over-specialisation in the profitable sugar trade. Bristol's trade was not linked to export industries that would probably have given a greater boost to industrial and demographic growth in the city and its hinterland, and as a result foreign and domestic demand were not linked effectively.

Inland towns that lacked good communication links were particularly poorly placed to benefit from the growth in foreign trade and some stagnated badly, for example Athlone and Hereford. Even inland river ports, such as Gloucester, could not compete with sea ports. Trade also interacted with changing domestic demand, especially the growth in consumption of goods designed to stimulate: groceries such as sugar, caffeine drinks – tea, coffee and chocolate – and tobacco. This was very much consumerism: none of these goods was 'necessary'.

Thus foreign trade was a crucial aspect of what has been termed the 'consumer revolution'. Indeed, critics of aspects of the commercial culture of the period frequently insisted upon the enervating effects of luxury, the emphasis upon consumption rather than conduct. The demand for imports interacted with the development of shops and provided the latter with crucial profit margins. The development of a retail infrastructure transformed the nature both of the domestic market and of townscapes. New covered markets were constructed in many towns. Bristol gained a new Market-House in 1745 and St James's market in 1776, Gloucester the Eastgate market in 1768, Lancaster the Shambles in 1774. Advertising reflected and sustained a pattern of changing retail patterns. Trade directories provided information. From 1755 lists of Dublin merchants and traders were published annually in *Wilson's Dublin Directory*; the first Birmingham directory appeared in 1767. Advertising was crucial for the press. The network of agents, who took in advertisements for individual newspapers, became more dense and comprehensive as the century progressed. Whereas in 1764 the *Chelmsford Chronicle* had six agents outside Chelmsford (as well as one London agent), the paper listed six London agents and another twenty outside Chelmsford in 1792.

There were more material goods, a rising demand for all types of goods, and a slowly changing material fabric of life. This was most obvious in the cities, where the ownership of new goods was more frequent, but was not restricted to them; itinerant retailers took goods throughout the British Isles. The probate inventories of the Warwickshire village of Stoneleigh indicate that around 1700 goods appeared there which were produced for mass distribution: Ticknall ware for the dairy and tin dripping pans for the hearth. The cotton fabrics imported by the East India Company were both attractive and could be used to provide for a mass market, the styles otherwise restricted to more expensive silks and brocades. Throughout the country, people consumed more medicaments, a process encouraged by longer average life-spans, for accumulation and expenditure both rose with life expectancy.

The pattern of improved communications and better commercial facilities was not restricted to England. In Ireland there were relatively few new markets in the first half of the century, but in the second half 200 market centres were granted patents so that little of Ireland was more than twenty kilometres from a market area. The number of fairs also increased. Hitherto remote areas, such as much of West Mayo, were, for the first time, provided with markets and roads. In County Tipperary there were market-houses in Fethard by 1712, Carrick by 1726, Tipperary (1737), Thurles (1743), Clonmel and Nenagh. Although average real wages were roughly stationary in England between 1760 and 1790, the rapid rise in population ensured that total demand rose; while in Scotland, where the rate of population growth was less than that in England and Ireland, average real wages themselves rose.

Trade and the related spread and intensity of the money economy in the British Isles could be seen as transforming the national character, and led to criticism. The radical writer, William Godwin, claimed in 1805, 'I saw that the public character of England . . . was gone. I perceived that we were grown a commercial and arithmetical nations . . . Contractors, directors, and upstarts, – men fattened on the vitals of their fellow-citizens – have taken the place which was once filled by the Wentworths, the Seldens, and the Pyms.'[4] Crime reflected the spread of the money economy. In 1784 Charles Price, nicknamed Old Patch, was able to circulate £200,000 in forged notes. He used high quality paper and inks and maintained three houses (and wives) to escape detection. The game trade, though illegal under the Game Laws, flourished in the second half of the century as game that had been poached reached urban markets, especially London, in increasing quantities, in part through the

Peasants Going to Market by Thomas Gainsborough. Much of the British Isles was within a day's journey of a market, and these markets acted as crucial foci for the local economy and for local society. Goods were traded, animals sold, servants hired, opinions exchanged. The markets acted as a link between localities and the wider world, a link where the influence of landlord and parson was less direct than in the parish.

developing network of coach services. Poaching, in part, turned from a craft into a business. The spread in tea and brandy consumption from the social elite to the middling orders encouraged and was facilitated by the development of large-scale smuggling, especially, by mid-century, in tea. Merchant capital financed much of the smuggling. Profit was also made from the struggle against crime. Thief-takers were paid a bounty while sites near the London gallows at Tyburn were let out to spectators.

Public agitation, and sometimes violence, frequently focused on food shortages and prices that, in part, reflected the subordination of local, to the exigencies of national, markets, and, in part, hostility to the role of middlemen. In 1740, after rain at harvest-time in 1739, the severe 1739 winter and then three months' drought, grain grew scarce and prices rose. The poor in the north-east of England suffered and some were convinced that large amounts of grain were being hoarded by Newcastle merchants in order to force up prices. On 19 June, about 300–400 marched and demanded cheap grain, and even though the merchants agreed to sell it for what it cost them and produced invoices to prove it (prodded by the Corporation), they broke into granaries, took much and paraded round the streets 'huzzaing and blowing horns, and were most of them well armed with cudgels'. On 26 June workmen several thousand strong took over much of the town, until intimidated by troops.[5] At Stockton the shipping of grain was blocked until the County Durham MPs settled the agitation by arranging for the grain to be purchased for sale to the poor at prices they could afford. In County Durham there were also seizures of wheat from farmers and demands of grain from merchants at lower prices than they were asking for it.

To suggest that the situation was one both of change and continuity, innovation and conservatism, is to draw attention to the variety in economic activity and regional fortune that characterised the British Isles. There are major problems both in measuring activity and in assessing how far change was feasible. The former posed difficulties for contemporaries, as it has done for modern scholars. In part there was only a limited consciousness of the value of statistics; in part the surviving figures are incomplete and pose as many problems as they solve. There was no national census until 1801, and information on land ownership and agricultural productivity was limited.

A CHANGING ECONOMY?

As with accounts of eighteenth-century politics and society, so with the economy, assessments depend on the basis for analysis. A theme of growing economic activity, specialisation and sophistication and of industrialisation, that might appear appropriate for much of England and the Scottish lowlands seems less well grounded if Highland Britain and Ireland are also to be considered. Much of Ireland's economy remained basically pre-industrial and many economic transactions took place outside the market context. However, as it was drawn more fully into the market economy, its agricultural sector experienced growing diversification and commercialisation and agricultural prices and rents rose substantially in the second half of the century, for example in County Wexford, where a malting barley economy developed, largely supplying the Dublin market. In County Tipperary there was a major expansion in cereal cultivation from the 1760s, reflecting and encouraging a more capitalised agriculture and leading to the spread of flour mills. More productive English strains of cattle, sheep and pigs were introduced into Ireland in the second half of the century. Textile production developed markedly there, while communications improved with the turn-piking of roads.

If the regional dimension is to be stressed, then it is clear that the industrialising regions of Britain were at the forefront of the process of economic change within the British Isles, and that a major discontinuity had occurred in a number of regions. On the other hand, the emphasis can be placed on the socio-politico-economic fundamentals of trade rather than manufacturing as crucial to the rise of the British economy between 1650 and 1850. A relatively stable political system, legal conventions that were favourable to the free utilisation of capital, especially secure property and contracting rights, a social system that could accommodate the consequences of economic change and an increasing degree of integration and interdependence, were all fundamental factors. Belief in the stability of political and economic arrangements encouraged the long-term investment that was crucial in many spheres, including transport. Taxes on manufacturing industry and transport were low or non-existent.

Greater national integration can be seen in the rise of Post Office revenues from £116,000 in 1698 to £210,000 in 1755 as new routes were founded – for example Exeter to Chester via Bristol from 1700 – or became more frequent, as the London to Bristol and Birmingham services were in the 1740s. London to Lancaster mail coach services began in 1786. Arthur Young claimed that better communications led to greater uniformity of prices; 'Make but a turn-pike road and all the cheapness vanishes at once', and indeed riots in the Bristol area against turnpikes between 1727 and 1749 stemmed from concern that food prices would rise.[6] A letter in the *Newcastle Journal* of 19 July 1740 referred to 'London (which place governs the value of all grain in England) . . . all the markets in England have a natural dependence on each other, and expect a mutual assistance'.

The national distribution of London newspapers depended on the mail service, initially horse-mail and then the mail-coach. Developments within existing infrastructures, improvements in the road system and in the provision of Post Office services, ensured that distribution by the traditional methods became more rapid and reliable. The first number of the *Newark Herald and Nottinghamshire and Lincolnshire General Advertiser* (5 October 1791) was keen to assert its national range and local circulation, clearly offering itself as an intermediary between nation and locality: 'Being published early in the morning, it will be dispatched by the South Mail of that day, to London, and all the intermediate market towns; and by the North Mail, and by-posts, at two o'clock, it will be forwarded to' a number of key cities, including Newcastle, Hull, Leeds, York, Liverpool and Birmingham. In addition, 'in the following villages in the counties of Nottingham and Lincoln, it will be regularly published every Wednesday, free of expense, by distributors employed for that purpose; and any orders given to them will be punctually executed'. Ninety-five places were listed. The provincial press had to be regional, not local, for commercial reasons. The *Salisbury and Winchester Journal and General Advertiser of Wilts, Hants, Dorset and Somerset* named agents in fifty-eight towns besides London in its issue of 23 February 1789.

The apparently transforming, or at least enabling, character of new communications was captured by George Colman in an essay published in the *St James's Chronicle* of 6 August 1761. He described past travel:

like the caravan over the deserts of Arabia, with every disagreeable circumstance of tediousness and inconvenience. But now, the amendment of the roads, with the many other improvements of travelling, have in a manner opened a new communication between the several parts of our island . . . stage-coaches, machines, flys, and post-chaises are ready to transport passengers to and fro between the metropolis and the most distant parts of the kingdom . . . the manners, fashions, amusements, vices, and follies of the metropolis, now make their way to the remotest corners of the land . . . The effects of this easy communication, have almost daily grown more and more visible. The several great cities, and we might add many poor country towns, seem to be universally inspired with an ambition of becoming the little Londons of the part of the kingdom wherein they are situated: the notions of splendour, luxury, and amusement, that prevail in town, are eagerly adopted; the various changes of the fashion exactly copied; and the whole manner of life studiously imitated . . . every male and female wishes to think and speak, to eat and drink, and dress, and live, after the manner of people of quality in London.

4 SOCIETY

Social relationships and attitudes reflected a clear cultural inheritance and a prevalent economic and technological environment. The Judaeo-Christian inheritance, clearly enunciated in the laws and teachings of the churches, decreed monogamy, prohibited marriage between close kin, stipulated procreation as a purpose of matrimony while condemning it outside, denounced abortion, infanticide, homosexuality and bestiality, made divorce very difficult, enforced care of children, venerated age and ordered respect for authority, religious and secular, legal and law-enforcing. The economy was technologically unsophisticated and much of it was agrarian. Economic productivity was low, there was little substitute for manual labour and the value accrued through most labour was limited; most of the population neither controlled nor produced much wealth and the principal means of acquisition was by inheritance. It is not surprising that the dominant ethos was patriarchal, hierarchical, conservative, religious and male-dominated.

WOMEN AND FAMILIES

It would be difficult to guess from many textbooks that women made up half the population; indeed that before the later eighteenth century the gender balance in the population was weighted towards women. They are often not deemed worthy of mention and seldom appear in indexes. It might be suggested that as they faced ecological challenges similar to those of men, any additional consideration is superfluous. However, women's biological role brought specific problems, while their treatment by society differed from that of men. The women working long hours carrying coal to the surface from pits faced gruelling labour and debilitating diseases identical to those of the men at their sides, but they were also in a society that awarded control and respect to men, and left little independent role for female merit or achievement. The economy of the poor was such that employment was the essential condition for most women. The arduous nature of most of the work, and the confining implications of family and social life, together defined the existence of the vast majority of women.

The basic unit of society was emerging as the nuclear family, a married couple and their generally non-adult children, although many couples lived together without getting married. Individual family structure was of course not constant. Birth, ageing and death ensured that the life-cycle of families was continually changing. It was necessary to adapt in order to survive periods when the family altered to include dependants, young children and invalid adults. As these groups consumed without working, they posed a challenge to the economy of individual families, just as they created formidable problems for society in general, and many other functions like education. The responsibilities of social welfare were left to families, communities, and private and religious charity. There was also the question of safety in a violent or lawless society: an isolated individual could be in a vulnerable position. Individual families coped with the problem of feeding children by defining childhood so that it included employment as far as possible and in so far as it was necessary. Many agricultural and industrial tasks, such as tending live-stock, were undertaken by children. Publicists approved of child labour, arguing that it prevented idleness and begging, educated children to useful employment and accustomed them to work. Most families, however, needed no such encouragement; their problem was to find employment for the children and to feed them until they were able to work.

The employment of as many family members as possible was essential not only to its well-being, but also to its very existence as a unit. The limited social welfare of the period offered little to families; parents who could not cope left children to foundling hospitals which were established from mid-century. Similarly, unmarried mothers turned sometimes to abortion and infanticide, both treated as crimes, and the former hazardous to health. The women, often very young, who were punished as a result of these desperate acts suffered from the generally limited and primitive nature of contraceptive practices, as did those exhausted from frequent childbirth. That unwanted children were not only an economic liability, but also, when born to unmarried mothers, the source of often severe social disadvantages, moral condemnation and legal penalties, made the situation worse. In a society where women sought mar-riage as a source of precarious stability, the marital prospects of unmarried mothers were low, with the significant exception of widows with children of a first marriage, particularly if they possessed some property. As a result unmarried mothers frequently became prostitutes or were treated as such.

Thus social and economic pressures helped to drive women towards matri-mony and also towards employment, whether they were unmarried or married. Employment in agriculture and textiles was very important, though by the end of the period female agricultural service was declining significantly in the south and east of England. Visiting Teignmouth in 1773, Fanny Burney recorded her surprise at the 'barbarous' fisherwomen who had the exhausting task of tending the nets while their men were away fishing.

A common form of work for unmarried women, as for unmarried men, was domestic service. In a society where household tasks were arduous and manual, the technological contribution minimal, service was the life of many. At least 12,000 female domestic servants were probably employed in the four largest Scottish towns in the late seventeenth century: possibly 10 per cent of the 16–25-year-old women in Scotland. Jobs such as the disposal of human excreta were unpleasant. Water-carrying, generally a female task, could cause physical distortion. Cleaning and drying clothes involved a lot of effort: the dirt had to be trampled or scrubbed out and early mangles required much muscle-power. Many servants were immigrants from rural areas and generally not members of collective groups and, lacking guilds, they were largely at the mercy of their employers. It was possible to gain promotion in the hierarchy of service, but in general domestic service was unskilled and not a career. Wages were poor and pay was largely in kind, which made life very hard for those who wished to marry and leave service, for married servants were relatively uncommon. For girls saving for a dowry, domestic service was far from easy, and they were often sexually vulnerable to their masters. The last was a central theme in two important early novels, Samuel Richardson's *Pamela* (1740) and, in this case a male servant pursued by a female employer, Henry Fielding's *Joseph Andrews* (1742). The notorious Colonel Francis Charteris was convicted of raping Ann Bond, a servant, in 1729, only to be pardoned by George II. Service was not only domestic, though that was the area in which female labour was most important. Agricultural servants were also vital. Generally living with their employers, they gave many nuclear families the quality, in part, of an extended family. The need for both men and women to go into service, and also the need for servants, varied geographically, seasonally and socially, and the contradictory needs produced difficulties, such as dismissals and migration in search of employment, producing a labour market filled with uncertainties. Servants, labourers and women could not aspire to the 'independence' so valued by the political theorists.

Another important source of female employment for both married and unmarried women was domestic manufacturing. Clothing was the biggest, though not the sole, form of employment in this area. Spinning-wheels featured frequently in British household inventories. Domestic manufacture could be a crucial contribution to family income, especially in areas where agriculture was poor and in households that had limited agricultural resources; either the women formed part of a family in which all members worked in domestic manufacturing or they supplemented income derived from other activities. As the value added by their work and that of children was generally greater than that derived from comparable labour in the fields, women and children generally made a greater contribution to family incomes if they engaged in domestic manufacturing. However, their opportunities were limited by the restricted nature of market-oriented domestic manufacture in many areas, and, to a lesser extent from the second half of the century, especially the 1790s, by the growth of factory-type employment which, by taking the worker out of the home, made it difficult to care for children. Particularly if combined with a move in the location of manufacturing, this change could destroy the basis of the family economy and lessened the chances of married women obtaining remunerative labour. It has been suggested that these economic changes had social consequences, including a rise in marital separation. Nevertheless, in some spheres job opportunities for women improved. In the north of England, for example, the production of women's outer garments was increasingly handled by local mantua-makers.

The most striking aspect of the female contribution to the labour force was its variety. Although women had only a small role in the churches, save as

Methodist preachers and in charitable works, and none in the armed forces, they were found in most spheres of employment, including those involving arduous physical labour. Thus women were employed as coal-heavers, taking coal to the surface, and as fish- and salt-carriers, and many worked in agriculture. Much reflected the expediency economy of the poor, and female opportunities were limited by the nature of the economy as well as the particular problems and restrictions that affected women. Literacy rates were lower for women in England, Ireland, Scotland and Wales; a result of the limited attention devoted to their education. Women were generally given the worse-paid jobs. In many industries, such as glove-making, women were given the less skilled jobs or their employment was defined as less skilled and therefore lower paid. In Scotland female wages in agriculture in 1791 were only 33 per cent of male wages, and there were also major differences in manufacturing wages: women's wages rose in the second half of the century, though at a far slower rate than men's. The majority of the poor were women. That was certainly true of lists of resident parish poor in Scotland and reflected the impact of widowhood, spinsterhood, unwanted pregnancy and differential job opportunities.

Nevertheless, not all women were confined to poor jobs and a tiny minority had interesting careers, some benefiting from the expansion of the commercial economy. Caroline Herschel was an astronomer, though very much her brother's assistant; the Swiss-born painter Angelica Kauffmann was one of the founding members of the Royal Academy in 1768; Sarah Siddons was the leading tragic actress on the London stage from 1782 until 1811; Catharine Macaulay was an active political pamphleteer who, in her pamphlets and her initially successful *History of England* (1763–83), advanced a radical Whig agenda of parliamentary and constitutional reform, the extension of the franchise and annual Parliaments. She applauded the execution of Charles I, criticised the Glorious Revolution for failing to be revolutionary and always refused to retire with the ladies after dinner. Women played an important role in the debating societies that developed in London from the late 1770s, although less so in enlightened societies in Scotland. There was also involvement in less 'genteel' activities. On 5 September 1759 *Lloyd's Evening Post* reported: 'On Monday night was fought at Stoke-Newington [London], one of the most obstinate and bloody battles between four noted bruisers [boxers], two of each sex; the odds, before the battle began were two to one on the male side; but they fought with such courage and obstinacy, that at length the battle was decided in favour of the female.'

Women were of great importance as consumers, and the need to satisfy their demands and fashions comprised a major aspect of the consumer revolution. This was also true, more generally, of their role. Rather than being subordinate agents, women played an important part in influencing developments. For example, the major shift from women-only midwifery to a situation by the 1770s in which increasing numbers of children were being delivered by male midwives reflected the choices of mothers, not the imposition of male structures of control.

Women played only a minimal role in politics, apart from those prominent because of their royal position such as William III's wife and co-ruler Mary II (1689–94), Queen Anne (1702–14), and the wives of George II and George III, Queens Caroline and Charlotte, and others influential because of their spouses or connections, such as Sarah, Duchess of Marlborough. She became influential as Groom of the Stole to Princess Anne and a Duchess as wife to John, Duke of Marlborough, and was left the effective head of the family on his death. Sarah was obsessed with politics, committed to the Whig cause and intelligent. Unusually for the period, Sarah was allowed by her husband to manage her dowry and retain her salaries from court posts, and she died the wealthiest woman in the country. Yet she wrote, 'I am confident I should have been the greatest hero that ever was known in the Parliament House, if I had been so happy as to have been a man.'

There were no women in Parliament, although some played a role in the management of parliamentary constituencies. Women also acted as political hostesses. The image of justice might be female but its formulators and executors were all male; there were no women judges, JPs or councillors. The use of the household as the basis for social organisation stressed the role of men, who were regarded as heads of households when they were present. The legal rights of women were limited, not least their rights to own and dispose of property. Legal devices circumvented common-law rules of inheritance that would otherwise have left more land inherited or held by women. Yet it would be mistaken to imagine that women lacked political consciousness. Women frequently participated in riots. This may have reflected the crucial role that women played in the purchasing of foodstuffs and the sense that women would receive more lenient punishments than men, but it may also argue for a degree of female political awareness. If this took the form primarily of hostile responses to changes in the price or availability of foodstuffs that were believed to be unfair, that was the politics of the poor in general.

Poverty was an experience to which women were particularly vulnerable. This was different from that of men for a number of reasons, particularly the responsibility of women, both unmarried and married, for children. It was women who were commonly held responsible for the birth of illegitimate children, while married men had a greater propensity than their spouses to abandon their families.

Seduced girls often had recourse to prostitution. The absence of an effective social welfare system and the low wages paid to most women ensured that prostitution, either full- or part-time, was the fate of many. Prostitution was seen as a threat to morals, both male and female, as well as to health and to population growth. The diseased prostitute, her hair and teeth lost in often fatal mercury treatments, was a victim of the socio-economic and cultural circumstances of the period. Her fate was more grisly than that of married women caught in adultery, and their circumstances were judged to be morally different by the community, but the situation was essentially the same. An economic system that bore down hard on most of the population, irrespective of gender, was nevertheless linked to a social system in which the position of women, whether relatively fortunate or unfortunate, was generally worse than that of men. The breakdown of marriage and desertion by the spouse frequently featured in accounts of women vagrants.

It has been argued that the period witnessed the rise of a pattern of family life that placed more weight on the wishes of individual members and in which affection rather than discipline, emotion rather than patriarchalism, bonded families together. This shift has been explained in part by demographic changes: an increase in the life expectancy of children and women encouraging a greater degree of emotional commitment. These changes have in turn been linked to a range of developments, including the rise of

distinctive fashions and the toy industry for children, the literary cult of the sentimental family and new pedagogic fashions that placed greater weight on the individuality of children and the need to socialise them without treating them as embodiments of original sin.

These suggestions have produced a debate that is complicated by the fact that the overwhelming majority of the population did not keep journals, leave correspondence or feature in any detail in relevant social records, other than in legal actions where their opinions were generally represented in the terms used by those who controlled justice. Furthermore, it is far from clear how one assesses, let alone measures, affection and changes in it. It is important not to mistake changes in style, such as modes of address within the family, for changes in substance. If marital experiences and expectations were related to economic circumstances, then it is difficult to see much reason for major change. In addition, recent work on sixteenth- and seventeenth-century family life has revealed that many of the suppositions supporting the ideas of subsequent periods as different were actually false. The idea that romantic love as a reason for and aspect of marriage was an eighteenth-century invention, whether a consequence of modernisation or not, has been rejected, as has the notion that children were brutally treated until then as a matter of course. Rather it seems clear that in the eighteenth century, as earlier, parents of all social and religious groups loved their children and that, in bringing them up, they saw the need to teach them basic skills, but regarded this correctly as for the benefit of children as much as parents. This was particularly the case when children were to follow the occupations of their parents, a tendency that limited education and opportunities, and inheritance practices made desirable. The degree to which families lived together in close proximity led to a need for co-operation and mutual tolerance that necessarily affected the nature of patriarchal authority. The inculcation of deference, discipline and piety by authoritarian parents was not incompatible with affection. The tension between individual preferences and social pressures was scarcely new.

It has been argued that male attitudes to women softened and became more sympathetic to female feelings in the period as a crucial part of the process by which more 'polite' and genteel social norms were encouraged. The good manners implied by the term 'gentleman' were thus redefined. Yet any stress on this politeness and on restraint in behaviour and attitudes has to address the question as to how far it was deliberately inculcated in order to cope with a very different way of life and expression. Vulgarities in private correspondence can illuminate the aspiration towards politeness that was a keystone of various public discourses in the period. A self-image of politeness might be understood as a cultural artefact, a socio-ideological aspiration designed to foster particular ends of moral improvement, Christian purpose and social order. Such a conclusion is also suggested by the contrast between the stress on sobriety and restraint and what is known about drinking levels in the period. Politeness can also be seen as stemming from the life and concerns of a large portion of the population, especially via Nonconformity and Methodism. The Reformation of Manners movements of the 1700s and 1710s and the 1780s were, in part, a response to the anxieties which coarse behaviour induced in religious and evangelical circles.

Eighteenth-century culture was highly ambiguous and descriptions of it in terms of 'a polite society' are insufficient. Politeness was part of the century's self-image, but a coarseness of utterance and indeed of thought was equally

Facing page: Catherine Macaulay (1731–91) by or after Mason Chamberlain. Catherine Macaulay was an active political pamphleteer who, in her pamphlets and her initially successful *History of England* (1763–83), advanced a radical Whig agenda of parliamentary and constitutional reform, the extension of the franchise and annual Parliaments. She applauded the execution of Charles I, criticised the Glorious Revolution for failing to be revolutionary, and always refused to 'retire with the ladies' after dinner. Her second marriage to a much younger man in 1778 led to much ridicule and abuse.

part of its image. Frequent campaigns against swearing, lewdness and profanity and the insistence on sabbath observance were of a piece with sexually explicit and forthright language.

Some of the private correspondence of the period offers a point of access to male attitudes towards male sexuality, at least in fashionable society. The casual attitude of many writers, their matter-of-fact acceptance of such problems as debt and venereal disease, is readily apparent. Many of the individuals concerned were, or were to be, prominent: 'Rigby is unfortunately clapt by Molly Henley and has unadvisedly employed Mr. Carey the surgeon to take off his inflammation', noted Thomas Winnington, MP, the Paymaster General, of Richard Rigby (1722–88) in 1744. Rigby was also to be an MP and Paymaster General. The following year, Charles Wyndham wrote of a fellow MP, Richard Edgcumbe, who was to rise to be a Lord of the Admiralty, Controller of the Household and a Lord Lieutenant, 'He did lately call at Olivers but finding no pensionaires he was obliged to bugger an externo [?] and has told all the particulars of the action in very publick companies.' Henry Fox, MP, Secretary at War, revealed his attitude to unmarried masculine sexuality five years later when he wrote to his 19-year-old nephew Harry Digby, later an MP, peer and Lord of the Admiralty, 'what signifys at your age whether a woman is handsome or ugly? Whenever you can, whomever you can, with safety; let that be your maxim'.

Another perspective was provided by Henry Harris's account of Mary, Dowager Lady Savile's attitude to her son, Sir George (1726–84). Lady Savile had herself separated from her husband in 1735, following her affair with William Levinz, MP, who in 1742 eloped with the wife of another MP, Soame

Matrimonial Fisticuffs attributed both to Paul Sandby (1725–1809) and to the engraver Hubert Gravelot (1699–1773). Notions of politeness, restraint, respect and deference, though important in the period, provide only a partial guide to conduct. Sandby was an important watercolour painter and engraver who was active in the Royal Academy and pioneered topographical art in Britain. Favoured by George III, Sandby became chief drawing-master at the Royal Military Academy at Woolwich. Born in Nottingham, he spent most of his adult life in London. Gravelot was a leading figure in the introduction of Rococo themes into Britain.

Jenyns. Sir George, who never married, was to be MP for Yorkshire, one of the most prestigious seats in the country, from 1759 until 1783, a prominent Rockinghamite Whig, and a supporter of conciliation towards America, the Yorkshire Association and parliamentary reform. He has a splendid funerary monument in York Minster. In July 1750 Harris reported from London,

> We have here a young, sucking Knight of the Bath, upon whom the fame of this curious taste will stick more closely. A very sober, demure, bible-faced spark he is – never misses the sacrament, and being well white-washed from all sin, last Whit-Sunday, he began a new score in a stable yard with the waiter at Mount's Coffee-House – his good mother, a most religious lady, is now wringing her hands, and bemoaning herself, that she kept so strict a hand upon him at home, and rather than he should have given way to such abominable, impure burnings, she now wishes he had fucked every Abigail about her, and had been indulged with the refreshing breeze of all the well twirled mops in her family.

Three months later, Harris added,

> Lady Savile has taken her young twig of Sodom into the country, and, by way of weaning him from that unnatural vice, takes great pains to coker him with every Abigail in her house, and all the milk maid cunts in the neighbourhood.[1]

The previous year there was an instructive exchange between Major Thomas Gage (1721–87), second son of Thomas, 1st Viscount Gage, and subsequently Commander-in-Chief in America at the time of the outbreak of the War of American Independence, and Captain Charles Hotham (1729–94),

Flying a Kite by Francis Hayman (1708–76). Hayman captured the world of children in such scenes from contemporary life, a series of which he produced in about 1741 to ornament the supper boxes at the London pleasure gardens at Vauxhall. Hayman also designed illustrations for books, was a portraitist, produced a set of historical works focusing on British history including *Caractacus* and *The Conversion of the Britons to Christianity*, and was one of the founders of the Royal Academy.

subsequently an MP and later a Major-General. Although Hotham's correspondence was quoted at length in A. M. W. Stirling's *The Hothams* (1918), there was no reference to either of the following letters. The first, undated but endorsed as answered on 12 June 1749, was sent from Dublin by Gage:

> I am glad Mr Slap Bang is so well and has got into such good Business; my compliments to him and desire he would send me Recommendations to some of his Female Acquaintances in this part of the World; where Slap Banging is on a very bad footing: the consequences of it, are either the small sword through your body, marriage, or clap, as I think the last the least evil of the three, my small dealings have been with the Ladys of that Order, tho' by the help of a Cuirasse, I have hitherto comme off unwounded.

On 19 August 1749, Gage wrote again from the family seat of Firle in Sussex,

> I have been in Sussex only about four or five days; tho' I made all possible haste to leave London; which was grown most intolerably stupid and dull. The only way I could devise to divert myself, was with a wench, who has obligingly given me a pretty play-thing to divert me in the country, in bestowing a most generous clap upon me, I call it generous, from its copious flowings; which I am endeavouring with the assistance of injections, and purgations to put a stop to . . . One Tomkyns a surgeon in London, advertises, to have medicines sent him by one Monsieur Daran, surgeon to the French King for the cure of Gleets, pray make enquiries after Monsr. Daran and his nostrum.[2]

Another instance of the suppression of material deemed obscene is provided by the diary of John Thomlinson. This manuscript diary is in the British Library and contains the thoughts of a young cleric in his search for a wife and living: he hoped to succeed his uncle as rector of Rothbury, but wanted a rich wife to fall back on. Thomlinson kept his diary intermittently from 1717 to 1721. Extracts from Thomlinson's diary were published by John Crawford Hodgson in *Six North Country Diaries* (1910). Hodgson referred to Thomlinson as 'sordid and . . . shameless', and his edition removed all the passages which contained anything of a vulgar nature.[3] Some of the missing entries are as follows:

> 3 March 1717 Sir John Brownlow's Lady[4] abused other women with her clitoris etc. . . . Dan. Burgess one rainy day complained in the pulpit of the absence of the ladies, saying they were afraid of spoiling their fine clothes etc. and so indulged themselves in bed – he wished he was with them, he would fuck them into devotion.
>
> 8 April 1718 I had tryed one woman and did not like her. I was to try another shortly for some overtures had been made etc., and if I found her answer the description etc. I intended to attack her very briskly and reduce her by storm etc.
>
> 13 December 1721 . . .Cousin Clarke said that Mr. Repington was clap'd and yet he lies with Sarah etc.
>
> 24 December 1721 . . . Arthur Grey condemned for burglary – his plea was that he got in drink and had a mind to see if Mr. Burnet [the Bishop's son][5] was not in bed with her, and he knew he would use him roughly if he was there and therefore he took pistol – it was proved by all the servants that he often stayed till morn and then one of the servants was called to let him out. She is niece to the Duke of Atholl.

Thomlinson's diary entries are often extracts from the letters he wrote to his brother, so they are part of that shared view of male sexuality seen in the correspondence already cited. They are also part of the 'news traffic' that passed between London and the North Country, and which seems to have been such a vital (in both senses) form of communication in the early eighteenth century. There was clearly a tension between the desire to entertain and communicate with one's family, and the wish to be perceived as polite and dignified. In Thomlinson's case this was overlaid by his status as a cleric, though he avoided this problem by framing the gossip as reports of other men's conversation. The tension suggests that eighteenth-century men may not have 'internalised' the politeness that they apparently valued in public, though this may also have reflected class divisions. Possibly this presaged the public morality and private vice of the Victorians and in part reflected the political situation which required the Tories to assume a veneer of support for the Hanoverians and the Whigs to overstate the stability and prosperity of Whig-governed Hanoverian Britain. If politeness and gentility, or at least a discourse of their value, are seen in the eighteenth century as 'middle-class' virtues and the discourse as characteristic of 'middle-class' writers, then eighteenth-century public restraint can be seen as evidence of the emergence of values which define the 'middle class' and of their greater importance within society. There are also ideas of moral and social superiority implicit in the attitudes to the objects of vulgarities. It is as dangerous to assume that politeness was simply a show as to assume that it was genuine. If politeness was a public act, that tells us something about changes in society that such a show was thought necessary.

Although even many of the more rakish members of the aristocracy accepted the new modes of behaviour, the use of a vulgar discourse can in some cases be understood in terms of a conscious rejection of 'middle-class morality' and more specifically of the moral authority of members of the elite. This can be seen in the 1713 tract *Terrae Filius*, an attack on the authorities of the University of Oxford. The tract questioned the paternity of the child of Dr Bernard Gardiner, Warden of All Souls and Vice-Chancellor, and printed a poem attributed to his 'nag', Mr. Ball:

'Since I' said Bag 'your nag have been
Han't I gone through both thick and thin;
F - - - d handsome, ugly, rich and poor,
Did I e're fail these twenty years
Except of Mr. Fulk's stairs?'

This intended tract was suppressed and burned on Gardiner's orders, but its author, John Willes, had it printed in London and it had a fairly wide circulation. Willes (1685–1761), later an MP (1724–37), Attorney General (1734–37) and Lord Chief Justice of Common Pleas (1737–61), was a notorious womaniser. Similarly, the obscene attacks on George I as a cuckold had a specific target.

Most obscene correspondence had no political target. Instead, it reflected the relaxed if not exuberant attitude towards male sexuality clearly felt within at least an appreciable portion of male society. Much focused on the celebration of priapic power, as with a letter of the polished 4th Earl of Chesterfield's that is not in the published edition of his correspondence. In 1728 he wrote to a fellow aristocrat-diplomat:

. . . your private pleasure; does that manly vigour and that noble contempt of danger, still continue? I am informed it distinguish'd itself at Paris; I hope it does so at Vienna too. As I know that both your rammer and balls are made for a

German *calibre*, you may certainly attack with infinite success, and I know your fortitude too well to suppose that you will decline the combat, let the danger be ever so great. So I expect some account of your performances. As for mine they are not worth reciting; you know I never was a great hero; and in this place[6] there are few provocations for courage, and the coldness of the enemy, even damps one's bravery; the warmest thing I have met with here between a pair of legs has been a stove; and they have not liked what I put in the place of it, half so well.[7]

The recipient, James, Lord, and later 1st Earl, Waldegrave, a widower, was a prominent womaniser, the 'King of the Belles', according to Thomas Robinson, his successor at Vienna. Among contemporary British diplomats, the Earl of Essex, Ambassador at Turin, shared Waldegrave's tastes, whilst Brigadier Richard Sutton, Envoy Extraordinary in Hesse-Cassel had an interest in laundry-maids, and Abraham Stanyan, Ambassador in Constantinople, was described by his successor, the Earl of Kinnoull, as a 'complaisant gentleman of an indolent temper . . . whose life here these twelve years past, as I am informed, has been upon a sofa with the women'.[8]

Before by William Hogarth, 1730–31. The clothes of the would-be-seducer reflect the extent to which showy garments were widely worn. The woman's clothes fall to the ground and her skirts are full.

A sense of male sexual confidence, if not self-satisfaction, reached its peak in an ode Sir Charles Hanbury Williams wrote in 1743 to Henry Fiennes-Clinton, 9th Earl of Lincoln (1720–94). This began:

> Oh! Lincoln Joy of Womankind
> To thee this humble Ode's design'd
> Let Cunt inspire the Song
> Gods! with what Powr's art thou indue'd

and included such lines as

> Tis Fucking now my Pen employs
>   [. . .]
> Prick and the man I'll sing
>   [. . .]
> Four times each Night some amorous Fair
> He swives, throughout the circling year.
>   [. . .]
> His Prick that always stands

After by William Hogarth, 1730–31. Moral disorder expressed through dishevelment. The multilayered dress reveals bare thighs above the knee-length stockings. The absence of elegance in the scene drives home a moral lesson.

That never baulks him with Delays
Its willing Lord alone obeys
And all the Fair commands
       [. . .]
With Whores be Lewd, with Whigs be hearty
And both in Fucking and in Party
Confess this Noble Race.[9]

This phallocentric approach was not untypical: the male approach to sexuality at least as evinced in private correspondence was clearly priapic. Men displayed their masculinity and virility by sexual conquests. This was the world of Sir Francis Dashwood's salacious club at Medmenham and of the obscene *Essay on Woman* (1763) attributed to John Wilkes. Far from this world being on the edge of political society, it looked to the court for a lead. Frederick, Prince of Wales, who shared a mistress with Lords Harrington and Hervey, the Duke of Cumberland and George III's sons were all, albeit to varying degrees, leaders of society. In 1717 George I felt able to use the standard pun of mounting women and horses when 'Mr de Johnston' presented his wife. George told him that if he 'connoissoit aussi bien en cheveaux qu'en femmes il ne pourroit manquer d'etre bien monté'.[10] Such remarks were more than an isolated counterbalance to 'polite' discourse: they were heard in off-the-record conversations as casually and often as the discourse of politeness might have been heard on formal occasions.

An explicit sexuality was hardly remote from a society in which large quantities of self-education sex literature was printed, while prostitution was also very important. The potentially explicit nature of the latter is suggested by the decorated titles of explicit sexual positions probably from a brothel or gentleman's club discovered following a fire at the Cheshire Cheese pub in London in 1962. One depicts a woman lying on the ground holding a rope that passes over a pulley and controls a wickerwork cradle in which a seated man is apparently being lowered on to his consort's waiting dildo. The private sexual language discussed here accords with the caricatures of the period as well as with its erotica. Thomas Rowlandson produced a series of explicit sketches designed for private circulation. An important homosexual 'subculture' also existed with its own vocabulary, dress-codes, rituals and geography. Many homosexuals were also husbands and fathers.

The humour in the eighteenth-century British press was often cruel: excremental jokes or verses directed against cuckolds were commonplace. Clearly they reflected popular interest. It is difficult to accept that only the idle wished to read the account of kissing in *Mist's Weekly Journal* of 24 July 1725, while the elopements and sexual scandals of the great were covered in great degree, helped by the often lurid nature of adultery cases in the House of Lords. The discovery of an admiral's wife in a Charing Cross brothel in 1771 was as good copy as Lady Abergavenny's adultery in 1729 and the Countess of Eglinton's in 1788. Robert Trevor wrote from London in 1729, 'Private persons have not escaped the notice and censures of our licentious press; nor can even the grave bury poor Lady Abergavenny's shame, every sillable of whose name, and every particular of whose life are hawked about the streets as articulately as old cloaths etc.'[11] The Abergavenny case can be held to illustrate double standards. Richard Liddell, who was caught in adultery with Lady Abergavenny by her husband, left the country in order to avoid paying the £10,000 damages awarded to the husband, but in 1741 he was returned to

Parliament and in 1745 became Secretary to the new Lord Lieutenant of Ireland, Chesterfield, and also became an Irish Privy Councillor.

The press was generally facetious on sexual matters. A correspondent of the *Reading Mercury* attacked women who wore cork round-abouts complaining that 'cork rumped devils' were harder to play with. The perils of provincial culture were brought home to a woman who had been to see a performance of the Shakespeare Jubilee Ode in Leominster when she came home to find her husband embracing their servant, an episode that helped to provide an amusing tale.[12] The often earthy nature of newspaper reports can be seen in an item in the *London Mercury* of 11 February 1721:

A certain Last-maker in Butcherhall-Lane being resolved to divert himself after a new Method, ran into the Sign of the Three Birds, and call'd for the Landlady, who immediately attending, he call'd her a Bitch and fell a laughing. The Woman, surpriz'd to know his meaning, stood mute, while Dick persisted in his Tone, calling her Bitch, and Bitch of Bitches, and as she kept such a House, ought to stand the Censure of her customers; the Woman, who was infinitely above the sawcy Language of his scandalous Tongue, resenting his ill Manners by calling him Rascal. Dick to prove to the contrary before 40 People, pulls down his Breeches to stand Search. The Gentlewoman of the House absconded with great Confusion; but a lusty Butcher Woman broiling her Supper, having more Courage than the former, she swore she would try the Event, and Catches fast hold by his Trickstaff with a pair of Stake Tongs with which she was turning her Meat, and shook him while he roar'd out like a Bull, and ran away as fast as he came, and hath been seen no more. The Woman swore she believ'd he was a Rascal by her manner of feeling; but whether she be a competent judge I cannot well determine.

An account of an eighteenth-century bedroom farce can be found in *Old England*, a London weekly paper, in its issue of 17 March 1753:

A few Days since, there happened a merry Affair at a certain Town in Buckinghamshire, not ten Miles from Windsor: A Barge [*sic*] of that Place being gone to London for some time, but returned Home sooner by three or four Days than he was expected by his Wife (who was formerly a Servant to a Gentleman of that Place) it was late when he came Home, and his Wife was gone to Bed, but soon let him in, and he went to Bed in the dark; soon after he was in Bed, his Wife complained of a violent Fit of the Cholick, and desired he would get some Gin: Accordingly the Man dressed himself and went to a Publick House in the Neighbourood and bought some, and gave the Landlady, as he thought a Shilling to change; the Woman told him it was a Guinea; he said it was not, for that he was worth only one Shilling in the World; but examining the Breeches, he found a Guinea and a Half more, and a Silver Watch: On his Return, he asked his Wife, how the Breeches came on the Bed, she told him a Gentleman had sent them to her to mend, which the good man believed and contentedly went to Bed; in the mean Time a Person made his Escape from under the Bed with the Loss of his Breeches, which occasions great mirth at all the Tea-Tables in that Neighbourhood.

Private and public sexual language also throws light on eighteenth-century medical opinion with its emphasis on the value of sex in accordance with natural drives and on the determination to present exemplary literature, as in Addison's essay warning about the dangers of 'obscene passions' in the *Spectator* of 13 June 1711; although his account of the sexual tempting of an immobilised gallant may also have had a titillating effect. Male observations of female sexuality were frequent. To give one recently-deposited archival reference that refers to a very notorious woman: in 1742 Lieutenant-Colonel

Decorated tiles of explicit sexual positions probably from a brothel or gentleman's club were discovered following a fire at the Cheshire Cheese pub in London in 1962. There were numerous prostitutes in London, but they and their patrons often suffered painfully from venereal disease. Thomas Steavens (*c*. 1728–59) noted: 'I was indiscreet enough to desire the enjoyment of Miss Sally Clerk, a young lady who sells oranges at Drury Lane Playhouse; and she cruel enough to consent to it, in short an unnatural flame on my side, and a still more unnatural one on hers had made such a bonfire of my body that I was obliged to apply to' mercury.

Charles Russell wrote to his wife from Ghent: 'The greatest Beauty we have here has followed us from England, which is Lady Vane who arrived here last Monday Night and in reality has follow'd the Brigade of Guards . . . walks about every Evening with an Officer on each side of her.'[13]

The extent to which there were changing meanings and styles for masculinity and femininity in eighteenth-century Britain is unclear. By European standards, British social conventions were not rigid. The Comte de Gisors was surprised, when visiting England in the 1750s, to find young women of quality paying visits alone without loss of reputation, but the French ambassador told him that it was the English habit to trust daughters to do this.[14] The emotional position of many women was difficult. The portrayal of marriage to a callous husband as imprisonment offered in Thomas Southerne's play *The Wives' Excuse* (1691) was not fanciful: Mrs Friendall, the perceptive and

Decorated tile from the Cheshire Cheese. The 4th Earl of Chesterfield wrote of his illegitimate son, Philip Stanhope, being put by a woman 'upon his haunches, by putting him frequently upon her own. Nothing dresses a young fellow more than having been between such pillars, with an experienced mistress of that kind of manège [riding]'. In spite of the actions of the Society for the Reformation of Manners, which initiated thousands of prosecutions, London was a hotbed of prostitution in the eighteenth century.

wronged protagonist, declared: 'But I am married. Only pity me', and later spoke of the 'hard condition of a woman's fate'. Prior to 1750 the majority of actions for divorce brought in the London Consistory Court were brought by women against their husbands for cruelty. After *c.* 1750 the notion of romantic marriage and domestic harmony came to prevail among the prosperous and the practice of divorce for incompatibility arose. Nevertheless, the custody of any children was generally invested in the father and divorced women generally lost touch with them.

The idea of equality was increasingly approved of, but the general notion of equality was one of respect for separate functions and development, and the definition of the distinctive nature of the ideal female condition was one that, by modern standards, certainly did not entail equality. Women, but not men, were expected to be virgins when they married and chaste thereafter. When in

1779 Parliament discussed the 'more effectual discouragement of adultery', it was of course an all-male body. Charles James Fox attacked the Adultery Bill 'on the doctrine of non-representation . . . the ladies totally unrepresented'. In English law men could divorce their wives if they were unfaithful, but women lacked recriprocal rights. In her *Vindication of the Rights of Woman* (1792), Mary Wollstonecraft pressed for equality in education and legal rights in order to give women a proper role and status. To a certain extent, however, such arguments were meaningless for most women. Their circumstances were generally bleak, because of their economic condition and the nature of medical knowledge and attention: Wollstonecraft died in childbirth in 1797 at the age of 38. It was to be subsequent changes in the last two factors that improved the position of most women.

THE ORDERS OF SOCIETY

The weight of the past was never more apparent in the eighteenth century than in the distribution of wealth, status and power. The influences that affected this distribution were similar to those of the previous century and there was little change in the methods by which the social position of individuals was determined or could be altered, although there was also considerable diversity of views about the nature of hierarchy in the eighteenth century. Furthermore, certainly in comparison with the following two centuries, the rate of social change was relatively slow, although that does not imply that there was little social change across the century.

Status and power were linked to wealth although not identical with it. Attempts were made to ensure that only those with a certain amount of land could become Justices of the Peace. A London report in the *Newcastle Courant* of 17 April 1742 that such provisions would be extended to lawyers serving as Commissioners of the Land Tax ended 'An excellent resolution'. The ownership of a significant amount of land was no longer an indication of noble rank, even though the (non-aristocratic) gentry enjoyed considerable social status. The very existence of social distinctions was seen as obvious, as arising from the natural inequality of talents and energies, and egalitarianism found favour with few writers on social topics. Social control by the elite was a fact, not an issue, in politics. Heredity and stability were regarded as intertwined. Snobbery was common. In 1744 John Phillipson, MP lost his seat on the Admiralty Board because the new First Lord, the Duke of Bedford, regarded him as a former clerk who lacked sufficient 'quality'. Though the son of a Wakefield linen-draper, John Potter, Archbishop of Canterbury from 1737 to 1747, disinherited his son for marrying a domestic servant. The desire to preserve family status and wealth in part lay behind Hardwicke's Marriage Act of 1753 which increased the power of parents, by outlawing clandestine marriages in England, though not Scotland. Twenty-four years later Robert Nugent attacked the Act in the Commons as 'tending to prevent an union of willing hearts, and to hinder young girls from giving their hands to such hearty young men as they could like and love, in order that miserly parents might couple youth with age, beauty with deformity, health with disease'.

Social differentiation was reflected in a range of activities and spheres, such as sport. Although there was elite participation in popular recreations such as bull-baiting, horse-racing, cock-fighting and fishing, hunting was restricted by the Game Laws. In addition, keeping horses was expensive. The seating arrangement in churches and the treatment of the dying and their corpses,

Facing page:
Eighteenth-Century Britain

Westminster Bridge under Construction, by Richard Wilson, 1744. Looking downstream from near Westminster Stairs, Wilson's painting shows the bridge as nearly complete on the Westminster side, but not on the Surrey side. On the left St Stephen's Chapel, then used as the House of Commons, and Westminster Hall are both visible. Barge-houses and timber-yards are to be seen on the Surrey side. The well-dressed couple in the foreground descending the stairs may have intended to cross by ferry to Vauxhall Gardens. The river is shown as full of traffic, and its muddy banks at low tide are also a scene of activity. Begun in 1739, Westminster Bridge was finished in 1750; it challenged both London Bridge, hitherto the only bridge in the London area, and the passenger traffic by ferry.

The Mad House from *The Rake's Progress*, *c.* 1733–35, by William Hogarth.
The Rake's Progress was a morally exemplary series of paintings that
achieved considerable popularity as engravings. The rake ended up
insane, presumably a consequence of his contracting syphilis. The
treatment of the insane was generally callous and they were often
treated as a form of curiosity: people paid to view them at Bedlam, here
shown, as it indeed was, overcrowded and with barred doors and
windows.

Penelope, 2nd Viscountess Ligonier by Thomas Gainsborough. Penelope, eldest daughter of George Pitt, Earl Rivers, was married to the second Viscount Ligonier. She had an affair with the Italian poet Count Alfieri and the two men fought a duel in Hyde Park in 1771. Ligonier obtained a divorce that year and in 1784 his former wife married an army trooper.

View of Dinas Bran from Llangollen by the Welsh painter Richard Wilson (1714–82), showing the Williams-Wynn estate, with earlier earthworks on the hill. The Williams-Wynns controlled rural Denbighshire: after Sir Watkin won the county seat in 1742 it was uncontested for decades. Best known for his Italian landscapes, generally of Classical themes, Wilson also painted Welsh and English scenes, such as *Snowdon*, as well as country seats, such as Houghton, Syon and Tabley.

also reflected social status and differences. Similarly, the provision of health both reflected and sustained social distinctions. Wealthy subscribers recommended poor dependants for admittance to infirmaries. Patterns and practices of crime and punishment, credit and debt also reflected social distinctions. Although the hanging of Earl Ferrers for murder in 1760 was cited as evidence of the universality of the law, it was rare for members of the elite to suffer execution or imprisonment unless involved in treason, while aristocratic debtors similarly escaped the imprisonment for debt that was a frequent consequence of the role of credit in society. The impact of social differences was clear at the hiring fairs where employers scrutinised the men and women who sought employment. Religion offered a degree of contrast, because the churches remained a career open to the talent of the humbly born, as was demonstrated by several bishops of the Church of England. Nevertheless, connections and patronage generally worked to the benefit of the well-born, and clerics from a gentry background received a disproportionately high share of the good livings.

The Wedding of Stephen Beckingham and Mary Cox by William Hogarth,
1729. A formal wedding portrait. It is possible that the figure on the left
standing slightly apart, represents the dead mother of the bride, which
would account for the funerary tablet behind her. Although the wedding
took place in St Benet's, St Paul's Wharf, the painting is based on the
recently completed interior of St Martin-in-the-Fields. The
Beckinghams were Kent county gentry with a tradition of going into the
law, and the painting was first recorded at their country seat at Bourne
Place, Kent.

If it is difficult to measure, there is none the less little doubt of the existence of tensions in eighteenth-century society. A degree of it underlay criticism of the social elite in the 1720s and 1730s for supporting foreign cultural movements and fashions, such as Italian opera and French cuisine. Fears of sexual corruption can be detected, as in 1779 when Robert Henley Ongley, a very wealthy London merchant, MP for Bedfordshire and ennobled in the Irish peerage as Lord Ongley, told the Commons that 'the French had contributed not a little to the increase of divorces, by the introduction of their petit maitres, fiddlers and dancing masters, who had been allowed to teach our wives and misses to allemande, and to twist and turn them about at their pleasure'. Great social and cultural value was placed on 'gentility', but it could be presented and interpreted in different ways.

In 1760–62, at a time when the Seven Years War was posing very heavy financial demands, the London press argued that the major burden of taxation should be borne by the rich, rather than the industrious poor, and that taxes should ideally fall on luxuries or the less useful elements in society, such as bachelors, dogs, footmen and public amusements, and not on the necessities of life or the useful and industrious. There was also social tension in rural areas. The Game Act of 1671, which made hunting the exclusive privilege of the landed gentry in England and Wales, was matched by legislation in Scotland in 1621 and 1685 and in Ireland in 1698 and 1763. Poaching was a form of resistance that was crucial to the livelihood of many. The game laws were widely seen as unfair, while the gentry viewed challenges to them as theft and as threats to the preservation of the social order. In the late 1770s game preserves were first protected by spring guns and mantraps. The nature of hunting was also affected by the reorganisation of rural space and control encapsulated in the enclosure movement. In the 1750s there was a serious dispute in Orkney as the 14th Earl of Morton was accused of illegally raising rents and a number of duties. Evictions as land was 'cleared' of much of the tenantry with the introduction of large-scale sheep farming and substantial rent rises led to tension between landowners and tenants in the Scottish Highlands in the second half of the century. The landowners increasingly acted as landlords rather than chieftains.

In England enclosures could lead to a violent response and it would be wrong to suggest that farmworkers were necessarily deferential or uninterested in politics. However, it would be misleading to suggest either that there was widespread criticism of the existence of a hereditary hierarchical society or that tensions were only apparent between as distinct from within social groups. Economic development and wealth can be seen as solvents of traditional notions of social organisation and behaviour, but this should not be exaggerated. Though satirised in figures such as Sir Novelty Fashion in Colley Cibber's play *Love's Last Shift* (1696) and Lord Foppington in Vanbrugh's play *The Relapse* (1696), fashions and opinions were shaped by the elite, became important and successful if it adopted them, and thus were emulated by other groups.

Educational access and provision reflected social power and assumptions. Because so many children worked, their access to formal education was limited. Education in England had to be paid for by the pupil's family, which was generally the case in grammar schools, mostly sixteenth-century foundations, or by a benefactor, dead or alive. It was not supported by taxation. The Society for Promoting Christian Knowledge, established in 1698,

The Porten Family by Gawen Hamilton, *c.* 1736. A grandiose setting for a
family scene. The gentleman is James Porten, a London merchant of
Huguenot origins; next to him is his only son, Stanier, who held minor
diplomatic postings at Naples, Madrid and Paris before becoming
Under-Secretary of State, Keeper of the State Papers and a
Commissioner of the Customs. One of the three daughters was the
mother of the historian Edward Gibbon. Britain's imperial position is
reflected in the tea being drunk and in the black boy in the foreground
trying to rescue a letter from a dog. Hamilton (*c.* 1697–1737) was a
Scottish painter of conversation pieces who moved to London in the
1730s.

81

Waistcoat. Sleeved English waistcoat made in Spitalfields, London in 1749. The silk was designed by Anna Maria Garthwaite (1690–1763) and woven by Peter Lekeux (1716–68). This rich blue silk with a figured effect in extended tabby, brocaded in three types of silver and with coloured silks was made for a man: the waistcoat was woven to shape, the adjustment for the wearer being made at the back by his tailor. The upper part of the sleeves, which would not normally show, were made from high-quality glazed worsted; the use of metal thread gave the waistcoat a sparkle. Garthwaite, the well-educated daughter of a Lincolnshire parson who came to London in about 1730, was one of the leading mid-century silk designers. She produced and sold an average of eighty designs a year, relying on a contrast between bright coloured floral motifs and a textured pattern in the ground, and from 1742 based her designs on flowers of correct botanical size and shape.

encouraged the foundation of charity schools. Girls and the rural population had fewer educational opportunities than boys and town-dwellers. In 1778 only about 5 per cent of the children in Cheshire were attending school. The elite also devoted more attention to boys than girls. Many of the former were sent to boarding schools, especially Eton and Westminster. From there those who wanted could move on, without difficulty, to the only universities in England and Wales: Oxford and Cambridge. Most of the elite did not bother to take degrees; they were generally taken by students who hoped to follow a career as clergymen.

In Scotland there was a stronger tradition of obligation to provide education. After the Reformation schools and universities in Scotland came under the control of local authorities, and under an Act of 1696 heritors (landowners) were supposed to build a school in each parish, half the cost of which they could recoup from their tenants. By the end of the century many parishes in the Lowlands had both school and schoolmaster, funded by fees and by landowners. Many heritors, however, did not build schools, for example in Galloway and the Highlands, so that educational provision and access partly depended on the presence of charity or Society in Scotland for Propagating Christian Knowledge (SSPCK) schools. Established in 1709 in order to found charity schools in the Highlands, the SSPCK had opened 176 schools by 1758. Free education was available to only a small minority of Scottish schoolchildren. In Ireland the absence of a system of parochial schools for the native population ensured that education did not serve to anglicise the people nor to convert them to Protestantism.

THE SOCIAL ELITE

It is not surprising that power and wealth were concentrated. The hierarchical nature of society and of the dominant political systems, the predominantly agrarian nature of the economy, the generally slow rate of change in social and economic affairs, the unwillingness of governments composed of the social elite to challenge fundamentally the interests of their social group or to govern without their co-operation, and the inegalitarian assumptions of the period, all combined to ensure that the concentration of power and wealth remained reasonably constant. The old order was under little threat from popular protest.

Across Europe those who enjoyed power and wealth tended to be noble by birth or creation. In Britain, however, it was the major landowners who constituted the most appropriate point of comparison with the continental nobilities, although special privileges (and relatively few of these) were attached only to the peerage. The small size and relatively closed nature of the peerage helps to make nobility too narrow a specification for any analysis of the English elite. At the beginning of 1710 there were only 167 male peers, the comparable figures for 1750 and 1780 being 187 and 189, and the many creations of the 1780s took the number up to only 220 in 1790. Of the 229 peers created during the century, only 23, 11 of whom were lawyers, had had no previous connections with the peerage. The inheritance of noble status by the eldest son alone was an important limiting factor. Other children were not released destitute into the world, but the combination of primogeniture and the restriction of noble status was largely responsible for the relative absence of poor nobility in Britain, and particularly England. There were, however, poor gentry, while in Scotland there were both significant numbers of poor nobility and gentry, and a higher percentage of the nobility and gentry were poor, a situation that conformed more to the position on the Continent than that in England. Yet the growth in employment in the armed forces, the bureaucracy, law and medicine can be seen as opening up major opportunities to the British gentry, at least to those who were conforming Protestant, and in helping to provide the social context of stability. Large estates rarely came on to the market and it was comparatively difficult to accumulate enough land to create a new one. This also ensured a measure of stability.

All adult, male, non-Catholic English peers were members of the House of Lords. The parliamentary representation of the Scottish peerage, however, was limited to sixteen, chosen by an election among them after the parliamentary union with England of 1707. Twelve years later the Peerage Bill sought to change this to 25 nobles who were to inherit the position at the same time as the size of the English nobility was to be fixed. The measure was defeated, not least because of the heavy representation in the House of Commons of gentry who aspired to ennoblement. This bill, the last attempt to alter dramatically the membership of the House of Lords for the rest of the century, was a British variant on the standard agenda of monarchical politics: it had been designed by the current ministry to limit the options of the heir to the throne, the future George II, who was bitterly opposed to his father's ministers. The absence of serious tension between nobility and gentry was an important feature of British society, a crucial aspect of stability. They formed a homogeneous group that intermarried and socialised together. Central government was dominated by this elite, as was local government; command of the latter reflected their supremacy in local society. Thus, Justices of the Peace (JPs) were the crucial figures in local government and law and order, and by law it was impossible to be a JP unless one held a certain amount of property. The gentry were also, as commissioners, the crucial figures in the local allocation of the Land Tax, a tax paid by all landowners including British peers, unlike the considerable tax immunities of much of the Continental nobility. Their role did not arouse the criticism encountered by the despised professional Collectors of the Excise. The gentry could use their resources and the law to harm other groups. Thus Sir George Downing, a Suffolk landowner and MP for Dunwich (c. 1685–1749), used his wealth to buy most of Dunwich, took a lease of the right to collect taxes for the Crown there, had the freemen who could not pay imprisoned for debt and allowed his tenants to fall into debt while requiring them to enter into bonds on the understanding that they would support him at elections. Most of the landed elite, however, preferred to gain their ends in a more consensual fashion and managed their localities in a more reciprocal manner.

There were moments of tension between nobility and gentry. The proposal that the government pay for the volunteer regiments that the nobility were raising and officering to resist the Jacobites in 1745 led to criticism in the House of Commons 'that it was a dangerous thing to give the nobility such an opportunity of influence in the country as might in time be fatal to the commons of England and destroy that proper balance between the two Estates in which our greatest security and happiness consisted'.[15] The Berkshire by-election of 1776 led to claims that wealthy peers were trying to override the gentry, charges that were raised on other occasions.

Such episodes were unusual and an absence of contention was far more

Prospectus Civitatis TAODUNI ab Oriente. The Prospect of y͂ Town of DUNDEE fromy͂ East.

39.

common. In other words, the principal institutional divide within the elite did not operate as a political fault line; nor did it reflect political or social division. The same was the case with relations between Crown and elite, court and Parliament: there were no rifts comparable to those that had occurred in recent centuries. The links between the magnates and the professional middling orders in Scotland were particularly long-term.

The nobility had great influence in many areas, although that was in part a matter of local circumstances. Thus in Wales the nobles were less numerous and important than in Northamptonshire. In Gloucestershire in 1783 the Duke of Beaufort 'and Lord Berkeley settled the peace of the country . . . by mutually agreeing' each to nominate one MP.[16] The dominance of both centre and localities by the landed elite was expressed by enclosure acts. In order to facilitate a reorganisation of the rural landscape that enhanced the control and profits of landlords, 1,532 enclosure Acts were passed between 1760 and 1797. The extent to which there was a peasantry with a proprietary interest in the soil was thereby reduced. Freehold tenure became more important and other 'rights' over land were downgraded. This loss of security of tenure, which characterised much of England and Lowland Scotland, increased uncertainty, not least by dislocating the senses of place and identity for many who worked on the land. This was taken furthest where settlements were moved, as when the medieval village of Nuneham Courtenay and its church were destroyed to make way for Earl Harcourt's new park in 1759. The village at Shugborough was moved by 1770 to accommodate Thomas Anson's building plans. The radical

The Prospect of the Town of Dundee from the East by John Slezer, showing, in the foreground, women washing and beating cloth. A German, who in 1671 became Chief Engineer for Scotland, Slezer was made a burgess of Dundee in 1678. Slezer travelled widely, making drawings of the major sights. In 1693 he was granted by Queen Mary a royal licence to publish a book of the views that he had recorded. Called *Theatrum Scotiae*, this was the first systematic pictorial record of Scotland, although the cost of producing it bankrupted Slezer.

Newcastle bookseller Thomas Spence wrote in 1800, 'Are not our legislators all landlords? . . . It is childish to expect ever to see small farms again, or ever to see anything else than the utmost screwing and grinding of the poor, till you quite overturn the present system of landed property.'

THE POOR

The labouring poor formed the vast majority of the rural and urban population and the largest general occupational grouping in the country, although it is problematic to describe all those not in the middling orders as 'the poor'. That term was used in broader and narrower ways, but quite often quite restrictively for those on relief or dependent on charity. When the phrase 'labouring poor' began to catch on in the later eighteenth century, some commentators, such as Edmund Burke, attacked it as newfangled cant. The vast mass of the population was in this category and it was far from undifferentiated: forms of status and security were attainable, although they were precarious.

The rural population was dominated by an economy of proprietary wealth, a system built around rent and poor remuneration for labour in the context of a markedly unequal distribution of land. The poor were badly affected by the decline in some rural industries, by enclosure and by any factor, short- or long-term, that pressed on real wages. Heavy rent rises led to the emigration of about 20,000 Scots to North America between 1769 and 1774, the Reverend William Thom reflecting in his *Candid Inquiry into the Causes of the Late and Intended Migrations from Scotland* (Glasgow 1771) that 'in whatever country the whole property is engrossed by a few, there the people must be wretched'. Demographic and economic change led both to a substantial increase in the number of those working for wages and to the growth of an 'underclass'. The increased numbers of those working for others found their economic relationship defined in part by other aspects of social dependence.

Social welfare provisions for the poor were limited and invidious. In order to try to avoid the birth of children who would be a burden on the rates, parish vestries in England sought to prevent the poor from marrying. William Russell (1740–1818), a Birmingham merchant and a member of Joseph Priestley's congregation, who was a keen supporter of reform, pressed the need for a law compelling every labouring man to become a weekly subscriber to a public fund in every parish providing relief in sickness and an annuity at a given period when they were past work, but the notion of legislation of this type was very much a minority view.[17] Nevertheless, by the end of the century a large proportion of the working population belonged to friendly societies, which provided a measure of welfare in need. Despite the development of charity schools, the poor, especially if female, had only limited access to education.

The poor were generally treated as objects or a problem, not as equal participants in the community. As the *Citizen* pointed out on 5 April 1757, 'They are called the vulgar, the mob, the rabble . . . and treated as if they were of some inferior species, who are designed only for labour'. The poor were particularly harshly treated or regarded if they could not earn their keep. Thus the philosopher John Locke proposed to the Board of Trade that the poor should be made to work and those who refused should be whipped and, if necessary, mutilated. His suggestions were not adopted but should not surprise us from an individual and society that profited from the slave trade. Wesley conspicuously adopted a different viewpoint, seeing the poor as industrious and a source of spiritual renewal. He saw the beggar as an image of the suffering Christ.

The poor were also all dependent on the environment, which helped to sustain a sense of fatalism, and also ensured that much employment was short-term or casual. Today it is difficult for a predominantly urban readership to understand a world in which the calamities of environmental mischance were matched by the incessant pressures of trying to scratch a living in adverse circumstances. Electricity, the internal combustion engine, and selective crop- and animal-breeding had not yet conquered the countryside and transformed both agriculture and agrarian life. Power was limited to human and animal muscles, with milling performed with the aid of wind and water. Furniture, utensils and foodstuffs were basic and rough, crop and animal breeds improved only by the watchful care of generations. And everywhere the awful extremes of climate and disease could always lessen or annihilate the prospects of crops, livestock and the humans who depended on them.

It was difficult for the poor to improve their condition. Although the political process was not impervious to public opinion and pressures, it was closed to any attempt to redistribute wealth and opportunities. Labour had only limited possibilities of improving its conditions in most branches of the economy. Nevertheless, there was widespread trade unionism, for example among the West of England clothworkers and the framework knitters of the East Midlands, and there were many industrial disputes, often defensively against unwelcome changes. In 1752 the combers in the Norwich textile industry struck in order to gain better wages and to prevent the employment of blackleg labour. In 1758 there was a major strike by check weavers in and near Manchester. They sought a return to the prices of the 1730s and recognition of the Manchester Smallware Weavers' Society, but their strike was defeated after a prosecution for illegal combination, a method also used to stop a worsted weavers' combination in Manchester in 1760. In 1764 the journeymen weavers of Carrick in Ireland conducted a five-month strike over the issue of substitute labour, and attempts to introduce a spring loom there in 1791 led to violent resistance. New technology in the textile industry in England was resisted by rioters in the 1760s, 1770s and 1780s, as seen, for example, in riots in Leicester in 1773 and 1787 against improved stocking frames; although there was also a degree of dialogue, albeit not from a position of equality, between employers and workers that facilitated the process of industrialisation in the West Riding. There was less common ground in the West Country, where the introduction of machinery into the weaving industry led to much unrest. In the case of the violent London silk-weavers strike of 1768–69, peace was restored only after the Spitalfields Act of 1773 brought an unuusal degree of outside regulation of wages. Apart from specific economic disputes, there was also an increasing amount of social tension between different social groups, especially after 1760.

THE MIDDLING ORDERS
It would be misleading to present society in terms of an elite and the bulk of the population if that detracts attention from those who can be

variously termed the 'middling orders', 'middle class' or 'bourgeoisie'. The bulk of this group lived in the towns and can best be considered under that head, although there was also an important middling order in rural society: tenant farmers and the agents of landlords. The former were greatly affected by the movements of the agrarian economy, encountering particular problems in the agricultural depression of the second quarter of the century. Thus, on 17 February 1739 the *Craftsman* noted that 'best shipping wheat' was selling in London for '£6 a load . . . which is so low that it is impossible farmers can live and pay their rents at such prices; and as wool likewise bears so low a price, unless some care be speedily taken, and the people eased of the present heavy taxes, most of the lands of the kingdom will be flung up into the landlords' hands'. The fate and fortune of tenant farmers, in fact, varied greatly and from mid-century the rise in grain prices due to the growing population brought more wealth into the rural economy.

The middling orders as a whole were a distinct social group, but many of the factors already discussed in terms of the structuring of society, such as concern with hierarchy, the role of birth, and snobbery, also played a major role for them, and there was a widespread aspiration among them to gentry status. Yet the middling orders also emphasised values of professionalisation, specialism and competence that helped to define their social presence. A stress on such factors was necessarily one of the individual rather than the family or dynasty.

The expansion and profitability of the commercial and industrial sectors of the economy led to a growth in the middling orders, who were increasingly difficult to locate in terms of a social differentiation based on rural society and inherited position. Their property and interests were as much protected by the general emphasis on liberty and property and by the ethos and direction of parliamentary government as were those of the landed order.

The middling orders played a considerable role in public affairs, generally co-operating with the landed elite to achieve their socio-political objectives. Property qualifications for many posts were relatively low, enabling the lower-middling orders to participate in the government of the localities. Subscription associations also gave them an important role, as, more generally, did public politics. The middling orders were also affected by the porosity of social boundaries. Social mobility was facilitated by primogeniture and the consequent need for younger sons to define and support their own position, and by the relative openness of marital conventions that in particular allowed the sons of land to marry the daughters of commerce. Partly as a result of this, the social elite in England was far less exclusive and far more widely rooted in the national community than was the case in most continental countries. In some counties, such as Durham, landed estates were frequently acquired by purchase, and acquisitions by previously non-landed men were frequent, and over half between 1610 and 1819 were by men from a professional or commercial background – over a quarter by the latter group alone. There was an active land market and status could also be readily acquired. Urban and rural elites shared cultural and leisure interests, such as visiting spas, and were linked by myriad patterns of subscription and other forms of social intercourse. The Birmingham Bean Club acted as a dining society to bring the town's leaders and the local gentry together. Fashions were rapidly transmitted and made accessible and affordable. By 1790 about one-fifth of the membership of the House of Commons came from backgrounds outside the social elite. Yet this mobility strengthened, rather than weakened, the social hierarchy. There were relatively few signs of the social tensions of a century later.

5 TOWNS

Urban life became more important in Britain, especially in England. The percentage of the population living in towns (settlements with more than about 2,000 people) rose from about 17 in 1700 to about 27.5 in 1800, and that at a time when the population was rising. In 1700 London had more than half a million people, more than all other English towns put together. There were only five of the latter with more than 10,000 people: Norwich (30,000), Bristol (20,000), Newcastle, Exeter and York. By 1800 there were more than twenty-seven, including important industrial and commercial centres in the north of England and the Midlands, such as Manchester, Leeds, Sheffield, Sunderland, Bolton, Birmingham, Stoke and Wolverhampton. Urban growth often happened in phases, but the general trend was of a marked increase towards the end of the century.

London's population had doubled, and in 1800 London had the largest population of any European city. It was over ten times larger than the second city in England. London attracted most attention in part because it posed the greatest problems of law and order and social conditions. It was also significant in influencing notions of urban life. Edinburgh had about 30–35,000 people in 1700 and was certainly then the second city in Britain, if not well before. The population of Glasgow by the mid-century was about 30,000, with 15,000 in Aberdeen, 12,000 in Dundee and 9,000 in Inverness. The urban population of Scotland grew by about 132 per cent between 1750 and 1800. Glasgow's population grew to match that of Edinburgh. In Scotland major industrial centres emerged: Paisley became the third largest town in 1801, Greenock the sixth. The New Town proposals of Sir Gilbert Elliott and Lord Provost Drummond, published in 1752, sought to make Edinburgh a fitting metropolis as the chief city of North Britain.

Wales was far less urbanised. Cardiff had fewer than 2,000 people in 1801.

The largest town then was Merthyr Tydfil, no more than a hamlet in 1750, but the first centre of the coke and blast-furnace based iron industry in South Wales. In Ireland urbanisation was overwhelmingly concentrated in Dublin, which grew from around 60,000 in 1685 to about 200,000 in 1800. Dublin was the centre of government and services. By 1800 only 7 per cent of Ireland's population lived in towns with over 10,000 inhabitants, a rather high threshold, compared with 17.3 per cent in Scotland and 20.3 per cent in England and Wales. The population in thousands in such towns in Scotland rose from 53 in 1700, when they had comprised 5 per cent of the total population, to 276 in 1800; in England and Wales from 718 (14 per cent of the total population) to 1,870. This level of urbanisation was far higher than that of Germany and France; in Europe only the Low Countries had a similar level.

The period is often associated with urban elegance, the squares of the West End of London, Bath, Liverpool and Dublin and the New Town of Edinburgh. 'Georgian buildings', constructed in a new regular, 'classical' style, often in terraces, lined new boulevards, crescents, squares, and circles. New houses were built in smart quarters in cities such as Norwich. Queen's square begun in 1699 set the fashion for brick-built houses in Bristol and was responsible for the growth of brickworks there. The very spacious Prince's Street followed in Bristol in 1725, King's Square and Brunswick Square were laid out between 1755 and 1769 and there was much similar construction there in the 1780s and early 1790s. The Priory Estate, centred on Old Square, played a major role in the gentrification of Birmingham. Occupants were not allowed to keep pigs, dump sewage or open butcher's or blacksmith's shops. Another area of select housing developed around the new St Philip's Church. In west-central Glasgow stone town houses in a neo-classical design, with balustraded roofs, entablatures and urns, were constructed from 1710. Genteel dwellings lined Charlotte Street (1779) and St Andrew's Square (1787). Stone, rather than brick, continued to dominate Scottish building. In Dublin, Luke Gardiner developed his estate on the north bank of the Liffey as a fashionable residential district centred on Sackville Street. Cork had about 80,000 people in 1800, Belfast, Drogheda, Limerick and Waterford between 12,000 and 15,000 each. The leading Irish towns were ports, their prosperity dependent on the growing commercialisation of the Irish economy.

The new and existing houses were decorated and filled with new products. Wallpaper became fashionable and carpets more common; plaster was whitewashed and furniture became more plentiful. Thanks to books of designs these fixtures, fittings and furniture became more standardised and thus more predictable for travellers.

Alongside light, roomy and attractive private houses numerous public and philanthropic buildings were built. Theatres, assembly rooms, subscription libraries and other leisure facilities were opened in many towns, alongside public outdoor space: parks, walks and racecourses. The first theatre in Lincolnshire, for example, was built in Stamford soon after 1718. Others followed in Lincoln (c. 1731), Spalding (c. 1760), Gainsborough (1775), Boston (1777), Grantham (1777) and Louth (by 1798). Bristol's Council House was rebuilt in 1704. In 1784 James Essex, the leading Cambridge architect, designed and built a new Guildhall (town hall). Nottingham had already replaced its medieval timber-framed Guildhall by a brick one with a colonnaded front in the mid-century. Coventry gained a new county hall (1783–84) and a new gaol (1772). Old gates and walls were demolished in, for example,

Covent Garden Market by Joseph van Aken, *c.* 1726–30. Market stalls in the seventeenth-century piazza. Social distinctions are captured in clothes and position, for example the drabness of the maid with the shopping-basket standing behind the lady buying vegetables in the right foreground. Born in Antwerp, Van Aken settled in London in 1720.

Newcastle, which also gained Assembly Rooms (1776) and a theatre (1788). In order to improve access, Nottingham's last surviving medieval gate was pulled down in 1743. Hereford's city gates were taken down in 1783–89 and the city – not a centre of industry or growth – acquired a new hospital (1709–10), a new school (1710), infirmary (1776), county gaol (1793) and lunatic asylum (1794). Norwich's city gates were taken down between 1791 and 1801. The city itself gained a lunatic asylum (1714), new shire hall (1749), assembly rooms (1754), theatre (1756), hospital (1771–72), public subscription library (1784) and new county gaol (1792–93). The first Exchanges in Manchester and Liverpool were built in 1729 and 1749–54 respectively. The total stock of public buildings in the West Riding of Yorkshire rose from about ninety in 1700 to over five hundred by 1840.

New construction was not restricted to England. In Carrickfergus in Ulster the wooden bridge was replaced in stone in 1740, a new market house was constructed in 1775 and a new county court house and jail in 1779. Whereas earlier buildings in the town had been defensive in character, there was no sense of menace in the new urban landscape. Carrickfergus benefited from the development of the Ulster linen industry, and many of its artisan houses were rebuilt in brick or stone with slate roofs. Market Street in Kells was rebuilt in the Georgian style: substantial houses with slate roofs and broad fanlights over the entrance doors. In 1694 the castle was converted into a market-house and court-house and in the late eighteenth century the leading local notable, the Earl of Bective, turned Kells into an attractive estate town. A fine court-house in classical style was built. The walls of many Irish towns, for example Carrick, Cashel and Clonmel, were breached.

Whatever the size of towns, they shared the inegalitarian and hierarchical nature of the rest of society. The smallest group were the wealthy and prominent, their power expressed in and deriving from their ability to organise others, generally economically and often politically. Their strength extended into the rural hinterland where they would enjoy influence as a result of their power as a source of credit, tend to own estates and, if merchants, control rural industry. Within the towns this group might be employers or landowners and generally enjoyed political power as a result of social status and the oligarchical nature of urban government.

The largest urban group were the poor, who tended to lack political weight. Their poverty stemmed from the precarious nature of much employment in even the most prosperous of towns and the absence of any effective system of social welfare. Most lacked the skills that commanded a decent wage and many had only seasonal or episodic employment. Day-labourers, servants and paupers were economically vulnerable and often socially isolated; a large number were immigrants from the countryside. As a result of poverty the poor were very exposed to changes in the price of food and generally lived in inadequate housing. As they could not afford much fuel, they were often cold and wet in the winter and the circumstances of their life made them prone to disease, though disease was also a social leveller.

In between these two groups, though not separated rigidly from them in economic terms and many of them coming from above or below, was a third one enjoying a more settled income than the poor. Many in this group were artisans, their economic interests and social cohesion frequently expressed through fraternities of workmen. In contemporary discourse they were the 'people', while the bulk of the poor were the 'mob'.

The relationship of the landed to the urban elite varied. There were signs of tension, but they tended to be overlaid by shared interests and increasingly a common culture. The purchase of landed estates by the bourgeoisie and professional men played a significant role in underlining the common aspirations of both groups, though on the individual level it could create tension. It was particularly important in Lowland Scotland. Intermarriage further facilitated links, though this was usually a matter of merchants' daughters marrying into the landed elite, transferring wealth and creating links without compromising social position.

The bourgeoisie did not usually want economic or political change. Rather than seeing themselves as the flag-bearers of a putative 'rising middle class', the bourgeoisie displayed little sign of what would later be termed 'class consciousness'. It has been argued that there were signs of a new ethos. The bourgeoisie read books and saw plays that portrayed a way of life emphasising the value of industry, discipline and professionalism, a conscious alternative to supposedly aristocratic habits of self-indulgence, but it is important not to exaggerate the significance of such ideas. They were neither new nor politically pointed and significant, and much of the landed elite would have accepted them.

Towns could be a major sphere of political contention and public disorder. Although many were dominated by rural landlords, most parliamentary seats were attached to boroughs rather than counties: 234 of the 300 members of the Irish House of Commons were representatives of 117 boroughs. The presence of political or quasi-political institutions in major cities, most obviously Parliaments, and their potential interaction with popular urban tension, could serve to increase urban political volatility; disturbances in London were linked to parliamentary opposition in 1733 and again during the Wilkite troubles in the 1760s. Edinburgh and Dublin were similarly centres of contention, but so also were other major towns; the malt tax riots in Glasgow in 1725 led to the dispatch of troops. Lady Burlington wrote to her husband in 1735 when the attempt to overturn Bristol's choice of anti-government MPs at the recent general election failed, 'There has been prodigious rejoicings . . . they do affirm, that if the House of Commons had gone on, and carried it against the town's choice, there would certainly have been an insurrection. It is a town of too great importance to be trifled with.'[1] Five years later food shortages led to major riots in Newcastle, as they did in Belfast in 1756. Concern about domestic radicalism led to the construction of new barracks from 1792, for example in Norwich (1792–93) and Coventry (1793).

Towns were not simply the source of potential political problems. They also, particularly the major ones, constituted the living space of the most articulate and informed members of society, and tended to house their associated paraphernalia: printing presses, newspapers, shops. Furthermore, towns appeared to be one of the principal products of human activity, the section of the environment most amenable to action, where society was open to regulation. Concern with air and light, public hygiene and open spaces led to an emphasis on wide streets and squares, and the introduction of pavements, attention to drains and street cleaning, as in Birmingham after Street Commissioners were appointed in 1769. One of the more symbolic acts in Birmingham was the sale and subsequent demolition of the Old Cross in 1784.

These priorities reflected common themes. The creation of a regulated environment was not simply functional in its rationale; it also reflected a moral vision, a spirit of change that was paradoxically in some respects as traditional in aspiration as it was progressive. The specific manifestations of this concept ranged from new drains to police forces, but the need for conscious improvement to the urban environment was accepted. Parliamentary Improvement Acts empowered individuals as commissioners to fund and implement schemes for improving the paving, lighting and cleaning of towns. The commissioners were permitted to levy rates and were separate from the municipal corporation. New Sarum (Salisbury) obtained such a commission for paving, lighting and watching the city in 1736, but the major surge in such commissions was begun by Liverpool in 1748 and became especially strong after the peace of 1763. They were established, for example, in Southampton in 1770 and in Cambridge in 1788.

The process of urban improvement was continual in the second half of the century and was much encouraged by emulation, Southampton following

Portsmouth's example. An Act of 1750 for enlarging the streets and market-places of Gloucester led to the removal of old market-places, as well as the pillory and the stocks. A Streets Improvement Act for Bristol was passed in 1766. Acts for Worcester of 1770, 1771 and 1780 permitted a new bridge, a better water supply and the first street lights. Under a Lamp Act for Hereford of 1774, town commissioners were appointed to improve street paving, lighting and cleaning. The open rubbish-filled brooks which ran through streets were covered over. The Bath Improvement Act of 1789 gave the city extensive powers of purchase and demolition which it used to rebuild the old part of the town. The City Surveyor, Thomas Baldwin, was responsible for the new broad and colonnaded Bath Street (1791–94). Paving Commissioners, responsible also for cleaning the city, were established in Chichester in 1791. In 1696 a company had been formed to provide a water supply for Nottingham. In order to keep dung out of the watercourses that provided the water supply, the council of Kells in 1706, 1712 and 1719 banned geese, ducks, and unringed swine from the streets, and pigsties in the town. The main streets of Lancaster were lit from 1738.

Action derived in part from the scale of the problems of regulation and control facing urban communities. Poverty and crime were concentrated in towns, as were problems of sanitation and health. The nature of urban life, with a relatively large number of people living in marginal circumstances, often in disrupted family situations and outside established patterns of hierarchical authority, all aspects exacerbated by the very growth of towns and by immigration, posed major problems.

Crime was extensive in towns such as London. The urban concentration of people provided criminals with opportunities for recruitment, activity and concealment. Refuse removal was another major and growing problem. Glasgow had no public sewers until 1790 and the situation thereafter remained inadequate for decades. In Leeds, public sewers passed downstream

The Old Town of Edinburgh from the West, by Philip Mercier. Edinburgh changed rapidly in the second half of the century with the development of the New Town and increasing social segregation in housing. The seat of the Scottish Enlightenment, Edinburgh was the beneficiary of the economic expansion of Scotland, especially the Central Lowlands, in the third quarter of the century. There was money to invest in building to cater for new demand and new tastes, not least in the form of new townscape. The Old Town became the more crowded, less healthy and poorer part of Edinburgh.

to water-collection points. Mary Scarth, the raker of the London parish of St Giles-in-the-Fields from 1705 to 1723, was paid £400 by the parish and employed twenty horses, four carts and five men. The scavengers paid by Lancaster Corporation only cleaned the major streets.

Poverty was another national problem that was particularly apparent in towns. The standard precept of care was that it should discriminate between the deserving and the undeserving. This religio-moral principle tended to be applied on grounds of age, health and sex, rather than on socio-economic criteria relating to income and employment. The sick, elderly, young and women with children were the prime beneficiaries of relief, while the able-bodied, whether in low-paid employment or unemployment, were denied it. There was scant understanding of the problems posed by unemployment, and under-employment, and such hardships were treated as self-inflicted and thus deserving of neglect or punishment.

A relatively flexible and well-established system of poor relief was available through the Poor Law. Compulsory poor rates had been introduced in England and Wales in 1572 and in 1598 the relief of poverty was made the responsibility of the individual parish, but able-bodied men unable to find work were treated as rogues and vagabonds. The Poor Relief Act of 1662 made the right to relief dependent upon the pauper being settled in the parish, a practice that led to the expulsion of paupers deemed non-resident. Individuals could only remain in a new parish if they had a settlement certificate stating that their former parish would support them if they became a burden on the poor rate. The rest were liable to be driven away unless they could find work. They were generally harshly treated and were frequently whipped as vagabonds.

From 1696 'corporations for the poor' were established in Bristol, Exeter, London and other cities to distribute poor relief through a system of work-houses. The first was John Carey's central workhouse, established in the Mint in Bristol (1696) and later named St Peter's Hospital. It represented a major advance in the treatment of the able-bodied poor. An increase in the number of the poor led Worcester in 1703 to establish a workhouse in which 'Beggars and idle people' could be compelled to work. The Workhouse Test Act of 1723 encouraged parishes to found workhouses to provide the poor with work and accommodation. All Nottingham's parishes built workhouses under the Act in the 1720s, Lancaster built one in 1730 and Birmingham another in 1733, but over the country too few were founded to deal with the problem, especially as the population rose from the mid-century. In many English parishes a 'P' stitched on garments denoted those in receipt of Poor Relief, but there was no equivalent to the Scottish licensed begging system, where a blue badge granted the right to beg in one's home parish. The general parish system of poor relief worked reasonably well in Scotland, and there was no equivalent there to the English Act of 1662, which helped to reduce long-distance mobility.

Growing public concern about the system led the House of Commons to establish committees of inquiry into the state of the poor in the 1770s and 1780s. Defects in the system were recognised in Gilbert's Act of 1782, which gave JPs the power to appoint guardians running Houses of Industry for the elderly and infirm. Workhouses, however, remained less important than 'out relief': providing assistance, and sometimes work, to the poor in their own homes. Under the Speenhamland system of outdoor relief introduced in

1795, though never universally applied, both the unemployed and wage-labourers received payments reflecting the price of bread and the size of their family. Payments to families were made through the male head of the household.

In Ireland the situation was less favourable. City corporations of the poor in the charge of workhouses were created in Dublin (1703) and Cork (1735). They were supported by local taxes and donations. The Dublin workhouse opened in 1706. In 1757 Belfast introduced a tax on all householders in order to fund outdoor relief for the poor. Dublin's problems were alleviated by a subsidy on the movement of domestic grain to it. Legislation of 1772 extended these corporations of the poor and their workhouses to the entire county and decreed that they were to be supported by subscriptions and county grants. The impotent poor were to be maintained and the deserving poor were to be licensed to beg, but begging without a licence was made a criminal offence. However, the Act of 1772 was in general inoperative, particularly outside the larger towns. There were major problems even there; the Dublin House of Industry, established in 1772 to care for vagrants and beggars, was unable to cope with the level of distress when it began to rise in 1777.

The general problem was the same everywhere, an absence of resources not only to deal with the poor *in situ*, but also with problems created by migration. There was neither wealth nor tax income sufficient to provide a widespread and comprehensive welfare system. However, as the government was not seeking to abolish poverty, but rather to alleviate it, or at least allay the fears created by the depiction of the poor, it is perhaps anachronistic to criticise it for failing to create an adequate system or for treating the effects of poverty rather than dealing with its causes.

The extent to which urban life had distinctive cultural and behavioural effects is open to debate. In some respects it offered freedom. If towns did not offer equality of opportunity, they did provide opportunity, and the sustained migration to them was a testimony to this. Each migrant represented an individual decision that life might be better in a town. For many this proved illusory: rural penury translated into urban poverty. Urban degradation was more pernicious, because of the absence of the social and community support that was more prevalent in rural parishes. However, the social system was more fluid in towns: mobility was greater and control laxer.

Urban populations were not on the whole radical in their politics or beliefs, but town life did provide the context for most new ideas, both elite and popular, and offered new experiences. It was also easier to bridge the divide between elite and non-elite in towns, whether in the dissemination of fashions, such as tea-drinking and the wearing of imported cloth, or of new political views. The concentration of people in towns, their higher rates of literacy and more marked traditions of political autonomy and independence of attitude helped to foster, at least in part, a consumer society the consumerism of which went beyond goods and services.

The dominant position of London increased during the period. This owed something to the enormous growth of the city's trade; it also reflected London's dominance of the world of print that became even more important as a shaper of news, opinion and fashion. Although a national Scottish press was emerging by 1800, London newspapers circulated throughout Britain and were also crucial sources for the provincial press. The annual sale of London

A View of the Mall from St James's Park, by Marco Ricci, *c.* 1710. A walk where fashionable society went to see and be seen, to intrigue, to flirt and to proposition. Ricci captures London on display, but this is also a world with cattle grazing, in order to provide the city with milk, and with people working. The large number of women depicted reflects the extent to which many public places were not segregated. The park contained three avenues for pedestrians and in the 1700s Queen Anne's gardener Henry Wise planted 350 limes to provide shade.

papers elsewhere in England rose from 1.09 million in 1764 to 4.65 million in 1790. The turnpike and postal systems centred on London. This dominance of communications reflected and sustained London's economic importance. Thus, for example, London-based insurance companies, such as the Sun Fire Office, and banks were able to organise insurance and banking elsewhere by delegating the work to agents in other towns with whom regular contact could be maintained.

London itself grew significantly, particularly at the beginning of the century when the West End estates of landlords such as Sir Richard Grosvenor and Lord Burlington were developed, especially as prime residential property. Thus Mayfair and St James's became the select side of town and the streets there still bear the names of the politicians of the period, for example Harley Street and Oxford Street. Leading aristocrats built or rebuilt grand London houses such as Burlington, Carlton, Chandos, Chesterfield, Derby, Devonshire and Spencer Houses. Buckingham House was bought by George III. Other areas further east, such as Clerkenwell and Hackney, became less fashionable, a process paralleled in Paris. Westminister Bridge opened a new route across the river and helped development on the south bank. It was followed by Blackfriars Bridge, opened in 1769 after nine years' construction. The ½d toll demanded from those who crossed led to a riot. London's squares were imitated in cities such as Bristol. London developed further as a centre of consumption and leisure; the amount of fixed specialised investment in leisure rose greatly with theatres, including the Theatre Royal, the King's Theatre and the Pantheon, pleasure gardens, picture galleries and other facilities, ranging from gambling-houses to coffee-houses.

Although some facilities were or sought to be exclusive, most were readily accessible to anyone with money to spend.

London, though large, was compact: it was still immune from the congestion and sprawl of the following century. The social basis of London's development was not only that the rural elite increasingly came to spend part of the year there, but also that the 'middling sort' expanded considerably. This was also true of regional capitals, such as Norwich, county centres such as Warwick, and developing entertainment centres, particularly spa towns, such as Tunbridge Wells and Bath. Thirty-four new spas were founded in England between 1700 and 1750, and even more in the second half of the century. Spas and resort centres, such as Moffat, were also founded in Scotland. The first Pump Room at Bath was built in 1706, followed in 1708 by Harrison's Assembly Rooms. The development of Bath as a city of orderly leisure owed much to Richard 'Beau' Nash, who in 1705 was appointed first Master of Ceremonies. His 'Rules' for the behaviour of visitors to Bath were first published in 1742, part of the process by which the codification of social propriety was expressed (and debated) in print.

The 'middling sort' were largely professionals and gentlemen merchants. Doctors, bankers, lawyers, clergymen and Customs and Excise men could all be found in major towns, and their numbers increased. They were largely responsible for new building and rebuilding, the replacement of timber-frame by brick in houses for the well-to-do, for example in Norwich from the late seventeenth century, and in Lancaster: service activities, rather than industrial expansion, were the basis of growth in many towns.

The economic basis of the shift was growing prosperity, especially in commerce, and this interacted with increased and differentiated consumption. Towns also benefited from the strength of the rural economy, providing not

Newcastle, by Thomas Girtin, 1796. Girtin (1775–1802) was a watercolour painter much influenced by a visit to the north of England in 1796 and a master in depicting light and shade, and in providing a poetic account of architectural subjects. Girtin's Newcastle is tightly packed beside the Tyne and dominated by its churches, particularly All Saints, rebuilt by David Stephenson between 1786 and 1796 with an oval body.

only a commercial but also a social focus. Chester, for example, had important race meetings in midsummer and autumn and the Lent and summer assizes.

It can be argued that a degree of urban–rural rapprochement and cohesion at elite level was an important factor encouraging stability. Furthermore, it is possible that this contributed to a degree of cultural merging. It is important not to exaggerate: differences remained, not least in politics and religion, and the landed magnates visited towns on their own terms. Yet there was a degree of interchange based on shared values that was arguably greater than that of the two previous centuries.

Any stress on towns as centres of culture, commerce and growth must take note of their variety. Apart from the centres of provincial culture, there were also important industrial towns, although their growth, as with Birmingham, owed something also to their role as centres of trade and distribution. Towns contained impoverished, squalid and dangerous areas. Some, such as Oxford and Hereford, were fairly static communities; others were affected by adverse economic circumstances. Gloucester's trade, sugar-refining and glass-manu-facturing could not compete with that of Bristol, and its cloth industry also declined. The Duke of Wharton wrote of York in 1721: 'The City itself is but poor, the Trade being very low.'[2] York, though hit by the growth of Leeds, was, however, to benefit as a centre for the local gentry and also to become in the mid-century the largest national collecting point of wholesale butter and the provincial source of London's butter. This reflected the prosperity of the Vale of York. The press is one index of urban success. Excluding London, the number of English newspapers rose from about 24 in 1723, 32 in 1753, 35 in 1760 and 50 in 1782 to over 100 in 1808. The provincial expansion was due both to the increase in the number of towns with papers and to more towns having more than one paper. Yet there were also failures. After the *Union Journal; or, Halifax Advertiser* (1759–c.1763) ceased publication, Halifax had no paper until the early nineteenth century. After the failure of the *Darlington Pamphlet* (1772–73), the needs of Teesside continued to be met by the Leeds, Newcastle and York press and no other paper was launched at Darlington until the *Darlington and Stockton Times* appeared in 1847.

The *Hereford Journal* (1739) was also short-lived, but the *British Chronicle; or, Pugh's Hereford Journal,* launched in 1770, lasted into the twentieth century. In Cumbria the *Kendal Courant* (1731–36), *Kendal Weekly Mercury* (1735–47) and *Whitehaven Weekly Courant* (1736–43) all failed, but the *Cumberland Pacquet; or, Ware's Whitehaven Advertiser,* launched in 1774, was successful.

Other towns only acquired their first papers later: the first in Montrose was in 1793, in Carlisle in 1798, Greenock and Arbroath in 1799, Falmouth – the first in Cornwall – in 1801, Ayr in 1803, Swansea – the first in Wales – in 1804, Inverness in 1807, Bangor – the first in north Wales – in 1808, and Barnstaple – the first in north Devon – in 1824. After two or possibly three failures in the eighteenth century, the continuous publication of papers in Plymouth began in 1808.

Other towns were less fortunate. Lieutenant Richard Browne wrote to his father from Enniskillen in Ulster in 1765 that it had 'but a miserable aspect, being small, the houses mean and thatched with straw'. Yet, as ever, variety was the keynote. Browne had written from the Isle of Wight in 1765: 'Newport is a very clean pretty town regular and well built, the Bath players are in it and we have plays every night.'[3] The growth in the numbers of schools, hospitals, dispensaries, infirmaries, theatres, reading rooms etc. in the

British Isles may not have been massive, but it was significant and changed the institutional and cultural landscape of most of the well-populated regions. This was important to the period's self-image as an improving society. Such self-understanding should neither be taken at face value nor regarded as descriptively or analytically sufficient, but it did reflect something of the realities of eighteenth-century life.

6 FAITH AND THE CHURCHES

To the casual observer of today the period may not appear a particularly religious age. Urban building is not generally recalled for its churches, any more than the British painters of the period are remembered for religious works. Religious warfare is seen as largely something of the distant past and the period is viewed as one of growing toleration. It is seen as a period of enlightenment and the Enlightenment as a secular movement. Faith is generally ascribed to superstitious conservatism or irrational religious enthusiasm; the serious anti-Catholic Gordon Riots of 1780 are seen as an anachronism.

Though such views are not found in most recent scholarly works, they are still widely held; and there are genuine problems of definition and methodology. The quality of the religious experience of the bulk of the population is difficult to assess, as is the source and depth of their faith.

It is similarly difficult to establish how far such personal and communal experience was affected by the politico-ecclesiastical changes of the period. The crisis of 1688–92 had led to major changes that were important not only in themselves, but also because of the role of the recent past in conditioning the understanding of developments. Religious antagonism provided a key to past, present and future.

In Ireland the crisis reimposed and strengthened an Anglican ascendancy, completing a process that had begun in the sixteenth century. Catholic officials and landowners were replaced. The percentage of land owned by Catholics fell as it had been doing for over a century, and anti-Catholic legislation was passed. Bishops and regular clergy were driven abroad under the Banishment Act of 1697. Transportations began in 1698 and at least 444 priests were certainly expelled. Banning the bishops prevented the ordination of priests in Ireland. Parish priests were obliged to register under the Registration Act of 1704 and compelled to renounce loyalty to the Stuarts.

Acts forbade mixed marriages, Catholic schools and the bearing of arms by Catholics, although the need to re-enact them suggests that they were evaded. The culture of power in Ireland became thoroughly and often aggressively Protestant.

Yet the Catholic percentage of the population did not decrease, because serious repression was episodic; instead the ratio of Catholics to Protestants rose from about 3:1 in 1731 to 4:1 in 1800. The draconian wartime legislation of 1697, 1703–04 and 1709 was inspired by fears of Catholic disloyalty and links with France, for example in response to the French invasion attempt on Scotland of 1708. Persecution slackened in peacetime. The Penal Code was designed essentially to destroy the political and economic power of Catholicism rather than the faith itself, although it was also an attempt to erode Catholic belief and practice. The ability of the Anglican establishment to proselytise in Ireland was limited by its general failure to communicate with a still largely Gaelic-speaking population. There were few clerics such as John Richardson (1664–1747), who frequently preached in Gaelic in his parish, published several books in the language, including an attack on pilgrimages, and played a role in the Gaelic translation of the *Book of Common Prayer,* which appeared in 1712.

In contrast, the Catholic colleges, such as the Irish College in Paris, stipulated a knowledge of the language as a requirement for priests in Ireland. The Catholics published many catechisms and devotional works in Gaelic. The church hierarchy survived largely intact and the Catholic clergy, wearing secular dress and secretly celebrating mass, continued their work, sustained by a strong oral culture, the emotional link with a sense of national identity, by hedge-school teaching and by a degree of tacit government acceptance. In 1719, for example, the government in London blocked an attempt by the Dublin Parliament to make castration a punishment for priests. The Convocation of the Church of Ireland, meeting in 1711, planned to establish a system of free compulsory education for Catholics in order to teach children Protestantism and the English language. The children were to attend school until the age of 16 and to be regularly examined by the parish minister in English and the catechism. The scheme, however, was ineffective. No church funds were forthcoming and the House of Commons was opposed to any plan involving higher taxation. A royal bounty, and from 1745 a parliamentary grant, finally financed a small-scale scheme launched by Primate Boulter in 1731 that established a system of primary schools to encourage Protestantism and the English language.

Anglican religious tests for public office in Ireland also handicapped the large Presbyterian community in Ulster until 1780, when the Dublin Parliament abolished tests for Protestant Dissenters as a wartime concession, while Presbyterians and Catholics had to pay tithes to support the Church of Ireland. To Presbyterians there was an Anglican, not a Protestant, ascendancy. The Presbyterian Church was not endowed like the Church of Ireland, but was linked to government by a small subsidy, the *regium donum* (king's gift), first paid in 1672. An Act of 1719 extended the 1689 Act of Toleration to Ireland. Many Irish Presbyterians emigrated to America.

In Scotland the Glorious Revolution led to a Presbyterian ascendancy. In 1689 the Scottish Parliament abolished Episcopacy and in 1690 a Presbyterian Church was established there; Episcopalian clergy were purged from their livings and from educational institutions. They created the basis of an

Monument to Archbishop Boulter, Westminster Abbey. Boulter (1672–1742), born in London and educated at Oxford, rose in the Church of England, becoming Bishop of Bristol in 1719, before being translated to the primacy of the Church of Ireland in 1724. Boulter was active in Irish government, repeatedly holding office as Lord Justice during the absence of successive Lords Lieutenant. He represented the 'English interest' and was opposed to the efforts of Irish Protestants to gain constitutional independence. Boulter was also keen on limiting Catholic rights, and was partly responsible for their exclusion from the legal profession. He died in London.

Episcopal Church in Scotland, which received limited legal recognition by the Act of Toleration passed by a Tory government in 1712. An Episcopalian culture of loss and loyalty was to underpin Jacobitism in Scotland, particularly in the north-east, and affected English Anglicans, some of whom, such as Bishop Samuel Horsley, championed the Scottish Episcopalians, partly because of their sense of isolation: they felt threatened by the Church of Scotland and by English Dissent. The Presbyterian settlement was confirmed, not reversed, by the Act of Union, although lay patronage, abolished in 1690, was restored in 1712, so that 1707 led to the creation of a multi-confessional state. The establishment and continuation of Presbyterianism was in some respects crucial to the success of the Union. The Act of Union contained a clause also safeguarding the privileges of the Church of England, and thus placed the Church of Scotland on a similar footing to the Church of England as an established Church. The Episcopal Church in Scotland declined during the course of the century. About 40 per cent of the Scottish population were Episcopalians in 1700, but only 5 per cent in the 1780s; they remained under disabilities until the early nineteenth century.

In 1779, when supporting the repeal of restrictions on Dissenters in England, Thomas Townshend, MP told the House of Commons that he 'rejected the idea of so essential a connection between our church establishment and our constitution, that any alteration in one must endanger the other. If that position had been true, how could the same legal government support two distinct church establishments, that of England and that of Scotland, which differed so very essentially from one another?' Catholicism was the third most popular creed in Scotland and was particularly strong in the Highlands and Islands. Concern about the Jacobite threat led to action directed against the Catholics. The Scottish Society for the Propagation of Christian Knowledge was granted a royal charter in 1709 to 'eradicate error and to sow truth, to teach true religion and loyalty and to strengthen the British Empire by the addition of useful subjects and firm Protestants'. From 1710 the Society erected schools and supplied teachers who also acted as catechists for the Church of Scotland until 1758. In 1723 and from 1725 the Crown gave an annual grant of £1,000 to the General Assembly of the Church of Scotland to assist in the struggle against Catholicism. The Royal Bounty was used to support catechists and missionary ministers. The Crown was represented at the General Assembly by the Royal Commissioner.

In England the Glorious Revolution ensured that the monarch would be a Protestant, but loosened Anglican hegemony. Under the Act for Exempting their Majesties' Protestant Subjects, Dissenting from the Church of England, from the Penalties of certain Laws, the concessionary but restrictive formulation of what is better known as the Toleration Act (1689), Dissenters (Protestant Nonconformists who believed in the Trinity) who took the oaths of Supremacy and Allegiance and accepted thirty-six of the thirty-nine Articles, and made the Declaration against Transubstantiation could obtain licences as ministers or schoolmasters, although these had to be registered with a bishop or at the Quarter Sessions. The Act was followed by the registration of numerous Dissenting meeting-houses: at least 113 in Devon by 1701. The Presbyterians, Congregationalists (Independents), Quakers and Baptists were the leading Dissenting Churches. A Presbyterian chapel was opened in Nottingham in 1689, followed by another in 1690 for the Unitarians, who were very influential in the city, and one for the Baptists in 1724. An Independent Meeting House was opened in Norwich in about 1693, followed by a Friends' (Quaker) Meeting House in about 1699 and a Baptist chapel in 1745. In Coventry a large Quaker meeting house was opened in 1698, a new Presbyterian chapel in 1701 and one for the Particular Baptists in 1724. Anglicanism declined in the city in the face of a strong challenge from the Presbyterians and the Unitarians. Unitarians, Catholics and non-Christians did not officially enjoy rights of public worship under the Act of Toleration, and Catholics were subject to penal statutes, as were Unitarians under the Blasphemy Act of 1697. There was no Toleration Act for Unitarians until 1813, and in Scotland the death penalty could be imposed for denying the Trinity. Trinitarian orthodoxy was strong and united Catholics and Protestants.

Apart from clashes between different Churches, there were also tensions within them, as with the Church of England. Some of its clerics were more hostile to other Protestant groups and inclined to see a threat in toleration, a threat not only to church attendance and religious orthodoxy, but also to the moral order and socio-political cohesion that the Church was seen as sustaining. The Toleration Act contributed to a sense of malaise and uncertainty. The lower clergy were frustrated that William III did not allow Convocation (the clerical assembly, there was one for each archdiocese) to meet until the last year of his reign. It was prorogued (postponed) continually from that of George I on (from 1717 with the exception of a brief session in 1741–42), as was the Convocation of the Church of Ireland. Dr Henry Sacheverell, a High Anglican cleric and a Tory, felt able to argue controversially in 1709 that the Church was in danger under the Revolution settlement, as interpreted by the Whigs. Indeed, Earl Wharton, the Whig Lord Lieutenant of Ireland, was sufficiently pro-Dissenter in this period, that the Irish House of Lords, where the bishops were influential, complained to Queen Anne and he was recalled in 1710. The Occasional Conformity (1711) and Schism (1714) Acts, designed respectively to prevent the circumvention of communion requirements for office-holding by Dissenters communicating once a year (occasional conformity), and to make a separate education for them illegal, both measures passed by Anne's Tory ministry of 1710–14, were repealed by the Whigs under George I in 1719. The Reverend Benjamin Robertshaw, Rector of Amersham (1728–44), recorded,

> About the year 1721 I was so unfortunate as to fall under the displeasure of my diocesan, Bishop Gibson [a Whig] . . . The occasion was my refusing to bury a Presbyterian's child, sprinkled in their unauthorised way, in my parish at Penn. Upon my absolute refusal the parents . . . carried it to Wycombe, where it was buried by one who I suppose would have given Christian burial even to Pontius Pilate himself, provided he had but in his lifetime used to cry 'King George forever!'[1]

Nevertheless, attempts during the years of Whig ascendancy to repeal the Test and Corporation Acts failed. These Acts, of 1673 and 1661 respectively, obliged members of borough corporations and office-holders under the Crown to take oaths of allegiance and supremacy and to receive communion in the Church of England, and these remained in force until 1828, although the Corporation Act was much diluted in 1719 so that many Dissenters were able to play a role in local government. The Test Act, however, remained much more effective at the national level. The Tories retained their control of Oxford, where many clerics were trained. The royalism of Oxford had been compromised during the reign of James II, when the Catholic king's attempts to improve the position for his co-religionists led him to clash with Magdalen College over its statutes, and as a result to purge the fellows. However, once the male line of the Stuarts had been driven out in 1688–89, the dynasty became a convenient symbol for conservatism, and several prominent eighteenth-century Oxonians were Jacobites, including James, 2nd Duke of Ormonde, Chancellor 1688–1715, and George, 3rd Earl of Lichfield, Chancellor 1762–72. In 1719, on 25 May, Restoration Day, the anniversary of the restoration of Charles II, Thomas Warton, the Tory Professor of Poetry, preached a pointed Jacobite sermon on the text 'Oh Israel, thou hast destroyed thyself, but in me is thine help.' The University had two MPs, elected by its doctors and masters of arts. All the MPs elected were Tories, including such prominent Anglican champions as Henry Hyde, Viscount Cornbury (1734–50) and Sir Roger Newdigate (1750–80), as the Crown did not possess the power of creating honorary doctors, by which a Whig majority was secured at Cambridge.

The Whig party had traditionally been associated with Dissenters. From 1722 a small *regium donum* was given annually to trustees from the Baptist, Independent and Presbyterian Churches, the funds used to supplement the incomes of their indigent clerics. The cautious Whig administrations of Sir Robert Walpole and his successors were unwilling to tamper with religious fundamentals, especially the sacramental test, not least because of the considerable ground swell of opinion in defence of the Church. Government control of ecclesiastical patronage – the Crown appointed all the bishops and about a tenth of the parish clergy – greatly influenced the senior ranks of the Church of England, and ensured that it was in alliance with the secular power. It also greatly affected the Church of Ireland. Appointments of all of its bishops and of many of its plum livings was vested in the Crown, and this led to the appointment of many Englishmen, including all the Primates of Armagh from 1702 until the Union. This was bitterly unpopular with Irish Protestants.

More generally, there was a close relationship between the Church of England and the landed elite. The appointment of much of the parish (local)

The Archbishop's Palace, Lambeth by J. M. W. Turner, 1790. The first drawing to be shown by Turner at the Royal Academy. Lambeth Palace was the London seat of the Archbishop of Canterbury and thus the political centre of the Church of England. The influence of archbishops varied greatly, not least because there was no system of retirement. For example, in his last years, William Wake, Archbishop 1716–37, was senile and Edmund Gibson, Bishop of London, was more influential. Apart from their administrative and political roles, several archbishops were also distinguished scholars. For example, Wake's successor, John Potter, Archbishop 1737–47, had been Regius Professor of Divinity at Oxford, and was a distinguished classical scholar, who also took part in theological controversies and wrote on church government.

clergy was directly controlled by the latter: 53 per cent by private individuals and 10 per cent by the Crown, a major cause of pluralism (the holding of several livings). In addition, one-third of English tithes were held by lay impropriators, while church properties were rented on favourable terms. Most tenants were too powerful to be exploited and resistance to episcopal rent increases was effective. Similarly in Ireland opposition to the payment of tithes also affected the Protestant landowning class which, after a long and bitter legal struggle, passed a series of resolutions in the House of Commons in 1735 that in effect declared pasture land free from tithe.

There was a degree of anticlericalism in the early Whig ascendancy, for example on the part of Viscount Stanhope who both brought in a bill to repeal the Schism Act in 1718 and wished to repeal the Test and Corporation Acts in 1718–19, but from the 1720s the hierarchies of Church and State moved closer together in England. Some prominent Whig politicians were personally devout. The Duke of Newcastle read a lesson every day and followed a course of theological reading. Lord Chancellor Hardwicke listened to daily prayers. Newcastle, the minister who was most influential in ecclesiastical appointments between 1742 and 1762, was concerned to ensure that effective and able men were appointed to positions of responsibility, although concern about the political consequences led him in the 1740s and 1750s to oppose the introduction of bishops into the American colonies. Though from 1726 Walpole obtained Indemnity Acts protecting the Dissenters from malicious prosecution, especially office-holders who had failed to take communion, each year except 1730 and 1732, and they were repeated frequently until 1757 and regularly thereafter, moves to repeal the Test and Corporation Acts were defeated in 1736, 1739, 1787, 1789 and 1790. The Reverend Thomas Brand wrote in 1790 to a fellow-Church of England clergyman, Thomas Wharton, rejoicing in 'the defeat of the Dissenters. Their success would have opened a door to every vile set of petitions which ambitious demagogues and disaffected spirits could have invented and the constitution must have been completely destroyed if the votes of Parliament could have been thus influenced by associations from without. Besides what would have become of our tithes, and our prebendal estates, our archdeacons, and our visitations.'[2]

If such events reaffirmed the identification of religion and state, in the form of government protection for the Church of England, they also sustained local tensions. In much of Britain animosity between Anglicanism or Episcopalianism and Dissent or Presbyterianism was a basic political axis, although the two rivalries were different in important respects and, in addition, there is much evidence that the fit between religious and political divisions was far from neat and uniform. In England Dissenters tended to support more radical political positions and their urban locale ensured that their activism was predominantely middle-class and had only limited reference to aristocratic leadership and interests. Whether the Church was in danger or not at the national level, Anglicans felt it necessary to protect it in the localities. Furthermore, in the absence of a modern structure of party organisation, ecclesiastical links provided the basis of community and sociability that was so important in the development of political alignments and the mobilisation of political support.

This was a society in which disagreements over how best to worship God and seek salvation, how to organise the Church and the relationship between Church and State, were matters of urgent concern. 'Polite' and 'religious' are not mutually incompatible, but the image of Hanoverian Britain as a 'polite' society is misleading if that is taken to imply the marginal nature of religious zeal. Despite the claims of other Protestant groups, the established Churches were not devoid of energy, their congregations not sunk in torpor. Hundreds of churches were built or significantly altered during the century. Although few new parishes were created, new churches were built in areas of expanding population, including Manchester, Lancaster, Birmingham, Bath and Leeds, and the problem of population growth did not become very serious for the Church until the 1780s. New churches included Thomas Archer's baroque St Philip's in Birmingham (1711–24), St Michael's (1734–42) and St James's in Bath (1768–69) and St Paul's in Bristol (1787). Churches were built at new fashionable watering places, such as Bristol Hot Wells. Many were rebuilt, for example in Cambridge, four in Worcester between 1730 and 1770 and in Bristol, St Nicholas's in the 1760s and St Thomas's in 1790. Most were kept in good repair. The creation of side aisles and the erection of galleries increased the seating in many churches, as at Saddleworth. In Ireland the growing numbers and greater wealth of the Catholics led to the erection of new churches, six in Dublin during the reign of George I. Economic growth and social challenges and changes also posed major problems for the Churches. Despite the construction of new churches, many growing towns, such as Leeds and Hull, lacked sufficient church accommodation.

Much recent work has stressed the dedication and diligence of clergymen, and the relative effectiveness of the Church's ministry. Clerical diaries of the period indicate faith and an attempt at self-examination. Because of toleration, the Church of England had to operate more effectively if it was to resist the challenge of other Churches. The duty of the Church to teach the faith was much emphasised: religious activism for clergy and laity alike was stressed in Anglican propaganda, not the soporific complacency of a stagnant establishment.

There were very few professed atheists, although they suffered prosecutions under the Blasphemy Act, and there was no necessary dichotomy of enlightenment and faith, the secular and the religious, scientific and mystical. Deism was influential in intellectual circles, but was not anti-religious. Deism was not a clear intellectual position or a movement, for it had neither creed nor organisation; it was a vague term used by polemicists that had a wide range of religious connotations. Eschewing the notion of a God of retribution, deistic writers, such as John Toland in his *Christianity not Mysterious* (1696), suggested a benevolent force that had created a world and a humanity capable of goodness, and a God not intervening through revelation or miracles. The universe therefore had origins, order and purpose, but there was no need for a priesthood.

It is unclear how far such a shift in religious sensitivity affected popular Christianity. Actions based on scriptural authority were treated with suspicion. The range of religious practice was extensive. Literacy, relative wealth and an urban environment enabled some to respond to new intellectual and spiritual currents, though it would be wrong to suggest that rural religion was necessarily unchanging. There was, as in practically every period, widespread concern about irreligion, leading, for example, to the foundation in 1698–99 of the Society for Promoting Christian Knowledge, an Anglican missionary society. The preamble to its charter in 1699 claimed that 'gross ignorance of the Christian religion' was responsible for a threatening 'growth of vice and

immorality'. An essay on preaching published in *Lloyd's Evening Post* on 2 February 1761 complained, '. . . it is very obvious that the Clergy are no where so little thought of, by the Populace, as here . . . the vulgar, in general, appearing no way impressed with a sense of religious duty ... pretty much neglected in our exhortations from the pulpit'. The writer complained that Church of England preachers stressed reason, not passion, and sent their listeners to sleep. Instead, he praised Methodists for the passion of their preaching. Similarly, the Evangelicals of the Church of Scotland criticised the Moderates of the Church for lacking enthusiasm in their sermons.

Nevertheless, there is copious evidence both of massive observance of the formal requirements of the Churches and of widespread piety. In many dioceses, for example London, the parishes were well staffed and services were frequent. Sunday schools and devotional literature, such as the chapbooks read by relatively humble people, fostered sanctity, piety and an awareness of salvation. *The Church Catechism Explained by Way of Question and Answer, and Confirm'd by Scripture Proofs* (1700) by the Kent cleric John Lewis (1675–1747) went through forty-two editions by 1812. Lewis also wrote a series of defences of the position of the Church of England. Popular piety was internalised, and there was a high level of introspective or 'internalised' faith. Concerns over the frequency of receipt of communion were caused by feelings of unworthiness; one reason for the infrequency was that many people felt unworthy of it. William Law's *A Serious Call to a Devout and Holy Life, adapted to the State and Condition of all Orders of Christians* (1728) enjoyed huge sales, and was influential in the development of Methodism. Bunyan's *Pilgrim's Progress* was widely read, and was praised by Dr Johnson.

The Church of England, as always, faced serious problems, especially in the distribution of its resources, but was in a less parlous state than is sometimes suggested. Standards of pastoral care were as good as in earlier periods, and were encouraged by the vigilance of the hierarchy. Benjamin Hoadly, who never visited his diocese while Bishop of Bangor (1715–21), was atypical. Thomas Herring, his successor between 1737 and 1743, regularly toured it in order to ordain and confirm, and to exercise a pastoral ministry among the clergy. Translated to York, Herring was again an energetic and conscientious diocesan who ordained with regularity.

The non-residence of clerics could be a problem, and certainly became more common. Herring's visitation return indicated that 393 out of the 836 parochial benefices in the diocese of York in 1743 had non-resident clergy; 335 out of 711 of the clergy were pluralists. In 453 out of the 836 parishes the required two Sunday services were not provided. In 1780 only about 38 per cent of English parishes had resident incumbents, and 36 per cent of Anglican clergy were pluralists. Pluralism often arose due to lay impropriation or clerical poverty arising from major discrepancies in clerical income and the inadequacy of many livings, but non-resident incumbents frequently lived nearby, and in general there were resident stipendiary curates. Pluralism was more common in areas where many parishes had poor endowments, for example on the Essex coast. Pluralism and non-residence were common problems among Church of Ireland clerics, and gravely limited their ability to undertake missionary work among the Catholic population. Thomas Percy, best known for his research on early English poetry, was so frequently absent in England when Bishop of Dromore (1782–1808) that the Archbishop of Armagh felt obliged to complain.

Facing page: Bishop Benjamin Hoadly (1676–1761) by William Hogarth. Hoadly, a low-churchman dreaded by the high-church faction as intending to level all barriers between the Church of England and Dissent, had his party zeal rewarded successively with the bishoprics of Bangor (1715), Hereford (1721), Salisbury (1723) and Winchester (1734). An active controversialist who wrote on religious and political topics, he was responsible for the Bangorian Controversy of 1717–20. This arose from a sermon preached before George I on 31 March 1717 in which he denied that there was a visible Church of Christ or any authority 'either to make new laws for Christ's subjects, or to impose a sense upon the old ones, or to judge, censure, or punish the servants of another master in matters relating purely to conscience or salvation'.

A Midsummer Afternoon with a Methodist Preacher by Philip James de Loutherbourg (National Gallery of Canada, Ottawa). Open-air preaching was characteristic of many Methodists, necessary because of their contentious ecclesiastical status and seen as subversive by their critics. Hostile clerics such as Bishop Lavington of Exeter prosecuted Methodists under anti-Conventicle legislation. Born in Germany, Loutherbourg (1740–1812) came to London in 1771 and became chief designer of scenery for Garrick at Drury Lane Theatre. A painter of landscapes in the Romantic style and of battle-scenes in the French Revolutionary War, Loutherbourg was interested in mysticism, claimed the power of prophecy and sought to heal illnesses by prayer and faith.

In addition, the Churches were not averse to religious campaigns, such as that waged in Wales in the early decades of the century by the Anglicans and the Dissenters against Catholicism, drunkenness and profanity, and for salvation and literacy. There was a major expansion of the printed word in Welsh and the majority of it was devoted to religious works. In 1746 the Society for Promoting Christian Knowledge issued an edition of the bible and prayer-book in Welsh. There was a stress on the public dimension of religion, on the spiritual health of the community. Piety and worship became fashionable and public practices, with charity sermons, fashionable services and fashionable churches, such as St George's, Hanover Square and St James's, Piccadilly in London.

The very nature of established Churches that sought to minister to all, in an age when religion was a social obligation as well as a personal spiritual experience, posed problems for some of those, both clergy and laity, who criticised anything that might compromise the latter. Believers sure of their faith could find the compromises of comprehension abhorrent, but the determination of clerics to ensure standards of religious knowledge and observance ensured that these compromises were not those of the lowest common denominator.

Dissatisfaction, however, reflected the importance of, and commitment to,

religion, the Church and the clergy. Few believed that they could or should be dispensed with, or doubted the close relationships of faith and reason, Church and State, clergy and laity, religion and the people.

Methodism was one consequence of religious enthusiasm. It was initially a movement for revival that sought to remain within the Church of England, supplementing the official parochial structure by a system of private religious societies that would both regenerate the Church and win it new members. However after Methodism's institutional founder, John Wesley (1703–91) died, it broke away completely, and his decision to ordain ministers on his own authority in 1784 marked a point of real division between Methodism and the Church of England. Wesley had begun his evangelical campaign in England in 1738, although George Whitefield, Howell Harris and Daniel Rowlands were already preaching a similar message. They used the same methods as Wesley, but preached Calvinism while Wesley preached Arminianism. Wesley combined concern for the church establishment with first-hand contact with

George II and Figures associated with the Protestant Moravian Church, attributed to J. Valentin Haidt. The Moravian Brethren, a pre-Reformation religious community, revived in Germany in the eighteenth century. A Lutheran, George II was interested in German Protestant religious developments; his wife Caroline was open to philosophical approaches to religion that struck some critics as radical.

continental Protestants, particularly the revived Moravian Brethren based at Herrnhut, a German religious community developed by the Pietist Count Zinzendorf. Methodism, initially intended by Wesley as a means to reawaken Anglicanism, was thus part of the 'Great Awakening', a widespread movement of Protestant revival in Europe and North America, and employed many of the organisational features of European Protestant revival, including itinerant preaching and love feasts.

Seeing his mission as one of saving souls, Wesley urged men to turn to Christ to win redemption and promised they would know that they had achieved salvation. He rejected predestination, asserted justification by faith and offered an eclectic theology that was adapted to a powerful mission addressing itself to popular anxieties. Wesley's Arminianism led him to stress that salvation was open to all. He combined traditional religion with Enlightenment thought processes. Wesley's belief in religion as an epic struggle, with providence, demons and witchcraft all present, and his willingness to seek guidance by opening the Bible at random, all found echoes in a growing popular following in many, though not all, areas. This was facilitated by the energy of the preaching mission, the revivalist nature of Methodism, with its hymn-singing, watch-nights and love feasts. In his *Enthusiasm of Methodists and Papists Compared* (3 parts, 1749–51), the hostile George Lavington, Bishop of Exeter, claimed that Methodism imitated the enthusiastic excesses of medieval Catholicism, with visions, exorcisms and healing, although Wesley in fact argued against excessive emotionalism and enthusiasm. Wesley was also flexible, well aware of the value of print, producing many tracts and much serial material. He was also tolerant, accepting men and women of all denominations as members, and from the mid–1740s using lay preachers because he could not obtain enough support from ordained ministers. This helped to increase clerical opposition, as did unease about Wesley's theology. Wesley had much sympathy for the poor and criticised some aspects of society, but was loyal to the dynasty and the political society. Thus Methodism did not pose a threat to the political elite. Wesley's loyalty and belief in divine intervention were reflected in a letter he sent to Matthew Ridley, Mayor of Newcastle, during the Jacobite rising of 1745. He felt bound to write, by the fear of God, love of his country and zeal towards George II, as he had been pained by 'the senseless wickedness, the ignorant prophaneness' of the city's poor and the 'continual cursing and swearing, and the wanton blasphemy' of the soldiers, and feared this would endanger divine support.[3]

Methodism was particularly popular among artisans and servants and responsive to the religious needs of such groups. In Nottingham its following was mostly among artisans, particularly those working in the stocking industry. Their first chapel in the city, the Octagon, was founded in 1764 and it was replaced by a larger chapel in 1784 and again in 1798. Methodism was also very popular among Cornish tinners and fishermen, both dangerous jobs. It developed rapidly in England and Wales, especially among artisans, though not unskilled workers, in manufacturing and mining areas, such as the West Riding of Yorkshire where the parochial structure was weak, but had little impact in Scotland or Ireland, especially among Irish Catholics. Wesley's Arminianism was resisted by the strong Calvinism of many Scots, although he made frequent visits there and there were independent Scottish revivals. Methodism won more support among women than men. Methodism was an important development, but it is necessary not to exaggerate its numerical significance. There were only around 100,000 Methodists in England and Wales by 1800.

Methodist meetings sometimes met with a violent response, as in Sheffield (1744), Exeter (1745), Leeds (1745), York (1747), Norwich (1751–52) and Birmingham (1764), although the degree to which the Church of England did not respond in an official fashion is striking. Wesley was not expelled from the Church of England. Thus there was an effective toleration of Methodism at the national level that was not always matched locally, although the local experience varied greatly. If Bishop Lavington of Exeter was very hostile in the 1750s, Bishop Ross was very friendly in the 1770s.

Religious issues were 'real', indistinguishable from political and social issues, and worth fighting over, literally so as the riots against Dissenters in England in 1710, 1715 and 1791, and against Catholics in Edinburgh and Glasgow in 1779 and in England in 1780, indicated all too clearly. There was a major riot in Dingwall in 1704 over the choice of a new minister. The fear among non-Anglican colonists that Anglican episcopacy would be imposed helped to fuel American hostility towards the British link.

Anti-Catholicism was a powerful force, throughout the period at the popular level and at least until the mid-century at that of the elite. Prior to then it was widely believed that Catholicism was on the increase in the British Isles and on the advance in Europe. Suspicions of Catholic disloyalty were increased by the Jacobite threat. There was an enormous amount of anti-Catholic material both in the culture of print – newspapers, pamphlets, prints and books – and in the public culture of anniversary celebrations, for example of the defeat of the Armada and the discovery of the Gunpowder Plot, and of other public rituals. The representation of Catholics was generally crude and violent: their intentions were seen as diabolical, their strength and deceit were frightening. The public ritual lent immediacy to the material in print, and both were further linked by sermons, as for the anniversary of the Gunpowder Plot. The wish of William Wake, Archbishop of Canterbury from 1716 to 1737, for closer Anglican relations with the French Catholic church (as well as with the Orthodox and Continental Protestants) was unrealistic, evidence of divergence between popular and clerical religion. Where landowners were Catholic, as on some of the Hebrides, the penal laws were generally not enforced, although the '45 led to a serious upsurge in anti-Catholic activity.

It has been argued that anti-Catholicism diminished during the period, especially after the suppression of Jacobitism; but it is unclear that this was so, especially at the popular level, although there is little doubt that at the level of the elite social relations improved. The stone with which the nave of York Minster was repaired in mid-century was the gift of a Catholic, Sir Edward Gascoigne. Catholic landowners, however, were hit by a double land tax.

As a result of the 1779 anti-Catholic riots in Scotland, the concessions given to English Catholics by the 1778 Catholic Relief Act were not extended north of the border, although John Wilkes told the House of Commons that 'when I am informed that the peaceable and loyal Roman Catholics of Scotland find no security, even in the capital, for their lives and property, I do not hesitate to assert, that there is a dissolution of all government'. Under the Act, officiating Catholic clergy were no longer liable to life imprisonment and the provision by which land had to pass over any Catholic heir to the next Protestant in line was repealed, in both cases so long as an oath of Allegiance was taken: Jacobitism and the temporal authority of the papacy had to be rejected. In addition, pressure for the repeal of the Act in England led to the activities of the Protestant Association, which culminated in the Gordon Riots in London and the provinces in 1780. These were a challenge to order in the centre of empire greater than anything hitherto seen that century. About 50,000 members of the Association marched on Parliament to present the petition for repeal. The JPs had only about seventy-six constables to control the crowds, but Parliament refused to be intimidated into repeal. The angry demonstrators initially turned to attack Catholic chapels and schools in Westminster and London before threatening establishment targets such as the houses of prominent ministers, politicians thought to be pro-Catholic, Anglican clerics, and those magistrates who sought to act against rioters. The prisons were stormed in order to release imprisoned rioters. The riots reflected a popular Protestantism that was deeply suspicious of elite tolerant tendencies. Nevertheless, in 1791 the Oaths of Allegiance and Supremacy were amended for Catholics after negotiation with the Catholic Committee.

In Ireland rising Catholic wealth in the second half of the century was important to the long-term process by which Catholics came to play a more central role in politics and a more active role in society. The legal position of Irish Catholics improved. In 1774 an Act allowed them to take the Oath of Allegiance; four years later, the Catholic Relief Act for Ireland removed restrictions on Catholics holding lands. Subsequent concern about the possible impact of the French Revolution led the government in London to extend this policy. William Pitt the Younger overruled the Lord Lieutenant of Ireland, the Earl of Westmorland, and the wishes of the Protestant Ascendancy, and bowed to Catholic agitation by granting better off Catholic freeholders the vote in 1793. The Place and Pensions Act and the Catholic Relief Act allowed Catholics to bear arms, sit on juries and hold minor civil and military office. Pitt was already thinking about the possibility of a parliamentary union between Britain and Ireland. The Irish Catholic Church, concerned about the hostility to the Catholic Church, and indeed to Christianity, of the French Revolutionaries, preached the religious duty of obedience to the government of George III. In 1795 the government began funding the Catholic college at Maynooth.

However, religious division and prejudice continued strong. Earl Fitzwilliam, Lord Lieutenant 1794–95, sought to remove the remaining legal disabilities barring Catholics from Parliament and government office, but was disavowed and recalled. Fitzwilliam had believed that concessions were necessary in order to prevent the spread of revolutionary sentiment; his failure helped in the alienation of Catholic opinion, and confirmed radicals in the view that the only means to achieve their aims was revolution. In 1795 the Orange Order was founded to reassert the Protestant Ascendancy in Ireland. The unsuccessful Catholic rebellion of 1798 reflected and sustained confessional bitterness.

Religious antagonism had other manifestations. The strength of popular Anglicanism was demonstrated in 1753, when a vicious press campaign of anti-Semitic hatred, with popular backing, forced the repeal of the Jewish Naturalisation Act of that year, which had made it easier to be naturalised by private act of Parliament, dropping the phrase 'on the true faith of a Christian' from the oaths of Supremacy and Allegiance. The *Salisbury Journal* of 7 January 1754 recorded the celebrations in Devizes:

Dancing Dogs by John Wootton, 1759. The painting hangs in the Staircase Hall at Wallington, then the home of Sir Walter Blackett, MP for Newcastle and a leading figure in the coal trade, who bred Bedlington terriers. Pets played an increasingly important role, an aspect of a wealthier society that did not need to adopt the former utilitarian attitude towards animals. There was a greater awareness of cruelty to animals. Wootton (1682?–1764) was noted as a painter of dogs and horses, but also tackled hunting and battle paintings, for example portraits of the Duke of Cumberland with the battles of Dettingen and Culloden in the background, as well as equestrian portraits.

Aerial View, Royal Crescent and the Circus, Bath. The Circus
was begun by John Wood in 1754 and finished in 1764; the
Royal Crescent was built by John Wood the Younger between
1767 and 1775. William Pitt the Elder paid £1,200 for 7 The
Circus in 1753 and retained it until 1770. Pitt was MP for Bath
between 1757 and 1766 and frequently went there for his
health. John Wood's design and decoration of the Circus
reflected his Masonic and druidical beliefs.

Facing page: The Tree of Life c. 1770, a
Methodist print showing the rewards
of faith and virtue and the wages of
sin. Belief in hell, sin and the Devil
was strong and biblical injunctions
were taken literally.

The TREE of LIFE.

which bear twelve manner of Fruits and yielded her Fruit every Month and the Leaves of the Tree were for the healing of the Nations Rev. Ch. XXII ver 2.

Likewise a View of the New Jerusalem & this present Evil World with the Industry of Gospel Ministers in endeavouring to pluck Sinners from the Wrath to come

Dr. Squintum's Exaltation or the Reformation, 1763. One of several anti-Methodist caricatures, this is an attack on George Whitefield, and argues that Methodist preachers are deceitful, motivated by greed and close to the Devil, and their congregations immoral and violent. Whitefield engaged in many missionary tours and much open-air preaching and was a powerful speaker; he gave over 18,000 sermons.

Last Friday the gentlemen and principal tradesmen of this borough, met at the Black Bear Inn to rejoice on account of the repeal of the Jew Bill; and though numbers of different persuasions were assembled on this occasion, yet party and prejudice were entirely laid aside, and all were unanimous in expressing their joy and highest approbation. The effigy of a Jew was carried through every street in town, attended with all sorts of rough music; several men had torches that the inhabitants might see the effigy, and read the paper that was stuck on his breast, containing these words:

NO JEWS!

Reformations to the B--ps [Bishops];

Christianity for ever.

They made a halt two or three times in every street, drank and repeated the above, amidst the acclamations of a great number of people: a large fire was made, and they burnt the body of the Jew, and set his head on the top of the pillory; the bells rang, and beer was given to the populace; several loyal healths were drank by the gentlemen, etc. and likewise variety of toasts, applicable to the occasion. The Thursday following (being Market Day) the head was again put on top of the pillory, which gave great delight to the farmers and other country people.

Dr Burgises Theater

The Sacheverell Riots, 1 March 1710, were provoked by the Whigs' impeachment of the Tory cleric Dr Sacheverell. Here Daniel Burgess's Presbyterian meeting-house in Carey Street, London, is wrecked by the mob. Sacheverell was a violently anti-Dissenter polemicist who in 1709 preached before the Lord Mayor and Aldermen of London on 'the perils of false brethren in church and state', and argued that the Church was in danger from toleration, occasional conformity and schism. The sermon was declared a seditious libel by the House of Commons, and the Lords impeached him, but his sentence was light and he was treated as a great celebrity. In 1713 Queen Anne presented Sacheverell to a rich London living.

The Times, 1780. Anti-Catholic propaganda produced by the Protestant Association, claiming that the Catholic powers are seeking to impose Catholicism on Britain. A dog is shown urinating on Magna Carta and there are references to Catholic cruelty, past and present. The Protestant clergy urge Protestants to remember past episodes such as the Gunpowder Plot, while a Scot is shown prepared to fight the Catholics. Anti-Catholic ideology served to unite Protestant opinion in Britain.

Religious issues were also an expression or aspect of other disputes, ranging from that over the succession following the Glorious Revolution, to the town –country tension that played a role in Anglican–Dissenter rivalries. Towns were often centres of Dissent, challenging Anglican religious–cultural hegemony just as they could seek to resist the attempts of the local gentry to control their parliamentary representation, and were also centres of a changing economy. Religious opposition to the Anglican world-view of George III's government was one of the factors responsible for the revolution in America. Dissent was strongest in regions where the parochial structure was weak, particularly in the West Riding of Yorkshire, where Quakers, Presbyterians and Baptists were numerous.

Religious tension is difficult to measure, because its classic product was not the violence that might attract judicial and military attention, but the prejudice that was expressed in endogamy (marriage within the group), discriminatory political, social, economic and cultural practices, and the acid of abuse and insult. Religious minorities cohered not only in order to practise their faith, but also for protection, employment, commercial links, credit, and the maintenance of their identity. Endogamy also served to preserve their strength and intermarriage led to criticism. Where today European religious groups generally face the challenge of the assimilation of their members into predominantly secular cultures, in the eighteenth century religious identity was maintained because assimilation on such terms was not an option. The role of clergymen and ecclesiastical and religious bodies in education, charity and social welfare furthered identification with confessional groupings, although it would be mistaken to give the impression that different religious groupings remained isolated from one another.

As ever, contrasting images of religious commitment and life can be presented. The strongest one of my schooldays was of the copious meals of a Norfolk Church of England minister, James Woodforde. Another is suggested by an account Richard Browne sent his father in 1765. He had visited St Patrick's Purgatory, an island in Lough Derg in County Donegal where each year over 10,000 Irish Catholics made a pilgrimage, a practice expressly forbidden under the Popery Act of 1704. He found

a multitude indeed of both sexes mostly indeed of the poorer sort . . . in one place there are built seven small places of a circular form like pounds in which place the penitents are obliged to run so many times round bare foot on sharp pointed rocks repeating so many ave marias etc., in commemoration of the seven deadly sins . . . in other parts they are obliged to wade to the middle in the water and stand there for a stated time repeating a certain number of prayers, when this is over the next penance is to retire to a vault made purposely, where they must remain 24 hours without eating, drinking, speaking or sleeping, for they are sure if they do either the Devil has a power of carrying them away, and to prevent sleeping, everyone that goes in there supply themselves with pins which they thrust into anyone they find dozing . . . the last ceremony is washing in the lake, when they wash away all their sins.[4]

7 ENLIGHTENMENT AND SCIENCE

The pre-Revolutionary eighteenth century in Europe is often referred to as the Enlightenment or the Age of Enlightenment, but the relationship of the British Isles to this movement is far from clear. It is generally agreed that there was a Scottish Enlightenment, but many writers do not discern or discuss an English one. This is mistaken, arising from the traditional concentration in Enlightenment studies on the writings of a small number of French thinkers, and reflects the difficulty of defining the term.

Rather than seeing the Enlightenment as a French-dominated movement, it could better be described as a tendency towards critical enquiry and the application of reason in which British intellectuals played a major role. Reason was a goal as well as a method of Enlightenment thinkers. They believed it necessary to use reason in order to appreciate man, society and the universe and thus to improve human circumstances, an objective in which utilitarianism, religious faith and the search for human happiness could combine. Certain thinkers, especially in France, believed that existing authorities were an active restraint on the quest of and for reason and accordingly adopted critical, even radical, views; but such a clash was untypical. Reason was believed to be the distinguishing mark of man, the insane commonly being regarded as monstrous. Reason was seen not only as the characteristic of the human species, but also of human development and social organisation. In contrast, the savage mind was held to be wild as well as heathen, obsessed by a world of terror, in which monstrous anxieties were projected on to nature.

Contemporaries claimed that reason freed men from unnecessary fears and could continue to do so. Thus, the great astronomer Sir Isaac Newton (1642–1727) had demonstrated that comets were integral to nature, not portents. God was believed to act through the normal laws of physics; not to

124

break them. Reason was seen as aiding human development by helping man to explore, understand and shape his environment, and it was argued that this was facilitated by a reliance on objective fact, scepticism and incredulity.

Reason led very few in Britain to attack Christianity. Instead, Reason was believed to support the established procedures of Christianity, not least in opposition to the claims of religious enthusiasts. Reason could be used to confirm revelation. If the Scottish philosopher David Hume (1711–76), in his *Essay on Miracles* (1748), challenged their existence, Thomas Sherlock, an influential Anglican bishop, was able in his *Trial of the Witnesses of the Resurrection* (1729) to come to an opposite conclusion. Sherlock's *Trial* was a counterblast to Thomas Woolston's *Discourses on Miracles* (1727–29), in which Woolston stated the deists' opposition to miracles. Sherlock tried to use reason and strongly empirical methods – the book was written as a trial with witnesses cross-examined – to argue the rational case for revealed religion. Thomas Clubb attacked Sherlock's *Trial,* and a response by Charles Moss, Sherlock's chaplain, reasserted the *Trial*'s view that the laws of man did not mean that miracles were 'incredible'.

In 1749 Conyers Middleton, a Church of England cleric, sought to reconcile history and religion with his *Free Enquiry into the Miraculous Powers which are supposed to have subsisted in the Christian Church*, which denied the credibility of the stories of miracles in periods subsequent to the first age of the Church. This was rejected by Wesley who, in his *Letter to Conyers Middleton*, stated that divine intervention had occurred throughout history. Wesley himself was interested in science as evidence of divine mysteries. The limited impact of scepticism was indicated in 1751, when widespread anxieties arising from English earthquakes led Hume's publisher to delay the second edition of his *Philosophical Essays*. In 1758, writing to his sister from London with a long account of comets, John Rolls struck a common note: 'Let not however any specious part of reason prevent our concern at such phenomena, but rather put us in mind of the end and final conclusion of all things . . . induce us to pay a more than common homage at the foot stool of the throne of our good Almighty God, who with a nod or touch or breath can hurl us with fury and terrible destruction to all eternity, or gather us up like a scroll in a moment.'[1]

Most intellectuals and churchmen shared John Locke's view that a rational appreciation of man's situation would lead people to be Christians. By treating reason as a divine gift and the universe as a divine creation, they established a framework in which observation need not be viewed as hostile to faith. Far from being compromises with tradition and religion, these views reflected the attempts of pious men in a religious society to comprehend the achievements and possibilities of scientific discoveries. In his unpublished *Essay towards an Abridgement of the English History* (1757–60), Edmund Burke ascribed the development of human society to Providence's role in providing suitable conditions. The hymn-writer Isaac Watts wrote *The Knowledge of the Heavens and the Earth Made Easy* (1726) in order to introduce beginners to astronomy. He believed that it would reinforce religious knowledge. Edmund Gibson and William Warburton, two of the most influential Anglican bishops, both defended John Locke from the charge of deism. They clearly felt that Locke's strongly rationalist stance was not inconsistent with Anglicanism. There was a powerful trend among Anglican clergy away from the mystical and 'spiritualistic' and towards strongly rational sermons. Sermons became analytical examinations of the meanings of biblical texts, sometimes quite explicitly championing the cause of reason. John Wynne, Bishop of St Asaph from 1715 to 1727 and of Bath and Wells from 1727 to 1743, published an *Abridgement of John Locke's Essay on the Human Understanding* (1696), which was praised by Locke, and in his *Sermon before the Society for the Reformation of Manners, January 1726* claimed that men and women needed to call on their reason and intelligence to overcome any sense of shame or embarrassment for their faith: reason had to conquer irrational feelings for the benefit of religion. This, more generally, was the theme of the Societies for the Reformation of Manners: reason harnessed to religion in order to overcome moral 'incontinence' and immorality. Knowledge was seen as a potent weapon against atheism and deism.

Yet, whatever their personal faith, the work of many scientists made little reference to God. His intervention in the world He had created, allowed for by Newton, was increasingly restricted by the explanation of supposed anomalies. Geological discoveries and theories threw doubt on the biblical creation story, the universal flood and Old Testament chronology, while astronomical work challenged received notions of the universe and the idea that it was static. Much medical experimentation and psychological speculation placed little weight on the idea of the soul.

The thought of the period was far from uniform. There were pessimistic and optimistic strains, and also humanitarian, liberal, moral and authoritarian dimensions. This diversity makes it doubtful whether the search for the origins or chronology of Enlightenment is particularly helpful. The origins have been found in a reaction against Louis XIV among English, Dutch and French writers, in a reaction against the Baroque, in the scientific revolution of the seventeenth century and in a crisis of conscience at the end of that period.

Abstract thought was important, most obviously in the work of Hume. He argued in his *Treatise of Human Nature* (1738) that only impressions definitely existed and that it was impossible to prove the existence of the mind and the nature of causality. Theoretical ideas were advanced from general principles in a number of fields. There was also a concern with the social context and with the relationship between theory and practice. Thinkers were as much concerned with discovery, whether through exploration, observation or historical study, as with speculation. Captain Cook charted the Pacific. Edward Gibbon based his masterly account of the *Decline and Fall of the Roman Empire* (1776–88) on massive scholarship. Experimental verification played a major role in the controversy over how best to measure longitude. The 1714 Longitude Act offered a reward for a successful solution, and John Harrison received the prize in 1773 for experiments which went back to the 1730s. Sir William Jones laid the groundwork for modern comparative linguistics when in 1786 he suggested that Sanskrit's affinity to Greek and Latin could be explained by suggesting a common earlier source. Though the nature and closeness of the relationship between discovery and speculation varied according to the individual investigator and to the subject investigated, it was crucial to the development and application of thought in this period. Methodism can in part be understood as a consequence of Wesley's stress on an individual's ability to understand and know salvation.

Publications were the main channel through which new ideas were diffused, and the strongly-developed culture of print was an important dimension of the British Enlightenment. The press played a major role in spreading knowledge. The *Leeds Mercury* of 26 December 1775 began an article: 'The present appearance of the grand planet, Jupiter, upon the meridian, at midnight, excites the curiosity of astronomers; we insert the following for the perusal of those less conversant in that science.' The book trade and the network of correspondents that lay behind scholarly journals provided the channels for ideas. The extent of the culture of print varied greatly; it was strongest in major urban centres and weakest in distant rural areas. Thus, whereas during most of the second half of the century Derby usually had four booksellers, no newspaper was printed in Wales and, apart from abortive secret Catholic enterprises, there were no printing presses there until 1718. Only towards the close of the century did literacy and prosperity combine to increase book purchases and allow the development of Welsh printing.

The culture of print was public, and spread knowledge rapidly. Although the protective value of cowpox against smallpox was not unknown before Edward Jenner experimented with, and in 1798 published his findings on the value of, vaccination, his publication turned folk wisdom into readily accessible knowledge. The corollary of the publications were the societies, ranging from the informality of coffee-houses to organised academies, that discussed ideas. Clubs and institutions, ranging from the subscription concert to the Masonic lodge, were a popular feature of cultural and intellectual life, the corporatist spirit being central in many spheres of eighteenth-century society.

The spread of new ideas was not simply a matter of the existence of the

Captain Cook witnessing human sacrifice in Tahiti, 1769. James Cook (1728–79) arrived in HMS *Endeavour* in Tahiti on the first of his three great voyages. The mission was intended to observe the transit of Venus across the sun in order to measure the distance between the sun and the Earth. Contemporaries, however, were more interested in the light his voyages threw on the remote civilisations of the Pacific and, in particular, on the character and life of the `noble savages'.

necessary channels of communications; in part, it reflected a conscious reaction against the past, as with the Scottish Enlightenment, but in England there was a less marked sense of discontinuity. The Scottish Enlightenment had many distinctive features, one of which was the application of reason to knowledge as a general principle. Important developments included the foundation of economics by Sir James Steuart (1712–80), whose *Inquiry into the Principles of Political Economy* (1767) was the first systematic treatment of the subject in English, and Adam Smith (1723–90), Professor of Moral Philosophy in Glasgow. Smith advised the government on economic matters between 1773 and 1776 and in 1776 published *The Wealth of Nations*, a work emphasising the value of the absence of government regulation in ensuring economic growth. Adam Ferguson (1723–1816), Professor of Pneumatics and Moral Philosophy at Edinburgh, helped to found sociology with his *Essay on the History of Civil Society* (1767). There were also important developments in psychology and history, and in geology with James Hutton's *Theory of the Earth* (1785). In epistemological and theological terms geology was one of the most significant branches of eighteenth-century science and, unintentionally, the most subversive. The jurist James, Lord Monboddo (1714–99) played a major role in the development of anthropology; his *Of the Origin and Progress of Language* (1773–92) treated the development of man in a social state as a natural process.

There was a renaissance in literature with the works of Scots such as Burns, Fergusson, Hogg, Mackenzie, Scott, Smollett and Thomson. The first professorship in English anywhere was founded at Edinburgh in 1762 and occupied by Hugh Blair (1718–1800), an Edinburgh cleric who was a prominent member of the Edinburgh Enlightenment. There was also a renaissance in painting in Scotland, with works by Ramsay, Raeburn, Nasmyth and Wilkie. A university curriculum focusing on philosophy was created. Legal codification proceeded with Stair's *Institutions* and Erskine's *Institute of the Law of Scotland* (1773). In England, the preservation of the control of the Church of England over higher education had an adverse effect by comparison.

Science was a major field of innovation both north and south of the border. The so-called Scientific Revolution of the late seventeenth century had seen major advances in discovering the operations of natural laws, particularly the developments in astronomy, mathematics and physics associated with Newton. For many people, however, such ideas and the standards of proof implied were little understood. The new science was ignored by much of the population, and the Copernican cosmology was not accepted by all; although traditional ideas had only a limited resonance in the culture of print. In 1728 the mathematician Joseph Morgan published *The Immobility of the Earth Demonstrated Proving the Earth to be the Center of the Universe*, a translation of a French work by Étienne Lecuyer de la Jonchère, but this work had little impact. About nine years later appeared a work that indicated interest in Newtonian physics outside 'polite' circles. Benjamin Parker, a Derby stocking-maker turned author, and sometime vendor of Restorative Jelly, published his *A Journal Thro' the World . . . An Explanation into the Beginning of our Existence*, which argued for the 'non-eternity of matter' and 'that the soul is immortal'. Although the book carried a London imprint it was probably printed in Birmingham.

It was still widely believed that astrological anatomies and zodiacs were keys to character and guides to the future, that extra-terrestrial forces intervened in the affairs of the world, particularly human and animal health and the state of the crops and weather, and that each constellation in the zodiac presided over a particular part of man, guidance to this process being provided by almanacs. Ptolemaic geocentricism continued to be important in this literature, while many almanac writers boasted of being anti-Newtonian. Astrology flourished at the popular level in rural areas and provincial towns.

Popular conservatism was not the sole factor inhibiting the diffusion of new scientific ideas and methods. There was no simple 'correct' line of scientific development which led smoothly to modern conceptions of science; unsound theories, such as the phlogiston explanation of combustion, could lead to greater clarification of the issues involved, and were not simply worthless. A form of history of science and medicine was emerging which identified a mainstream tradition stressing observation, experiment and careful deduction of laws, but the very looseness of the processes involved made this difficult to apply to separate 'sound' from 'unsound' science. The sense of a great tradition, correct approach and recent important breakthroughs in the investigation of the nature of light and gravitation gave a rough framework for what was and what was not scientific. There was confidence that knowledge was increasing and better understood. In his *History of the Present State of Electricity* (1767), Joseph Priestley claimed that recent discoveries of electrical phenomena would extend 'the bounds of natural science . . . New worlds may open to our view, and the glory of the great Sir Isaac Newton himself, and all his contemporaries, be eclipsed by a new set of philosophers.' The notion of an age of progress became well established.

However, the creative tension in eighteenth-century science, of experimentation and speculative systematisation, did not simply foster one approach to any particular problem. Instead, a wide range of approaches was adopted and conclusions drawn. It was difficult to establish any individual interpretation in an age where standards of scientific proof were not always rigorous and the facilities for the necessary experimentation often absent. The amateur and commercial nature of much scientific activity possibly exacerbated the problem, though the world of scholarship, too, was not free from serious error. The belief that man could come to understand much about himself and the world through his own reason and through empirical investigation had played a major role in the Scientific Revolution. However, science was a process, rather than a set of answers, and this belief encouraged not only the activities and acceptance of charlatans, but also the continued intertwining of metaphysics, theology, human interest and scientific thought and experimentation that had been so important in the previous century.

There was no shortage of charlatans, but, in putting scientific interest and methods to personal profit, they also revealed the varied relationship of both of these to the widespread desire, at the individual and the social level, to understand and control the environment. This desire was only imperfectly catered for by existing formal institutions. Quack-doctors won fame and fortune with their remedies. Joshua Ward (1685–1761), for example, gained tremendous popularity and a considerable fortune from 1734 and was patronised by George II, despite the fact that his remedies killed as many as they cured. There was a tar-water mania according to which it was regarded as a remedy for all ills. One wild claim was that tar-water could heal amputees in three days. In 1786 Dr Katterfelto, a travelling lecturer who claimed mystical powers, was regarded by some in Yorkshire as the devil and by others as able to cure troublesome spirits. Alchemy continued to be important. Giuseppe Balsamo, 'Count Cagliostro' (1743–95), began his career as an alchemist by seeking to transmute excrement, hair, herbs, minerals, urine and wood into gold in London in 1776–77. Some scientists were interested in alchemy; the eminent chemist Peter Woulfe (1727?–1803), who developed an apparatus for passing gases through liquids, also pursued alchemical investigations, fixing prayers to his apparatus.

The idea of direct divine intervention was not only held by the populace. Newton himself argued that God acted in order to keep heavenly bodies in their place. The idea that personal fault or the malevolent intentions of others were responsible for mishap proved difficult to dispel whatever the current teaching on cosmology, physics and medicine. Medicine was a particular field of misapprehension, because much about both body and mind was not understood. It was widely believed for example that masturbation was the specific cause of mental and physical diseases, and there was much ignorance about menstruation. Mary Toft, the 'rabbit-woman of Godalming', who claimed to have given birth to rabbits, was believed by many, including several prominent physicians, in 1726.

Much scientific work advanced inaccurate theses that were contested, but, as it often used principles of hypothesis and experimentation similar to those employed by its critics, it was difficult to disprove. Thus scientific activity and experimentation did not necessarily advance knowledge. John Needham (1713–81), the first Catholic cleric elected a fellow of the Royal Society of London (1747), published in 1749 his experimental proof of the theory of spontaneous generation, the idea that inanimate matter could come alive, and thus that mutations and the creation of new species were possible. The fallacy of his experiment was demonstrated in 1760. A polymath in the manner of a period where modern distinctions between branches of knowledge had little meaning, Needham also published on ants, the Alps, electricity – one of the great interests of the period, his correspondence with Voltaire on miracles, and in 1761 a widely discussed, but speedily refuted, book that sought to interpret an Egyptian inscription by the use of Chinese characters. On his circumnavigation of the world in 1764–66 John Byron inaccurately reported the existence of Patagonian giants.

Experimentation, even if designed to sustain established views, reflected a determination to expand on received information, while through taxonomy scholars sought to classify and organise knowledge, in part so that it could be better applied. Exploration played an important role, especially in botany, astronomy and geology; the botanist Joseph Banks (1743–1820) sailed round the world with Cook and also collected plants on expeditions to Newfoundland and Iceland. Succeeding George III's favourite, the Earl of Bute, as Director of the new Royal Botanic gardens at Kew (founded in 1759), Banks helped to make them a centre for botanical research based on holdings from around the world. Nevil Maskelyne (1732–1811), Astronomer Royal from 1765, was sent by the Royal Society to observe the transit of Venus of 1761 on the island of St Helena. While on his way he experimented in taking longitudes by lunar distances and while there kept tidal records. In 1766 he began the annual production and publication of the *Nautical Almanac and Astronomical Ephemeris*, a book of tables of the predicted positions of celestial bodies at a series of times, that was of great value to navigators and at once sold 10,000 copies. Maskelyne also improved the accuracy of astronomical instruments. Sir William Jones, who made his reputation translating Persian works in the 1770s, issuing a *Grammar of the Persian Language* in 1771, mastered Sanskrit in the following decade, and translated several Hindu classics. Founding the Bengal Asiatic Society in 1784, he studied Indian languages, literature and philosophy.

The British played a major role in exploration, especially in the South Seas. In 1767 a naval officer, Samuel Wallis, discovered many islands in the Pacific, including King George the Third's Island, better known as Tahiti. The collaborative international observation of Venus' transit across the sun in 1769 took another naval officer, James Cook, to Tahiti, whence he conducted the first circuit and charting of New Zealand and the charting of the east coast of Australia. Here in 1770 Cook landed in Botany Bay and claimed the territory for George III. In 1772–75 Cook's repeated efforts to find a great southern continent, including the first passage of the Antarctic circle, failed. Cook, however, discovered New Caledonia and Hawaii, and in 1778 he proved that pack ice blocked any possible 'north-west' passage from the Atlantic to the Pacific.

Land exploration received less government support and faced an often hostile environment. Much of the interior of North America was explored by the British, French and Spaniards. The first crossing of the continent from the Atlantic to the Pacific was made in 1792–93 by Alexander Mackenzie. Mackenzie, building on the discoveries of Pond and Hearne, had earlier followed the river, subsequently named after him, to the Arctic. In Africa, James Bruce rediscovered the Abyssinian source of the Blue Nile in 1770, while Mungo Park discovered the course of the Niger in 1796.

The Reverend John Walker (1731–1804) was typical of many clergymen in his interest in botany and geology; a friend of Kames, and from 1779 Professor of Natural History in Edinburgh, he met Rousseau and Franklin and corresponded with Linnaeus. He won medals from the Edinburgh Society in the 1750s for his collections of natural manures and in 1761–64 his mineralogical researches led to the discovery of Strontianite. Walker helped to organise the Royal Society of Edinburgh and its Natural History (1782) and Agricultural (1792) Societies. Walker was not only a pillar of the Edinburgh enlightenment, but also an avid collector of geological and botanical specimens. As professor, Walker emphasised laboratory work, and he and his pupils established Scottish geological studies.

Major works of classification included Pennant's *British Zoology* (1766–68) and John Lightfoot's *Flora Scotica* (1778). Lightfoot, the Oxford-educated son of a Gloucestershire yeoman who became librarian and chaplain of the Dowager Duchess of Portland, arranged his work on the Linnaean system. He also first described the reed warbler. The naturalist Thomas Pennant (1726–98) also visited Scotland, publishing a *Tour in Scotland* (1771, 5th edn 1790) that increased English awareness of its customs and natural history. Pennant was a correspondent of the Reverend Gilbert White, whose *Natural History of Selborne* (1788) threw much light on the conduct of the natural world, particularly birds. William Withering (1741–99), an Edinburgh-educated doctor, who was physician to the Staffordshire County Infirmary (1767–75) and subsequently Chief Physician to the Birmingham General Hospital, published *A Botanical Arrangement of all the Vegetables naturally growing in Great Britain . . . with an easy Introduction to the Study of Botany* (1776) and subjected digitalis to scientific study, writing *An Account of the Foxglove and some of its Medical Uses* (1785).

Though measurement played a major role in the experimentation of the period, there were major problems. It was difficult to make standard instruments and replicate laboratory results, and research in chemistry was hindered by the difficulty of quantifying chemical reactions. Vulcanised tubing did not appear until the mid–1840s. The astronomer William Herschel (1738–1822), who, from Bath, identified Uranus in 1781, the first planet discovered since antiquity, encountered numerous failures in 1773–74 in the construction of his first telescope. Yet in 1706 Francis Hauksbee was able to construct the first machine to generate electricity. John Harrison invented an accurate chronometer that measured latitude; one of his chronometers was used by Cook. The mapping of the far side of the earth was one of the great European achievements of the century.

The virtues of experimentation were widely praised in scientific circles, and this led to a number of major advances, such as those in chemistry and medicine. Stephen Hales (1677–1761), a clergyman like many of the scientists of the period, was typical in his wide-ranging interests. Besides inventing artificial ventilators and quantifying various aspects of plant physiology, Hales opened the way to a correct appreciation of blood pressure, thanks to his conception of the living organism as a self-regulating machine, and his experiments. The surgeon John Hunter, who rebelled against the predominant European medical training which then consisted of the study of classical texts and refused to 'stuff Latin and Greek at the university', was typical of many leading surgeons in his willingness to try new methods, even when their theoretical explanation was unclear. In his *Medical Sketches* (1786), John Moore discussed the transmission of impressions from one nerve to another, illustrated by the fact that eating ice-cream causes a pain in the root of the nose. Typical of the interrelationship between experimentation and application was the work of Chester Hall (1703–71), a lawyer whose study of the human eye convinced him that achromatic lenses were possible. His success (*c.* 1733) in making them laid the basis for an improvement in the performance of almost all optical instruments. In 1750 the optician James Ayscough published an account of the nature of spectacles, in which he recommended a tinted glass to reduce glare, and in 1755 an *Account of the Eye and the Nature of Vision*.

Medical research became more important. The appointment of physicians to the London charity hospitals turned them into centres of research, and in Edinburgh the modernisation of the curriculum strengthened the role of hospital-based research. In England the training of surgeons was increasingly conducted in hospital schools rather than through apprenticeships.

There were major advances in chemistry; William Brownrigg (1711–1800) formulated the concept of a multiplicity of chemically distinctive gases. Joseph Black (1728–99), professor of chemistry at Glasgow and later Edinburgh, discovered latent heat and first identified the compound carbon dioxide. Henry Cavendish (1731–1810), a master of quantitative analysis, was in 1766 the first to identify hydrogen as a distinct substance and in 1781 the first to determine the composition of water by exploding a mixture of hydrogen and oxygen in a sealed vessel. Priestley (1733–1804) discovered a number of gases and oxides and carried out experimental work on astronomy, electricity, optics and respiration; he also made considerable advances in the equipment for studying gases.

Much chemical research was directly intended for practical purposes. The Edinburgh doctor Francis Home (1719–1813), who first called attention to croup as a distinct disease in 1765, tested water for bleaching and in 1756 published *Experiments on Bleaching*. In 1746 the English doctor John Roebuck (1718–94) revolutionised the manufacture of sulphuric acid, reducing it to a quarter of its former cost, by substituting lead chambers for glass globes for the purpose of condensation. In 1779 Bryan Higgins, an Irish-born doctor who in 1774 had opened a school of practical chemistry in London, patented a cheap and durable cement.

However, the chemistry of such operations as brewing and iron-making was far from understood. The chemistry of industrial processes was still largely traditional, arrived at by a long process of local trial and error. In brewing the processes varied from region to region, with top- or bottom-fermentation and the evolution of local yeast strains. Some of these methods were doubtless better than others at excluding the contaminated air, but all were vulnerable, as the underlying biochemistry was not yet understood. Pasteur's work on yeasts was not done until the 1850s, and enzymes were not discovered until the end of the nineteenth century. Consequently, when large-scale brewing began later in the eighteenth century, the hazards of sudden losses of huge and costly batches of porter were great. The big London brewers only used their fermentation vats in the winter.

Leather-tanning was in the same state. Processes were technically developed, but not capable of easy change and experimentation, since no distinction existed between the truly important and the accidental elements in the process. Iron-making also was largely unscientific, at least at the level of ordinary practice; when to add the handful of sand to the furnace, when to tap the ore and how much blast to permit tended to be skilled judgements resting in the person of the workman. Dyeing was mainly with vegetable products and often centred in local specialisms and processes, again with little possibility of improvement because of uncertainty about the active principles. Similarly, bleaching of cottons and linens was a long-drawn-out process which occupied much space and time, with comparatively little change. Sulphuric acid was used only for vegetable fibres. Woollens were quicker to bleach with a mixture of washing in stale urine, and then 'storing', which effectively meant giving them a mild sulphuric acid bath by burning sulphur in a large closed chamber and letting the products condense over the cloth. There was little pressure to develop a complete understanding of the process, or to apply new methods. The introduction of chlorine for rag bleaching in the paper industry began only in the 1790s.

The growing prestige of science reflected the sense not only that it could have practical value, but also that by increasing the sum of man's knowledge it was worthy of praise and was both a civilising influence and a cultural resource. Dissenting academies introduced the teaching of experimental science as a means of understanding the wisdom of God. George III patronised astronomy, although he did not understand the complex mathematics that played an increasing role in it. As Prince of Wales, George visited the house of William Watson (1715–87) in order to see his electrical experiments. Critical and rational approaches to the world became the fashion. Public awareness of science increased; a big market developed for scientific textbooks and works of popularisation, including books for women and even children. Francesco Algarotti's *Il Newtonianismo per le Dame* (1739), which explained the theories of light and gravitation in a series of dialogues, was translated into English in 1739. James Ferguson's *Astronomy explained on Sir Isaac Newton's Principles* (1750) achieved great success because he used familiar language; 'Tom Telescope's' *The Newtonian System of Philosophy, adapted to the Capacities of young Gentlemen and Ladies* went through many editions. The Scots-born and educated Birmingham chemist and industrialist James Keir published the first part of his *Dictionary of Chemistry* in 1789.

Museums of natural history were created, public scientific lectures developed, with lecturers such as J. T. Desaguliers, John Harris, John Horsley and William Whiston, and societies of enthusiastic amateurs were founded, such as the Linnean Society of London, established in 1788, but without women fellows until the 1900s. Knowledge and science became genteel and a focus for sociability. In Norwich a Natural History Society was founded in 1746, a Norwich Botanical Society in the 1760s and two general scientific societies in the 1750s and 1780s. The Manchester Literary and Philosophical Society was founded in 1779. Lecturers were not restricted to the major towns; in 1775 John Banks published at Kendal *An Epitome of a Course of Lectures on Natural and Experimental Philosophy*, a manual for a series of scientific lectures, with sections on hydraulics, hydrostatics, pneumatics, optics and electricity. Accounts of exploration, for example of the voyages of Anson and Cook or Dalrymple's *Collection of Voyages to the South Seas* (1770–71), were very popular. Experimentation became a theme of art, most powerfully in Joseph Wright of Derby's *A Philosopher giving that Lecture on the Orrery, in which a Lamp is put in Place of the Sun* (1766) and in his *An Experiment on a Bird in the Air Pump* (1768). This was a culture which Enlightenment values permeated perhaps more deeply than anywhere else in Europe.

If science became public, fashionable and a matter of cultural status in some areas, the level of scientific knowledge was rarely profound and much of the interest was dilettante and restricted to display rather than theory. The mathematisation of science possibly made theories harder to grasp. Instead it was the phenomena themselves that attracted attention because they appealed to the imagination as well as or rather than to the intellect. This was true of star-gazing, mesmerism and electricity.

Interest in phenomena and the environment reflected in part the belief that man was actively shaped by outside forces. Locke's *Essay Concerning Human Understanding* (1690) argued that all knowledge consisted of ideas which originated in sensation. Psychological theories suggested that man, both as an individual and as a social being, could be improved by education and a better environment, bringing and reflecting progress. Activity, rather than the passive acceptance of divine will and unchanging universe, was stressed. Locke's theory of personal identity challenged traditional Christian notions of the soul, though this was not seen so at the time.

Few, however, were led towards the idea of evolution. Most writers clung to the notions of the fixity of individual species and of a static natural environment. Knowledge concerning human conception and the origin of man's characteristics, both as individuals and as a species, was still too limited to help to clarify theoretical speculation. Among scientists there was a reluctance to abandon the notion of a ladder of nature with species

Facing page:
Gibside Chapel. Begun in 1760, the work of the architect James Paine, though not completed and consecrated until 1812; based on buildings of Roman antiquity and churches of Palladio which Paine had seen on a visit to Italy. A Classical building on the plan of a Greek cross, with a double portico closing the vista along the avenue; six Ionic columns line the entrance facade. Above the portico is a pediment in front of a parapet carrying urns. The work on the estate in the eighteenth century was funded by the coal wealth of George Bowes (1701–60), MP for Durham County, who died leaving a fortune estimated at £600,000. He left one daughter, Mary Eleanor, who married the 7th Earl of Strathmore in 1767.

occupying fixed positions, and to probe the world of plant- and animal-breeders and their attempts to enhance particular characteristics, for example by hybridisation. The relationship between experimentation and theorisation was not always close or productive, and theoretical advances were not always easy to apply. Possibly more important was the establishment of the idea that we could understand and influence our environment, even altering the calendar by switching from Old to New Style in 1752. The ideology of scientific advance was well developed by the end of the century, even if most people knew nothing of it and understood their lives, jobs and environment through the teaching of their predecessors.

Facing page:
Gibside Chapel, Domed interior, that focused on the preacher, with a three-decker pulpit, with staircases on each side leading up to an oval pulpit with an umbrella-like sounding-board raised over it. There are box pews in side apses with curved seats for servants and visitors and square box pews for the owner, agent and chaplain. All joinery is in cherry-wood. The lightness of the interior is achieved by use of tall windows at the corners of the chapel and by slightly bowed windows at a high level. A dramatic interior space with restrained, elegant furnishings.

John Locke by John Greenhill. Locke (1632–1704) was a leading philosopher with radical opinions. Close to Whig opponents of the Stuarts, Locke took refuge in Holland in 1683. He emphasised the role of reason. Major works included *Two Treatises of Government* (1690), the *Essay Concerning Human Understanding* (1690) and *Some Thoughts Concerning Education* (1693), which were banned from Oxford in 1700–03. Locke argued that a rational appreciation of the human situation would lead people to be Christians.

8 CULTURE AND THE ARTS

There is no single approach to the culture of eighteenth-century Britain. It is possible to focus on developments in style and artistic movements, from Baroque to Romanticism. It is also possible to focus on spheres of patronage, more particularly the nature of the so-called consumer society, which has become a much studied theme of late. Much recent scholarship, following the lines established in the seminal work of N. M. McKendrick, J. Brewer and J. H. Plumb, *The Birth of a Consumer Society: The Commercialisation of Leisure in Eighteenth-Century England* (1982), has associated the cultural patterns of the century with the various forces of social and economic change. Above all this branch of scholarship has tended to link cultural development with the new forms of leisure and recreation in the period. It has been suggested that cultural diffusion can be seen as one way of accounting for the so-called stability of eighteenth-century England, the growth of leisure and refinement helping to defuse the political tensions of the previous century. Yet caution is needed in seeing society as consumer-led, with culture as just a response to market forces. A more complex relationship existed between producers, suppliers and the market. Far from being primarily an offshoot of middle-class leisure activity, cultural activity was often closely bound up with the worlds of local politics and religion. The spread and diffusion of culture could have more to do with political and religious crises than with consumption. Those who agreed on an ethics of politeness and a morality of moderation might disagree on much else. Culture could become an expression of conflict rather than a panacea for strife.

One area of potential conflict was the divide between popular and elite culture. The late Edward Thompson focused attention on the world of 'plebeian', as opposed to 'patrician', culture. His work has been crucial in alerting historians to the social and political messages of ritual within society, showing the unwritten cultural and political assumptions behind the 'moral economy' of the crowd. It is, however, also possible to modify this analysis of a bi-focal cultural world by seeing, instead, cultural gradations and/or a world that encompassed populace and elite. Furthermore, it is probable that the oft-cited dichotomy between written and oral culture, the former progressive and the latter conservative, should be replaced by an emphasis on gradations within a cultural world that encompassed both written and oral forms.

Apart from problems in analysing causes and patterns of cultural diffusion and patronage, there are also problems in describing changes in style, particularly since these developments can be perceived fully only through an appreciation of specific texts, objects and performances. Rather than thinking in terms of competing styles and influences, it is more appropriate to emphasise their coexistence, even though public criticisms were part of the establishment of an identity for newer styles. The appropriateness of the accepted stylistic vocabulary is also open to question: a vocabulary or chronology that might suit portraiture is not necessarily appropriate for opera. Movements such as the English Baroque are open to very different definitions. If common themes can be discerned in some fields it is more appropriate to write in terms of stylistic tendencies, rather than to suggest that distinct uniformities can be discerned.

It is possible to discern several important sources of patronage and artistic market-places, though it would be inappropriate to suggest that they were necessarily distinct and unrelated. The situation varied not only by artistic form, the churches featuring as patrons of music but not of novels, but also by place: towns formed a different cultural world compared to heavily rural areas.

By European standards, the British monarchs were not great patrons. Their courts were settings of elegance and sometimes splendour, but not to compare with their Continental counterparts, and they were not centres of high culture. William III demolished earlier work and built essentially new palaces at Hampton Court and Kensington, both carefully integrated with their gardens. Sir Christopher Wren remodelled Hampton Court with scant concern for the Tudor fabric. Anne, however, was not a great builder. The accession of the Hanoverian dynasty did not have a dramatic cultural effect, because of the relatively small scale of their royal patronage and the absence of a strong indigenous Hanoverian culture. George I had Kensington Palace expanded, but he, George II and George III did not compare in their building with George IV or such Continental monarchs as Elizabeth I and Catherine II of Russia. Indeed, George III chose rather to purchase than to build, a new London residence – Buckingham House. Though keen on the music of Handel, and a patron of the architect Sir William Chambers (1726–96), who had taught him architectural drawing, George III was more interested in astronomy and farming than most of the arts. His grandfather, George II, was also not a noted sponsor of culture, certainly far less so than his son, Frederick, Prince of Wales, who was a significant supporter of music, gardens and literature and an important patron of Rococo art in England. Frederick's widow Augusta employed Chambers to adorn the gardens of her house at Kew and between 1757 and 1762 he erected a number of buildings in oriental or classical style that had a great impact. As Prince of Wales, the future George IV reached his majority in 1783 and within a year had expensively remodelled Carlton House.

Elevation of The Great Pagoda - as first Intended

Kew Pagoda, engraving by William Woollett. The pagoda was the work of the architect Sir William Chambers (1726–96), who studied in both Italy and Paris and travelled to China. Through the patronage of the Earl of Bute, he built a number of structures in oriental styles in the grounds of the Princess of Wales's palace at Kew. Chambers taught architectural drawing to the future George III, who made him Comptroller of His Majesty's Works; Somerset House was his major work. He spread knowledge of Chinese styles in *Designs of Chinese Buildings* (1757) and *Dissertation on Oriental Gardening* (1772).

George Frederick Handel by Balthasar Denner. Handel (1685–1759), was born in Germany and worked there and in Italy before moving to London in the 1710s, becoming a naturalised British citizen in 1727. The leading composer of Italian operas in England, fourteen alone written for the Royal Academy of Music, of which he was Music Director, Handel created the form of the English oratorio, with *Deborah* and *Athaliah*, both in 1733, and, more famously, *Saul* (1738), *Messiah* (1741), *Samson* (1743) and *Judas Maccabaeus* (1745). Handel's other works included organ concertos, chamber music, and the *Water Music* (1717) for George I.

Handel produced and conducted the coronation anthems for George II's coronation and had been awarded £200 annually for life by Queen Anne as a reward for his birthday ode of 1713 and his thanksgiving for the Peace of Utrecht; but his livelihood depended on the commercial success of his works on the London stage. More generally, the history of theatre during the century revealed the declining significance of royal patronage. George II preferred hunting and drilling soldiers, although the established routine of court festivities and the embellishment of palaces helped in general to ensure that portraits were painted and furniture and porcelain purchased. This was an important ingredient in the shift from 'grand' culture to 'domestic' culture which was more accessible to the middling orders.

In Britain the landed elite played a greater role in artistic patronage than the monarchy. 'Taste' came from outside the royal court. This was particularly the case with architecture and portraiture. The stately homes of the period were a testimony to wealth, confidence, the profits of agricultural improvement, the greater social stability that followed the Restoration of Charles II in 1660 and the increased political stability of the eighteenth century. In some cases social stability was more directly linked with elite culture: portraiture and architecture promoted stability by emphasising the power and immutability of the elite leadership of society. The Duke of Montagu had his coat of arms and family tree carved on his staircase to promote the idea of an unchanging family succession. Stately homes such as Wentworth Woodhouse were monuments of ostentation that dominated the countryside.

Sir John Vanbrugh (1664–1726), a leading exponent of the English Baroque and a playwright of note, displayed at the Duke of Marlborough's seat at Blenheim, the Earl of Carlisle's at Castle Howard and Admiral Delaval's at Seaton Delaval, a degree of spatial enterprise similar to that of the architects of princely palaces on the Continent. He also pioneered informally laid out gardens and parks. In contrast to the heaviness of Vanbrugh's architecture, the Scottish architect Colen Campbell (d. 1729) was influenced by Palladio and Inigo Jones, as was his principal patron Lord Burlington, who was responsible for Chiswick House. Both sought to encourage what they saw as a distinctly British style in contrast to the Baroque of Wren, Vanbrugh and Hawksmoor. Campbell's works included Wanstead House, Mereworth, and Stourhead. There was also a vogue for Palladianism in Ireland until about 1760. Sir Edward Lovett Pearce was responsible for the Parliament House in Dublin and for Castletown, while Francis Bindon worked on Russborough House. Palladianism also influenced the extension of Bath with John Wood the Elder's Queen's Square (1728–34) and Circus (1754–64), and his son's Royal Crescent (1767–74).

Other major figures proclaimed their prominence with new or greatly rebuilt mansions, such as Sir Robert Walpole's at Houghton, the Duke of Chandos's at Canons, the Earl of Hardwicke's at Wimpole, Sir George Lyttelton's at Hagley Hall, the Ansons' at Shugborough, and William Duff, 1st Earl of Fife's, at Duff House. The last was designed by the Scot William Adam, whose brother Robert (1728–92) rebuilt or redesigned many stately homes, including Culzean, Kedleston, Luton Hoo, Osterley, Mellerstain, Syon House for the Duke of Northumberland and Kenwood for the Earl of Mansfield. William Kent (1684–1748) remodelled Esher Place for Henry Pelham.

Alongside Palladianism, there was also a continuing interest in the Gothic style, which influenced both domestic and ecclesiastical architecture. Thus Henrietta Howard, Countess of Oxford, rebuilt Welbeck Abbey in the Gothic style from 1752. Alnwick Castle was remodelled in a Gothic fashion from 1750. In 1742 the first English book on Gothic architecture appeared, Batty Langley's *Ancient Architecture Restored and Improved by a Great Variety of Grand and Usefull Designs, entirely new in the Gothick Mode for ornamenting of Buildings and Gardens*. However, the Gothic was not used for new seats, only for rebuilding, and Horace Walpole's Gothic suburban villa at Strawberry Hill, Twickenham, was unusual in being a new house. Gothic was not seen as a style equal to Classicism until the work of architects such as James Wyatt at the close of the century.

Landscape gardening, closely linked to wealthy landed patronage, flourished and was influential on the Continent where a vogue developed for the 'English Garden'. New developments in horticulture, especially imports, mainly from America, greatly extended the range of possible trees, shrubs and flowers, while classical texts provided inspiration. Newly-introduced plants included the rhododendron (1736), magnolia grandiflora (1737), camellia (1739), buddleia (1774), strelitzia (1780s), Rugosa rose (1784), hydrangea macrophylla (1789), chrysanthemum (1793), geranium (1796) and dahlia (1798). The architect William Kent developed and decorated parks (grounds of houses) at, for example, Stowe, Chiswick and Rousham, in order to provide an appropriate setting for buildings. He used the 'ha-ha', a ditch, sunk from view, to create a boundary between garden and park that did not interrupt the prospect. Sunken fences were employed to conceal the limits of the property.

Trained under Kent, Lancelot 'Capability' Brown (1716–83) rejected the rigid formality associated with geometric Continental models, contriving a setting that appeared natural, but was, nevertheless, carefully designed for effect. His landscapes of serpentine lakes, gentle hills, copses on the brow of hitherto bare hills, and scattered groups of newly planted trees swiftly established a fashion. Brown laid out or remodelled the grounds of 180 houses, including Kew, Blenheim, Kirtlington, Chatsworth, Eywood, Ingestre, Audley End, Trentham, Nuneham Courtenay, and Burton Pynsent for Pitt the Elder. His work brought him substantial wealth and, having begun work as a kitchen gardener, he became High Sheriff of Huntingdonshire. Brown and Kent's

The East Front of Erddig, Clwyd. The splendour of landed wealth; a late seventeenth-century house with eighteenth-century additions; a gravel path leads up to the east front. The garden has a formal design.

system was criticised for formalism by Sir Uvedale Prince, who argued in favour of a wilder, more natural and 'picturesque', beauty that would accord with 'all the principles of landscape-painting'. This influenced Humphry Repton (1752–1818), who transformed about 220 gardens and developed Brown's ideas in accordance with the concept of the 'picturesque' which stressed the individual character of each landscape and the need to retain it, while making improvements to remove what were judged blemishes and obstructions and to open up vistas. Many landowners displayed a close personal interest in the landscaping of their own and their friends' parks. Prominent examples included Burlington, Lord Cobham at Stowe, George Bowes at Gibside, the 5th Lord Byron at Newstead, William Pitt the Elder, and Thomas Jones at Hafod, which was landscaped in the 'picturesque' style by 'Warwick' Smith. The 3rd Duke of Bridgewater, famous as the 'Canal Duke', also, between 1759 and 1768, employed Henry Holland to work on his seat at Ashridge and Brown to landscape the park.

A Perspective View of Denham Place, Buckinghamshire possibly by John Drapestier *c.* 1700. British gardens in the early decades of the period were designed in the formal, geometric patterns that characterised Continental gardens. There was a clear segregation between gardens and the surrounding estate. Gardens were an opportunity for ostentation and display; flowers became a commodity.

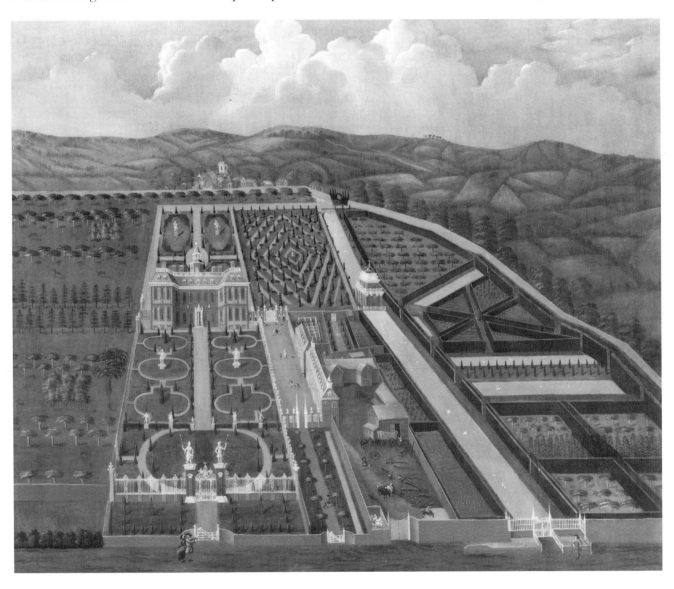

Though park landscape was not without economic value, sheep serving as more than natural lawnmowers, the labour required to excavate basins for artificial lakes or to create hills was considerable. Landscape gardening reflected and created a new aesthetic that was interested in nature, albeit an altered nature. In her poetic account of an English country house, *Crumble Hall*, Mary Leapor, a kitchen-maid, wrote of climbing up to the roof to view the 'beauteous Order' of a landscaped park. The new fashion entailed stylistic conventions and derived from artistic models, for example the presentation of the landscapes of Roman Italy in the paintings of Claude Lorraine, which influenced the banker Henry Hoare when he laid out the gardens at Stourhead which he inherited in 1741. The imitation of the Temple of Theseus (or Hephaestus) at Athens designed for the grounds of Hagley Hall by James 'Athenian' Stuart in 1758 was the first copy of a Greek Doric temple. Parks were embellished with grottoes, follies, shell-houses, columns and classical statues.

The new fashion was, however, less rigid and formal than its predecessor, and this permitted a more personal response to the tamed natural environment that was presented, a direction that led towards the more personal response to nature that was to be such a major theme in Romanticism. In 1762 Lord Lyttelton revealed a sense of confident cultural competitiveness at Stourhead:

> The Pantheon [by Flitcroft] is finished, and is an abode worthy of all the deities in Olympus . . . I think I never saw the Graces of Sculpture and all the power of that divine art, before I saw them there. I would have every Frenchman that comes to England be brought to this place, not only that he may see the perfection of our taste, but to show him that we have citizens who have a truer politeness in their manners, and a nobler elegance in their minds, than any Count or Duke in France.[1]

The stately homes that were built had to be decorated and furnished. This led to a massive amount of patronage ranging from frescoes to furniture. Thomas Chippendale (d. 1779) from Worcestershire, who became one of the leading furniture-makers in mid-century London, dedicated his book of designs for furniture, *The Gentleman and Cabinet-Maker's Director* (1754), to Hugh, Earl of Northumberland. Publication brought his work to the attention of an elite readership, and new editions appeared in 1759 and 1762. Patronage was also a means to establish, in the public mind, the unassailability of the 'taste' and position of the Earl, who was concerned about his social position: he was only an in-law of the Percys, obtained the title by a curious creation and much of his behaviour was aimed at striking the pose of a 'real' nobleman – he employed more flambards to light the route of his carriage than royalty. The Earl, Duke from 1766, had Alnwick Castle extensively decorated with coats of arms of the Percys and related families.

A lighter, less ornamented and simpler style than that of Chippendale was developed subsequently by Hepplewhite and Sheraton. Thomas Sheraton (1751–1806) from Stockton, established himself in London in about 1790 and began publication of a series of manuals of furniture design.

Apart from furniture, the new houses required large numbers of books for the libraries which became an established feature, and of portraits for the large spaces created in their public rooms, particularly the grand, often two-storied entrance-halls, as at Seaton Delaval and Beningbrough. Many members of the elite were keen collectors of paintings. An important theme was aristocratic recreations, particularly horses and hunting, as in the works of

George Stubbs. The classical interests of patrons and artists combined in the depiction of classical landscapes and stories, the heroes of ancient Rome being suitable companions for the portraits of modern aristocrats. At Petworth the Duke of Somerset invited artists and craftsmen to 'design' pieces for particular places and spaces in the house. The Lowthers patronised Mathias Read (1669–1747), a Londoner who spent most of his life in Whitehaven, which the Lowthers were developing. Read painted many of the Cumbrian country houses for their owners and was one of the first native painters of English landscape, painting Cumbrian mountains and skies. In Ireland, Scotland and Wales the landed elite responded to and shaped the same cultural impulses as their English counterparts. Their patronage of distinctive cultural traditions, such as bardic poetry, declined, and these traditions suffered; Roderick Morison (c.1656–c.1714) was the last famous bard/harper of Gaelic Scotland.

Master's Chair of the Fruiterer's Company, anonymous, 1748. A masterpiece of English Rococo furniture-making; light, swirling, sinuous and decorated. The acanthus cartouche shows the Company's Beadle making an annual presentation of fruit to the Lord Mayor of London; the cabriole legs rise from lion-paw feet and are headed by men-of-the-woods masks.

William Congreve, studio of Sir Godfrey Kneller. Born in Yorkshire, Congreve (1670–1729), studied at Trinity College, Dublin and trained for the law in London. He made his name with a number of comedies, *The Old Bachelor* (1693), *The Double Dealer* (1693), *Love for Love* (1695) and *The Way of the World* (1700). These are studies of social values with a strong accent on relations between the sexes; witty dialogue is used ably to depict character. These mannered works, based firmly in the fashionable society of contemporary England, dwell much on the role that marital practices offer for intrigue and deceit. Congreve's work was attacked by Jeremy Collier in his *Short View of the Immorality and Profaneness of the English Stage* (1698).

The role of wealthy landowners as patrons and leaders of fashion ensured that they played a crucial role in the artistic world. Display was a major part of the nature of patronage, and the conspicuous consumption and display of culture emphasised social status. Major stately homes, such as Houghton, Castle Howard and Stourhead, were open to respectable-looking visitors and acted as display models for architectural, artistic and landscape styles. Guidebooks for the most notable were published from the mid-century. If less affluent gentry could neither emulate the patronage of the elite nor share in their role, they were nevertheless of considerable importance in rural regions. Their influence has received insufficient scholarly attention, not least because they could not afford to patronise major artists; however, they were arguably a central means by which new styles, whether in clothes or portraits, buildings or gardens, were disseminated.

The Churches were also important patrons, while religion continued to be a major theme of the arts. What was judged immoral or sacrilegious in lay culture could be condemned. There was strong criticism of the alleged profanity and immorality of the stage, for example by the non-juror cleric Jeremy Collier in his pamphlet *A Short View of the Immorality and Profaneness of the English Stage* (1698) and this led in February 1699 to government pressure on London playhouses, and to Congreve and Vanbrugh making some alterations in their plays. In 1712 the Society for Promoting Christian Knowledge asked Collier to write a pamphlet discouraging the teaching of lewd songs and the composing of music to profane ballads. Thomas Herring, later Archbishop of York and then Canterbury, condemned John Gay's *Beggar's Opera* (1728) for immorality. The Methodists were strong critics of theatres; in 1766 Wesley, who in 1764 had praised the conversion of Birmingham's first theatre into a Methodist chapel, criticised the building of the new theatre in Bristol.

The Churches, however, regarded the arts, especially music, as important means for the glorification of God; although fear of accusations of crypto-Catholicism led the Bishop of London in 1773 to block attempts by the Dean of St Paul's to commission religious paintings for the interior of the cathedral, and in general church patronage of art was less fulsome than that for music and popular prayer-books. The enjoyment of religious art was suspicious to most divines. The construction and decoration of churches and chapels involved much activity, although far less than in the next century. The

Oxford showing the Radcliffe Camera and the Hawksmoor Neo-Gothic towers of the north quadrangle of All Souls College. The Camera, a library endowed by the will of a leading London doctor Thomas Radcliffe, was built between 1737 and 1747 to the designs of James Gibbs. It is a masterpiece of the English Baroque, heavily influenced by Classical architecture. Gibbs was a Catholic, also responsible for the Senate House at Cambridge and for the west side of the quadrangle at King's College, Cambridge. The more eclectic Hawksmoor designed the Classical Clarendon Building in Oxford.

episcopal and parochial organisation of the country did not alter, so there was little call for new construction. When the Commission for Building Fifty New Churches in London and Westminster, established in 1711, was abolished in 1758, owing to the inadequacy of its principal source of funds, the coal duty, it had authorised the construction of only twelve churches. Yet there were important buildings, and the careers of several architects reflected this. Nicholas Hawksmoor (1661–1736) was responsible for several of the London churches and for the west towers of Westminster Abbey. James Gibbs (1682–1754), an Aberdonian who studied in Rome and settled in London, was responsible for important work in Cambridge and Oxford, including the Radcliffe Camera (Library) in Oxford, but also for St Mary-le-Strand, St Peter's, Vere Street and St-Martin-in-the-Fields in London, Allhallows in Derby and St Nicholas, Aberdeen. Henry Flitcroft (1697–1769), a protégé of Burlington who became Comptroller of the Works and worked on Wentworth House for the Marquis of Rockingham and Woburn Abbey for the Duke of Bedford, was also responsible for the new church of St Giles-in-the-Fields in London, which cost over £10,000, the church of St Olave in Southwark, that of St John in Hampstead and for rebuilding the church at Wimpole. The decoration of churches was also important. In 1741 William Kent designed a pulpit and choir furniture in York Minster and a choir screen in Gloucester Cathedral. Much effort was put into funerary monuments; John Flaxman (1755–1826), for example, decorated grand tombs and monuments for Chichester and Winchester cathedrals.

Religion also provided patronage and themes for music, while the Churches provided training and employment for many musicians. It was a great age of hymns and psalms by masters such as William Cowper, John Newton, Christopher Smart, Isaac Watts, Charles Wesley and William Williams. They offered clear and attractive expressions of religious tenets and messages. The greatest English musician of the period, Henry Purcell, was employed as organist of Westminster Abbey between 1680 and 1695 and composed a large number of anthems, hymns and services. He had a vast influence on the next generation. John Weldon (1676–1736), another successful composer of much sacred and secular music, was organist of New College, Oxford and later of the Chapel Royal, St Bride's, Fleet Street and St Martin-in-the-Fields. Religious art and music were determined by the elite but also enjoyed by the congregations; they were at once elite and 'mass' culture.

Religious literature was also of importance, and popular religious works sold incredibly well, although the percentage of works published in London on religious and theological topics declined. Nevertheless, devotional verse and religious poetry were of importance, sermons were a major branch of literature, and some novels, such as those of the firm Anglican Samuel Richardson, can be seen in part as Christian fables.

The patronage of the middling orders was of growing importance. Unable individually to provide sustained patronage, they participated through attending public performances of works and by forming public markets for the arts; these expanded considerably during the century. There was an increasing dissemination of new cultural works. Most of the means of diffusion, such as engravings, newspapers and books, were far from new, but there was a definite expansion in the scale and variety of the culture of print. The reproduction of paintings for wealthy collectors had commonly taken the form of having individual copies painted, but there was now a considerable increase in their mass reproduction in the form of engravings, for example of the works of William Hogarth (1697–1764). This created copyright problems. Print shops displayed such works in windows for public entertainment and 'consumption'. About 15,000 satirical prints were published between 1740 and 1800.

The public sale of paintings and production for such sales, rather than in response to a specific commission, was far from novel, but there was a considerable expansion of the art market in London. The expansion of art dealership and middlemen led to an enormous market for fakes; economic expansion helped to fuel this market, as did widespread interest in artistic issues, which extended to a development of printed art criticism. Jonathan Richardson's *Essay on the Theory of Painting* (1715) both developed art criticism in England and argued that the English could equal Italian 'old masters'. The ethics of 'politeness' affected ideological justifications for art. Painting increasingly addressed public audiences, at the same time that economic and commercial progress enabled the creation of public spaces and places for the enjoyment of art, such as Vauxhall and Ranelagh Gardens in London, as well as the foundation of clubs and societies. There were also new points of connection between artists and patrons, such as the London Foundling Hospital, where both artists and aristocrats were governors. Art was seen as a public medium that could improve society, rather than as a private luxury. Paintings were also used as furniture; there was a tendency to hang particular kinds of paintings in certain rooms, for example still lifes in the dining room to remind people of food, and hunting scenes in the main entrance-hall of country houses such as Althorp.

Though many musical productions were still private, the musical world was becoming more public. The opera-houses were centres of fashion, and public concerts became more frequent. In Dublin foreign composers such as Francesco Geminiani and Handel as well as Irish counterparts such as Garret Wesley (1735–81) enjoyed great success. In Edinburgh, weekly concerts were held throughout most of the year by the Musical Society, established in 1728. In Hertford there were subscription concerts in a specially built concert-room from 1753 to 1767 and in the 1770s concerts in the new Shire Hall, completed in 1771, which had assembly-rooms built for such functions. In Francis Lynch's play *The Independent Patriot* (1737) a character complained, 'Music has engrossed the attention of the whole people. The Duchess and her woman, the Duke and his postilion, are equally infected.' Singers at the concerts in the London pleasure-gardens at Vauxhall in the second half of the century knew that their future engagements depended on the number of their encores: the patronage of an anonymous public was crucial and affected both works and performers chosen. Mozart visited London in 1764 and Haydn came there in 1791 and 1794 to give very successful public concerts for which he wrote his London symphonies; such concerts encouraged and reflected the more frequent performance of popular works. Haydn also set a number of Scottish songs in the 1790s.

It was easy for amateurs to participate in instrumental music: William Felton (1715–69), a cleric attached to Hereford Cathedral, wrote thirty-two keyboard concertos, more than anybody else in Britain, as well as popular practice pieces. Chamber and solo works thus enjoyed considerable popularity, and instruments, music and manuals were produced accordingly. An idea of the scale of activity can be grasped from the accounts of Thomas Green (1719–91), a Hertfordshire organist, tuner of musical instruments and teacher of music. Between 1755 and 1765 he tuned about 180 different harpsichords, 115 spinets and 40 pianofortes, nearly all within eight miles of Hertford. Music teachers came to play a major role. Instruments were displayed and played in the fine rooms constructed in so many houses during the major rehousing of many of the better-off in both town and countryside. New houses also had more furniture, especially chairs, tables, dressers, clocks and looking-glasses, as well as plastered ceilings, curtains and fireplaces. All provided opportunities and employment for craftsmen.

Musical journalism developed in response to the increase in public interest in music, and provided a forum for a stylistic debate that opposed new operatic forms to the dominant *opera seria*, a world of classical mythology, serious heroism and solemn music brought to life in London by Italian singers. The ballad opera, exemplified by John Gay's popular *Beggar's Opera* (1728), offered popular tunes and songs and scenes from 'low life', in a deliberate attack on the Italianate operas patronised by the cosmopolitan court and composed by Handel, among others. These operas were driven out of fashion. Handel produced his last in 1741, but he went on to enjoy a great success with his *Messiah*, an oratorio that revealed the commercial possibilities of sacred music.

Middle-class patronage was also crucial in the theatre, which developed both in London and elsewhere: purpose-built theatres opened in Bath in 1705, Bristol in 1729 and York in 1734. The Orchard Street Theatre at Bath opened in 1750, the New Street Theatre in Birmingham in 1774, the fourth in the city but the first to be a long-standing institution, and the first permanent theatre building in Lancaster was constructed in 1781.

The amorality and bawdy of much late seventeenth-century comedy was moderated by the rise of sentimentality. Many plays encouraged a bourgeois consciousness equally opposed to indulgence, whether decadent 'aristocratic' mores or popular ignorance and vice. In Sir Richard Steele's *The Conscious Lovers* (1722) virtue and sensitivity are rewarded. Virtue was similarly identified with the middling orders in George Lillo's *The London Merchant* (1731), in which a weak apprentice commits murder and then undergoes an exemplary repentance. This popular work represented a major change in tragedy in that it was written in a prose idiom and given a bourgeois setting and values. Such a work can be seen as a moral counterpart to Hogarth's satires and Richardson's novels. It is indicative of the cultural importance of the London stage that Lillo's play made his name, while the court masque he wrote in 1733 for the marriage of the Princess Royal was not performed because of the postponement of the marriage, and made no impact. As Henry Fielding noted in the prologue to Lillo's tragedy *Fatal Curiosity* (1736):

> No fustian Hero rages here to Night
> No Armies fall, to fix a Tyrant's Right:
> From lower Life we draw our Scene's Distress:
> Let not your Equals move your Pity less.

In the 1740s the leading actor and theatrical entrepreneur David Garrick (1717–79) sought to raise the moral tone of the theatre. The sentimental comedy that resulted generally lacked bite, and British theatre did not greatly flourish in the second half of the century, but its moral tone reflected audience wishes.

If morality was increasingly prescribed and indulgence proscribed this represented not a bourgeois reaction against noble culture, but a shift in

sensibility common to both. For every decadent aristocrat depicted on the stage in the second half of the century there were several royal or aristocratic heroes. Hogarth similarly criticised aristocratic mores, but most painters depicted aristocrats in an exemplary light. Thus, rather than seeing the commercialisation of leisure as a triumph of bourgeois culture, the role of the middling orders was largely one of patronising both new and traditional artistic forms rather than developing or demanding distinct styles. The rise of the novel can best be seen as an important instance of the embourgeoisement of culture, if that is regarded as a matter of patronage rather than content. Novels created and responded to a large readership, Henry Fielding's *Joseph Andrews* selling 6,500 copies in 1742. The growth of circulation, proprietary and subscription libraries as well as the serial publication of books permitted those who could not afford to purchase them to read them. A new public library opened in Bristol in 1740 and the first in Lancaster in 1768; Manchester gained its first circulating library in 1757. The first of the many proprietary libraries whose members owned shares was the Liverpool Library,

The Pantheon at Stourhead, built 1753–54. The gardens were laid out between 1741 and 1780 by Henry Hoare, the owner of the house, and were planned as a Neo-classical scene, an English realisation of the classical landscapes of Roman Italy as presented in the paintings of Claude Lorraine. The Pantheon was designed by Henry Flitcroft, as was King Alfred's Tower, a folly built in 1772 at the edge of the estate. The house was completed in about 1712, also in Neo-classical style, by the Scottish architect Colen Campbell, who was influenced by Palladio.

Monuments on Easter Island by William Hodges. Hodges (1744–97) was draughtsman on James Cook's second voyage to the Pacific. After he returned, he was employed by the Admiralty in finishing his drawings, and in superintending their engraving for the published account of Cook's voyages. He first exhibited at the Royal Academy with Pacific views. Hodges painted in India between 1778 and 1784 thanks to the support of Warren Hastings, and in 1793 published an account of his Travels in India. His Indian paintings had already been engraved for a British market fascinated by distant lands. Hodges was less successful as a painter of British landscapes and allegorical pictures and retired from the profession, becoming a banker in 1795.

formed in 1758; membership was already 140 in 1758, 300 by 1770 and over 400 by 1799. Between 1758 and 1800 the library acquired an average of almost 200 books annually. There were about 1,000 circulating libraries by the end of the century.

Far from conforming to a common tone, form or intention, novels varied greatly, a trend encouraged by the size and diversity of the reading public. Thus Richardson's first novel *Pamela* (1740), a very popular book on the prudence of virtue and the virtue of prudence, was countered by Fielding's satirical *Apology for the Life of Mrs Shamela Andrews* and his *Joseph Andrews*. John Cleland employed the epistolary style of *Pamela* in his pornographic novel *Fanny Hill; or, The Memoirs of a Woman of Pleasure* (1749). By the end of the century about 150 novels, 90 of them new, were being published annually.

Publishing expanded greatly. As there were few technical innovations, profitability depended on increased sales, and publishers such as William Strahan in London, producing sizeable editions, had to be sensitive to the market. The Edinburgh-born Strahan (1715–85) was publisher to Blackstone, Blair, Cook, Gibbon, Hume, Johnson, Robertson and Smith, made a lot of money and became an MP. The growth of the reading public affected literature. In the field of history authors such as Gibbon, Hume and William Robertson, and hack writers, such as Richard Rolt, were able to write for a large and immediate readership, producing a clearly commercial product, in contrast to the classical model of writing history for the benefit of friends and a posthumous public. Gibbon and Robertson both made substantial sums. Works were produced to supply new and developing specialisations; for

An *Excrescence*, by James Gillray, 20 December 1791. Gillray (1767–1815) was one of the masters of what was a great age of British caricature. At first he concentrated on engraved caricatures of social subjects but from 1780 until he stopped work in 1811 he concentrated on political topics. Working in London, Gillray was at the cutting edge of a commercial and politically aware society. He produced about 1,500 caricatures, many very savage.

The *Excrescence* depicts William Pitt the Younger, showing him as an outgrowth of royal power. A pointed attack on corruption in the body politic, this cartoon is only one in a series which attacked Pitt. In 1797 Gillray was given money by a junior minister to produce less critical cartoons of the Prime minister.

the popular world of horticulture, Peter Miller's *The Gardener's Dictionary* (1724), Robert Furber's *Short Introduction to Gardening* (1733), James Lee's *Introduction to Botany* (1760), William Hanbury's *A Complete Body of Planting and Gardening* (1770), John Kennedy's *Treatise upon Planting* (1776) and Loddiges's *The Botanical Cabinet* (1777) were followed in 1786 by *The Botanical Magazine*.

Authors sought to make their writings as comprehensible as possible to the anonymous, expanding literate population. Books, magazines, newspapers and dictionaries assisted the spread of new ideas, transmitting the grand themes of artistic and intellectual life. Treatises on taste (aesthetics), were designed to guide appreciation and patronage. Thus James Granger's *Biographical History of England . . . adapted to a Methodical Catalogue of Engraved British Heads. Intended as an Essay towards reducing our Biography to System, and a help to the knowledge of Portraits* (1769) was intended to assist portrait collectors and indeed led to a rapid rise in the price of portraits. Ephraim Chambers's *Cyclopaedia, or an Universal Dictionary of Arts and Sciences* (1728) attempted a classification of knowledge. Johnson's massive *Dictionary of the English*

Language (1755) sought to clarify meanings and included an English grammar; 2,000 copies of the folio edition were printed and the price was £4 10*s*. John Walter published an English–Welsh dictionary in parts between 1770 and 1794.

The spread of new ideas was easiest in an urban setting, the principal context of cultural patronage by the middling orders. The London pleasure-gardens were showpieces for all kinds of art and music, and they, and the walks and assembly-rooms of London, were emulated in other cities and towns. The ethos of polite society helped to blur culture and leisure, spectator and performer. Many cultural institutions, learned societies, periodicals and theatres helped to create a cultural climate more sensitive to new ideas; reviews such as *The Critical Review* and the *British Magazine* guided book purchasers. In Norwich, for example, where there was a very active musical life, both public and performers were ready to accept quite rapid change, and at the end of the century, concert-goers were able to hear the latest Britain and German works. Although the century saw a major increase in public cultural activity outside London, it was very much dominated by the metropolis. In 1782 the Belfast printer John Tisdal published *Flora's Banquet,* a collection of Irish poems he had edited. He stated: 'it does not follow, that works of merit can *only* originate in the metropolis of England; and that, unless a new book is distinguished by a *London* title page, and character in the review, it is beneath the notice of the curious. There have been some instances to the contrary in *this* kingdom.' However, the promised second volume did not appear. There was, though, a strong Scottish publishing base by late century.

High and popular culture are frequently sharply differentiated and then presented in terms of a 'battle of cultures'. Popular culture is often presented as being under assault from the moral didacticism of the secular and ecclesiastical authorities and middling orders. It is not only in the artistic sphere that this tension has been discerned and that the analysis of relationships has been coloured by the use of words and phrases such as 'oppressive', 'control' and 'protective mechanisms'. Indeed the discernment of artistic duality is but part of a wider sense, or allegation, of cultural control, of clashing *mentalités*, of worlds in collision, which has also influenced the assessment of popular religiosity. New intellectual and artistic fashions and codes of behaviour are held to have corroded the loyalty of the upper and middling orders to traditional beliefs and pastimes, and it is claimed that religious activity, the Scientific Revolution, the Enlightenment and the cult of sensibility marginalised the common culture and pushed it down the social scale. Given such an analysis it is unsurprising that attention has been devoted to the contrast between popular and elite culture and that this is held to have inspired initiatives to 'reform' popular practices. In 1791 the *Leeds Intelligencer* printed a letter attacking bull-baiting 'as a disgrace to a civilized people', that produced depraved manners rather than amusement: 'Tis pity, then, but those who make this a practice merely from *custom* would reflect upon the cruelty of it, and, by substituting any harmless diversion in its stead, do themselves a most permanent credit, and render a true service to the rising generation'. Other papers of the period attacked such popular practices as wife-selling, gambling, the shooting of street lamps for fun, boxing, swearing and cruelty to animals, although all except wife-selling were also popular with the aristocracy. The Mayor of Lancaster banned the sale of alcohol on Sunday mornings in 1787; the following year the attempt by the Stamford authorities to end the local

Mrs Siddons as the Tragic Muse by Sir Joshua Reynolds, 1784. Mrs Siddons (Sarah Kemble 1755–1831), was from 1782 the leading tragic actress in the country. Reynolds's rich, dark painting with its figures of Pity and Terror looked forward to Romanticism. The painting was a great success, praised by James Barry as 'The finest picture of the kind, perhaps in the world, indeed it is something more than a portrait'. After the appearance of the painting, Mrs Siddons was wheeled along the stage at Drury Lane as the tragic muse in a 1785 production of Garrick's *Jubilee*.

custom of bull-running, in which a bull was hunted to death, led to disturbances and was unsuccessful.

However, it could be argued that the idea of a sharp distinction between the culture of the elites and that of the bulk of the population is misleading. It is possible that the notion of a common culture, albeit one with different styles, is more appropriate: that there were not contrasting *mentalités* but rather a shared currency of interests, notions and idioms, and mutual interchange of ideas. Performers and public sought to investigate and express common problems and emotions, to make sense of a common world in a number of different styles and formats. There was noticeable overlap between the amusements of the 'best people' and the rest at the theatre, and at such entertainments as public executions, horse-racing, bear-baiting, cock-fighting and boxing. Far from 'art' and 'folk' music being distinct and antithetical, the folk music being conservative and transmitted almost solely by oral tradition, there is considerable evidence of interrelationship and change, both thematic and stylistic. If for the bulk of the population music meant ballads, hymns and primitive instruments, that does not mean that popular music was necessarily unsophisticated or unchanging.

In part the relationship between sections of elite and popular culture derived from the greater interest in popular culture displayed by artists and intellectuals. By the 1770s there was more interest in the supposed lifestyle of the peasantry, a process that matched growing fascination with landscape. However, the routine grind and miseries of rural life were generally ignored and, instead, an idealised view presented, as in the stylised charm of Gainsborough's cottages.

The folk tales of the peasantry were also of less interest than those of older times. Much attention was devoted to the latter in what is termed the 'Pre-Romantic' period, which stretched from the 1760s and 1770s to whenever the Romantic period is held to begin. To the antiquarian tradition of interest in early literature, such as the Anglo-Saxon studies of the English clergyman Edward Lye (1694–1767), and Sean Ó Neachtain's preservation of old Irish manuscripts and the invention of much Welsh folk law, was added a fascination with early 'folk' literature which was presented as offering an imaginative perspective capable of reviving culture. James Macpherson (1736–96) published poems which he claimed to have translated from the Gaelic of a third-century Highland bard called Ossian. His *Fragments of Ancient Poetry collected in the Highlands* (1760) brought him fame and were followed by *Fingal* (1761), dedicated to George III's favourite, the Earl of Bute, the preface of which proclaimed the superiority of Celtic to Greek heroic poetry, and by *Temora* (1763). These works, in part his own creation, in part based on genuine Gaelic poems and ballads, enjoyed a phenomenal success and made primitivism popular, although they were bitterly criticised by evangelical Highland Church of Scotland ministers and by Johnson.

Impressed by Macpherson, Thomas Percy (1729–1811), a grocer's son who sought to show his descent from the medieval Earls of Northumberland, published *Reliques of Ancient English Poetry* (1765, four editions by 1794), an edition of old ballads which promoted a revival of interest in the subject. An interest in traditional Scots tunes led to the publication of a series of works beginning with *Orpheus Caledonius* (1725). Evan Evans edited *Some Specimens of the Poetry of the Antient Welsh Bards* (1764) and Rhys Jones *Gorchestion Beirdd Cymru (The Masterpieces of the Welsh Poets)* (1773). 'Medievalism' also led to the success of Thomas Chatterton (1752–70) who invented and wrote the works of a fifteenth-century poet, Thomas Rowley. William Stukeley (1687–1765) developed enthusiasm for medieval antiquities. If the peasantry appeared less interesting and uplifting as an artistic topic than ancient Celts and medieval Britons, it was also the case that very few peasants became artists enjoying elite patronage. Stephen Duck (1705–56), the 'Thresher Poet', was an agricultural labourer who, thanks to the support of the local clergy, won fame and in 1730 Queen Caroline's patronage. John Bancks (1709–51), the 'Weaver Poet', failed to emulate his success. Gaelic poets included Robb Donn Mackay (1714–78), a Highland cattle-drover, and Duncan Ban MacIntyre (1724–1812), a gamekeeper. Such individuals were not typical, however.

While popular culture is a subject that is still largely uncharted, and in which generalisations about peasant conservatism and cultural borrowing from the elite are still too common, there are also problems in assessing the relationship between cultural cosmopolitanism and xenophobia, the history of which is still largely unwritten. Cosmopolitanism was aided by travel, patronage, the role of cultural intermediaries and the process of emulation. Travel helped to spread knowledge of present, as well as past, artistic developments among patrons; as the Grand Tour became fashionable, increasing numbers travelled for pleasure and, at a formative period, were exposed to foreign culture. Artists, such as the painters Allan Ramsay, Joshua Reynolds and Richard Wilson, and the architects Matthew Brettingham and William Kent, also travelled in order to acquire training, employment and inspiration; Ramsay spent a total of eight years in Italy.

Patronage was inspired by and sustained an elite cosmopolitan culture. Variations in the distribution of artists and performers were especially marked in certain elite cultural forms, particularly opera, and there was an additional sense that certain regions were characterised by innovative artists. The role of cultural intermediaries was facilitated by the appreciable number of foreigners in London, especially in the first half of the century by the number of Huguenots (French Protestant refugees), who had close links with both France and the United Provinces.

Emulation and fashion were significant. At the level of elite culture, particularly in the early decades of the century, there was a strong sense of inferiority to the cultural life and products of France and Italy. This sense of inferiority took a number of forms and had a variety of consequences, including the attempt to implant foreign fashions and the patronage of foreign artists. France was a major leader in fashion, including women's clothes, and behaviour. The morning levée and the umbrella were introduced into Britain from France. France's position in fashion encouraged the demand for French clothes, hairdressers, cooks, food and wine in elite circles in London.

Britain was part of a European culture. All the major stylistic and thematic changes occurred on a continent-wide scale, though there were significant national variations and differences in chronology. Just as the Baroque and Rococo styles struck resonances and Chinese and Turkish motifs were repeated across Europe, so the discussion of the arts in different countries tended to be similar and critical tendencies, towards sentimentality in the mid-century or Romantic from the 1770s, were generally international in their scope. Cosmopolitanism implied neither similar circumstances nor identical developments, but it did encourage eclecticism.

British influence abroad was strongest in intellectual life, literature and

gardening. The Adam style of interior decoration was paralleled in Paris in the 1780s, a period in which significant numbers of the French elite were affected by an Anglomania, the effects of which included an interest in horse-racing and a male fashion for English clothes. While some aspects of British culture became more influential abroad, there was also a shift in attitude towards Britain's cultural relations with the rest of Europe. Thanks to a burgeoning economy, an apparently successful political system and a great and powerful world empire, there was less of a sense of inferiority than there had been in the seventeenth century; at that time, to its own people, Britain had seemed superior in little apart from its Protestantism. By the eighteenth century, in spite of the popularity of Batoni, Mengs, Piranesi and other Rome-based artists, it appeared that the country of Newton and Sloane, Reynolds and Watt, had little to learn from modern Italy. In 1720 James Thornhill became the first English artist to be knighted. Prior to that the great names in British portraiture had been foreign, Van Dyck, Lely and John de Medina becoming

Facing page: The Painted Hall at Greenwich

By 1663 Charles II had decided on a major rebuilding of the Tudor Palace at Greenwich. The initial work was carried out by John Webb. The scheme was transformed into one for a Royal Hospital for Seamen and this was executed by Sir Christopher Wren; the result was a masterpiece of British Baroque architecture.

In 1708 James Thornhill was commissioned to paint the Great Hall. His rich painting of the ceiling (1708–12) was a triumphant work, proclaiming British power. The painting represents William II and Mary bringing Peace and Liberty to Britain and Europe. The painting at the end of the hall makes reference to Britain's naval success and power.

Thornhill, who became Serjeant-Painter to the King and the King's History painter in 1720, was the first native artist to be knighted. He made a fortune through his art and re-purchased and rebuilt his ancestral seat at Thornhill in Dorset.

John Henderson as Macbeth, by George Romney (1734–1802). Romney painted several of the leading actors and actresses of the day. His portrait of Henderson captures the intensity that tragic actors increasingly sought.

Alexander Pope (1688–1744). The son of a London linen-draper, Pope was debarred by his Catholicism from attending university, but became one of the leading literary figures of the first half of the century. His varied works, informed by a subtle intelligence, were written in a style that was urbane and civilised. Closely attuned to the classics, he wrote many of his works in conscious imitation of classical genres. A translator of Homer into heroic couplets, Pope also produced the satirical *Rape of the Lock* (1714), *The Dunciad* (1728), a satire on dullness in contemporary English culture, and the *Essay on Man* (1733–34), which was more philosophical in its subject and tone.

knights and Kneller a baronet. Thornhill's masterpiece was his painting of the Great Hall in Wren's Royal Hospital at Greenwich (1708–12), an explicitly British grand state painting. Hogarth advocated a specifically English style.

In the mid-century Canaletto, with his splendid canvases, used talents developed to depict Venice in order to show the glories of modern London. A neo-imperial, modern pride of London was expressed in his views with new buildings such as Greenwich Observatory, Somerset House, Westminster Bridge and the rebuilt towers of Westminster Abbey. In contrast, Italy was increasingly seen as a decayed civilisation, and there was greater interest in Classical, not contemporary, Italy. British commentators claimed Rome's mantle of civilisation, and the spectre of the fallen Roman empire emphasised, in contrast, Britain's present potency. Modern Britain was held to define civilisation, an assessment that owed much to the Whig myth; this was more successful and lasting in creating standards by which Britain appeared superior to foreign countries than in sustaining a coherent and united viewpoint on domestic politics. It was no coincidence that 'God Save the King' and 'Rule Britannia' both emerged in the mid-century. British self-regard and condescension towards foreign countries was not dependent on contemporary foreign praise for Britain as a country of liberty and progress, although, in so far as British commentators were aware of it, it could not but have contributed.

Similarly, there was a greater interest in aspects of England's cultural past, part of the process by which a more self-confident nation focused on native values and models. Shakespeare was praised as the national poet with his monument in Westminster Abbey. He was the most frequently cited authority in Johnson's *Dictionary*, and no less than six major editions of his complete

Silver Swan Automaton, workshop of James Cox, *c.* 1773. A fascination with mechanisms was an important theme in the culture of the period, most obviously with interest in technological developments, but also in other respects, as with this beautifully-carved automaton. A London goldsmith, Cox, active from 1749 to 1797, made toys and automata, many in Rococo style, and published a *Descriptive Inventory of the several exquisite and Magnificent pieces of Mechanism and Jewellery . . . For enabling Mr. James Cox . . . Jeweller, to dispose of his Museum* (1773).

works were published in the century: by Rowe (1709), Pope (1725), Theobald (1733), Warburton (1747), Johnson (1765) and Malone (1790). Garrick was responsible for his plays being staged more frequently, and actively promoted the Shakespeare Jubilee in 1769. Similar views lay behind the interest in earlier English music, particularly Purcell and Handel, that led to cathedral festivals of music, the Academy of Ancient Music, the fashionable Concert of Ancient Music established in 1776 by aristocrats led by the 4th Earl of Sandwich, and finally the mighty Handel Commemoration celebrations in 1784. The last were so successful that they were repeated in 1785–87, 1790, and in 1791 with over 1,000 performers and in the presence of George III.

The domestic cultural tradition became stronger in the second half of the century, in part thanks to the institutionalisation of art, not least through the Royal Academy. Artists and craftsmen developed products of excellence in areas formerly dominated by foreign work: English silverware gained in importance and ceramics produced in London and Staffordshire were admired for their beauty. For design, Wedgwood called on the artistic skills of Flaxman and Stubbs. In painting, a modernised classical style was popularised by Reynolds and taught at the Royal Academy, founded in 1768. Garrick developed a naturalistic school of acting believed to be superior to Continental acting methods. The painters who accompanied Cook on his voyages, such as William Hodges and John Webber, provided a powerful visual image of the South Seas. Between 1777 and 1783 James Barry produced a set of paintings to decorate the Great Hall of the Society for the Encouragement of Arts, Commerce and Manufactures, a body that produced decorative medals and premiums which rewarded innovations in various fields, including the arts. The array of philosophers, scientists and others displayed by Barry reached back to the ancient world, and culminated with modern British talent, for example poets from Homer to Goldsmith. To Barry and to his patrons, the British could be seen as the new Olympians, equal to the greatness of the past.

Worcester porcelain of the 1760s. Drawing on Japanese *Kakiemon* designs and colours, the skilled painters of the Worcester factory produced more elaborate versions. Richly coloured and flamboyant, depicting dragons, phoenix and ho-ho birds, as well as exotic vegetation such as chrysanthemums and bamboo, this pottery reflected interest in the Orient. Gold was used for details and highlights. Teaware patterns, for example *Rich Queen's* and *Jabberwocky*, were very popular.

The Distribution of Premiums in the Society of Arts
by James Barry. Painted *c.* 1778–1801. Founded
in London in 1754, the Society for the
Encouragement of Arts, Manufactures and
Commerce was designed to pursue both
pragmatic and artistic goals. The Society
sponsored a range of activities, including new
county surveys, whaling, not least through the
successful search for a more effective harpoon,
gem-engraving and wood-engraving, the last
seen as a cheap illustrative medium for the
dissemination of knowledge. Its gold medals
and premiums rewarded entrepreneurial
initiatives as well as new inventions. For the
period 1760–1820 it represented a spur to
industrial experimentation. Art was seen as
aesthetic capital that would benefit the nation.
The painting depicts members of the society
including Samuel Johnson and Arthur Young.
The Prince of Wales, a potential patron of the
Society, is painted in his Garter Robes.

9 AUTHORITY, THE STATE AND ADMINISTRATION

Societies are structured by patterns of authority. For most individuals this is primarily a matter of relations within the family, at the workplace, and in the local community, but the context framing these relations is commonly provided by the state, and in some spheres, particularly law and order, individuals are brought into direct contact with the state. The state itself, however, should not be seen as an abstract force outside society and rarely impacting upon it. Rather the state, though possessing its own autonomous institutions and conventions, is also an expression of social and economic structures and values which it helps to shape and is, in turn, shaped by.

Authority took many forms in eighteenth-century Britain, some of which are discussed in other chapters. Within the family there was the authority of age and the power of patriarchy. In the local community there was the power of landowners and employers, the authority of Justices of the Peace (JPs) and in Scotland sheriffs, generally the same people, and the pressure of neighbours and colleagues. In the wider polity governmental power and authority was widely distributed, but primarily in accord with the structure of the social system. This was an inegalitarian system of authority in which the representative dimension was slight. It is unclear whether non-governmental aspects of authority weakened in this period, possibly leading to an increase in lawbreaking. Patriarchy, religion (and ecclesiastical discipline and courts) and the 'moral economy' of the community were all under stress from socio-economic developments, while the Act of Toleration encouraged an ecclesiastical pluralism that challenged religious authority. These shifts may have led to a crumbling both in important external pressures, particularly those of the established Church, and in the internalisation of authority, so that the agencies and pretensions of the state were increasingly left to resist criminality and to establish social norms.

The nature of government, however, was such that any concentration on the administration and its officials can be misleading. Government was the function and privilege of a large number of individuals and institutions who were guided by their own conventions and ideas. This posed a political problem for central government in the event of non-co-operation, but it also vastly extended its range; the relationship involved a persisting pattern of definition and compromise, rather than antagonism and conflict. By modern standards many government functions were 'privatised', including most of social welfare, education and health. Prisons, for example, were private businesses whose keepers bid for leases and expected to make a profit from the fees that prisoners paid for accommodation and food.

The production and distribution of gunpowder was a matter jointly for private manufacturers and for the Ordnance Office. Whether in government or in opposition, politicians were unwilling to extend the powers of government in this crucial field, even though they were aware of their inadequacy. At the outset of the Seven Years War (1756–63) the makers failed to provide the required and agreed amount, so that the war effort in 1756–58 depended partly on substantial imports from the United Provinces. In the winter of 1761–62 some warships had to sail from Portsmouth and Plymouth without their full complement of powder. In addition, much of the powder submitted

John Howard visiting a Lazaretto, by George Romney. Art Gallery of Toronto, Ontario. Gift of Professor T. A. Heinrich, 1980. Howard (1726–90), a Londoner who settled in Bedfordshire, became interested in the state of prisoners while High Sheriff in 1773. As a prominent prison reformer he was responsible for the acts of 1774 that abolished gaolers' fees and pressed for improvements in the health of prisoners. Author of the *State of the Prisons in England and Wales* (1777), Howard travelled extensively abroad visiting prisons and died in Russia. In 1778 he gave evidence to a Commons select committee on the greater suitability of buildings rather than ships for imprisonment.

to the Ordnance Office did not meet its high standards of quality. The government did not own any mills until 1759, when it purchased those at Faversham, but their performance was never distinguished.

The press-gang was a harsh way to raise sailors for the largest navy in the world. The formation of a reserve of seamen proved ineffective: the Register Act of 1696, which provided for a voluntary register of seamen, proved unworkable and was repealed in 1710. The press-gang was not only arbitrary (although by law it applied only to professional seamen), but also only partially successful. Perhaps there was no better option, in the absence of any training system for the navy, and given the difficulty of making recruitment attractive when length of service was until the end of the war. The government never seriously considered paying sailors more, and in light of contemporary concern about naval expenditure this is not surprising. However, on numerous occasions naval preparations and operations were handicapped by a lack of sailors. A deep reluctance to embark on fundamental change characterised government policy both in this field and more generally.

Clear hostility to the idea of despotism, and conventions of acceptable governmental behaviour, limited the possibilities for state action by setting restrictive parameters of consent, although the constitutional and political expression of the latter varied. Government was expected to operate against a background of legality and tradition, and this made new initiatives politically hazardous and administratively difficult. When in 1762 the Commissioners for lighting Westminster claimed the right to standardise lamp-irons and remove non-standard ones, this was bitterly attacked in a periodical, the *Contrast*, of 2 November:

> The security of property in this happy kingdom is held so sacred, that the Parliament cannot divest an innocent subject of any part of his effects, without giving him a valuable consideration, and that not to be determined by a state tool, but by a jury; and even this has never been done by compulsory laws, except in cases of the greatest necessity, such as the making new or enlarging old avenues, road-acts, and the acts for building Westminster and Blackfriars bridges etc. Though road-acts give a liberty to cut new roads through any person's lands, it is never without paying them to the utmost, and repairing all kind of damages.

Apart from the ideology of limited government that arose from the defeats that royal authority had suffered in the seventeenth century, there were also practical problems in exerting control. The number of trained officials was limited, communications were poor, the government was short of money and, in a generally pre-statistical age, it was difficult to obtain adequate and accurate information. Thus the most effective way to govern was in co-operation with those who wielded social power and with the institutions which had local authority. The crucial figures were the JPs, about 8,000 in number in 1760. They were the linchpins of local administration, the central figures in the law and order of the localities. They were responsible for the implementation of social policy, a field in which the central government played little role, but, in doing so, had to respond to local factors.

A stress on the problems facing government and on its co-operative nature provides the best basis from which the initiatives of the period can be assessed. The extent to which initiatives such as changes in taxation or the calendar should be seen as reforms is questionable. Though the opponents of reform could be stigmatised as selfish protectors of particular interests, such an analysis ignored the ambiguity of reform. Instead of reform being the cutting edge of the modern state, most administrative agencies were not particularly effective, but rather represented fresh and unpopular fiscal demands and novel interventions in proven existing practices that were frequently more responsive to local interests and needs.

Government was expected to protect people and their property, provide justice and suppress disorder. Crime was regarded as a major problem and casual violence was indeed endemic. Crime was likely to run in families, was committed by the middling orders as well as the working classes and worsened as transportation links improved: the criminal's ability to evade justice grew in direct proportion. There was much brutality and cruelty in everyday life. In his speech opening Parliament on 15 November 1753, George II declared that he was appalled by the rise in murders and robberies. The repression of crime was often brutal, especially in England and Wales. Deterrence through execution or transportation, rather than incarceration, was generally favoured, imprisonment being seen as an expensive method commonly used principally for those who were suffering civil action, in particular, debtors. Conditions in many gaols were also very poor: food was meagre, sanitary arrangements primitive and water supplies limited.

Concern about rising crime after the War of the Spanish Succession (1702–13) led to the Transportation Act (1718) which, for the first time, allowed for transportation not only as part of the pardoning process in the case of capital offences, but as a penalty for a wide range of non-capital crimes, including grand larceny – the theft of property valued at between a shilling (5 new pence) and £2. Parliament went on to pass another sixteen acts between 1720 and 1763 that established transportation as a penalty for crimes from perjury to poaching. As many as 50,000 convicts were transported from England to America and the West Indies between 1718 and 1775, but, after the War of American Independence, transportation came temporarily to an end and a substantial number of major offenders were released back into the community, leading to a crime wave. After transportation to Africa had been considered, Australia was founded as a penal colony in 1788. At least 10 per cent of those transported to America were expected to die on the convict ships, a counterpart to the cruel treatment of Africans sent to the New World as slaves.

The extent of crime is difficult to evaluate, not least because of uncertainty as to how the percentage reported varied. Crime seems to have risen after wars were ended, because men accustomed to fight were demobilised without adequate provision in a labour market in which unemployment and underemployment were chronic. Transported felons were mostly poor young men, typically those who had found it difficult to gain employment in the major cities. After the War of the Austrian Succession, there was a crime wave in the early 1750s. The long-serving Austrian agent Zamboni reported that due to the rise in thefts and murders it was unsafe in London, both in houses and on the streets at night. He also claimed it was dangerous to go into the provinces, and that policing was negligent.[1] Post-war demobilisation led to another crime wave in 1783–84.

The Scottish criminal justice system, from which there was no appeal to London, differed not only in punishments, but also in other respects, including fifteen-strong juries, more limited use of jury trials and the not proven verdict. The poet Robert Southey thought crime was less rife in Scotland because the disparity in wealth was less and there was less envy.

Policing was weak. Landowners could rely on their own 'police' of estate-workers and employees, who could surround a household with some degree of security. In Ireland under an Act of 1715 only Protestants could be constables, but in many districts it was difficult to find men to fill this unpaid office. The weakness of formal policing mechanisms in the British Isles ensured that informally raised forces were used on an *ad hoc* basis; locally controlled urban forces generally entailed part-time and poorly armed watchmen who were unable to deal with major outbreaks of crime. The use of thief-takers was rife with abuse, as in London between 1745 and 1754 where they fabricated crimes in order to collect rewards. Rising levels of household theft in Lancaster in the 1780s led the Corporation to open a subscription for a town watch, and in 1790 a private watchman was hired by individual subscribers to patrol the main streets. Policing agencies responded to what was urgent or particularly violent, and a certain equilibrium that offered a reasonable amount of peace tended to reign, but this did not free the population from fear and the need to consider their own defence, while the agencies ignored the non-observance of much of the law. Serious breakdowns of law and order could only be dealt with by calling on the army, a method that was generally unpopular and was fraught with complications and legal hazards.

New initiatives were launched. John Fielding, an active JP, organised mounted police patrols in and around London in the 1750s. A prosecution society was established in London in the late 1750s and *Drewry's Derby Mercury* reported on 8 October 1773, 'The frequency of all kinds of felonies is complained of by all degrees of people, and some counties have (in order to lighten the burden from an individual) laudably formed associations for apprehending and prosecuting all offenders.' The paper urged that the same be done in Derbyshire. Aside from Associations for the Prosecution of Felons, there were also Watch and Ward Societies. In the early 1780s Yorkshire magistrates led moves for the increased regulation and policing of the bulk of the population. In 1785 a bill was introduced in Parliament to create a single centrally-controlled force for London, in place of the existing local ward and vestry constables and watchmen. Though it was defeated, due to fears about the consequences for liberty and opposition from local interests, similar legislation was passed for Dublin by the Irish Parliament in 1786. The Corporation opposed the new force without success and a local rate was introduced to pay for it, while the force, unlike the parochial watchmen, was given arms.

Punishment could be harsh. The judicial system has sometimes been presented by modern scholars as an aspect of social control by the elite. The Riot Act of 1715, passed in order to deal with Jacobite disturbances, made rioting and riotous assembly felonies. The number of capital offences increased greatly in England, and the method of hanging was fairly primitive, so that a quick death was not always obtained; when the famous pirate, Captain Kidd, was executed in 1701 the rope broke. Pressing to death for refusal to plead to an indictment was only abolished in England in 1772; branding and nailing by the ear to the pillory were penalties both still in use in Scotland. The large increase in sheep-stealing in 1740 as a result of the dearth of that year led to it being made a capital offence in 1741. However, the number of those hanged in London was far lower in the late eighteenth than in the early seventeenth century; in the 1730s and 1740s almost half of those condemned to die in England received a royal pardon. Many criminals were sent to America to be

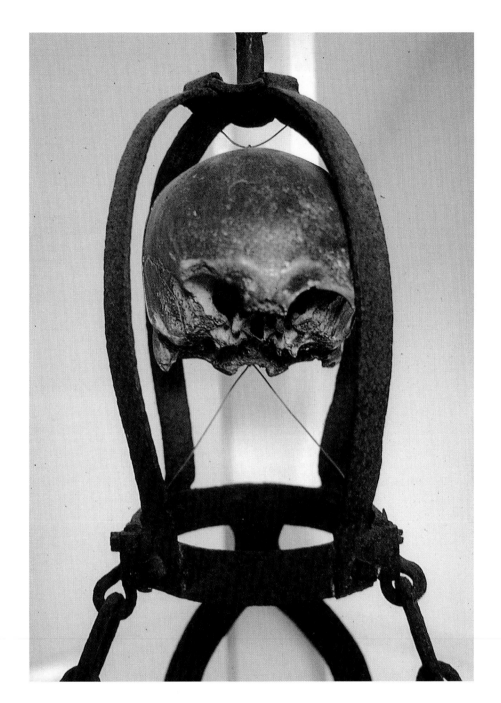

The Force of the Law. The skull is all that remains of John Breads in his gibbet cage. In 1743 he murdered Allen Grebell, mistaking him for James Lamb, Mayor of Rye.

Fort George, near Inverness. The '45 was followed by improvements in
the government's military position. In 1746 William Skinner was sent to
Scotland as Chief Engineer of North Britain, to build defensive works
that could control the Highlands. His proposals included a major new
fort near Inverness at Arderseer Point, which would control the
northern end of the Great Glen and block any foreign intervention
there, and be reinforceable by sea. Fort George, begun in 1749, took a
decade to construct, costing over £100,000. A 'state-of-the-art'
bastioned fortification, it never heard a shot fired in anger.

indentured servants; local juries frequently acquitted minor offenders. In Ireland a high proportion of criminal trials ended in acquittal, and there was a relatively low number of capital sentences and executions. Legal procedure rather than legal terror was predominant until the 1790s.

However, there is also evidence that the law served all social groups, albeit without equal access and favour. The use of legal redress in civil disputes was widespread. In Surrey an appreciable percentage of prosecutions were initiated by labourers or servants. Courts of Requests were founded in England to get people to pay their debts at a time when the central common law courts were pricing themselves out of business. They were, in effect, small debts courts. Birmingham's was founded in 1752. Many JPs sought to resolve disputes by informal mediation and sanctions, rather than the penalties of the law, although in this, as in other respects, the attitudes and styles of JPs varied greatly. The unemployed, unconnected and immigrants were generally the most badly treated by the judicial system; they were most likely to be suspected of crimes. Although there was much criticism of the cost and processes of the civil law, especially in the 1690s, 1720s and 1790s, the common law faced less hostility, particularly before mid-century and outside London, possibly because, prior to a trial, the criminal law was essentially a local process run by constables and JPs.

It would be misleading to suggest that the norms and practices of institutional justice were accepted by all. It is possible that much of the population settled their own problems without recourse to judicial agencies. Feuds, attempts to enforce particular norms of behaviour, generally eluded control by the authorities and were common. Gangs of poachers became more active and more violent from the mid-century, but were already prominent in southern England in the 1720s, leading to the 'Black Act' of 1723 which made killing game, breaking down fences, arson, trespass and going in disguise capital offences. Crime literature presented prominent criminals, particularly highwaymen such as Dick Turpin, in a heroic light. It is difficult to assess popular attitudes towards the law and its enforcement.

Authority was defied both at the centres of power and on the margins. City crowds rioted against unpopular policies, while in more distant regions the law was openly defied. When in 1703 Maurice Donnellan, the Catholic Bishop of Clonfert, was arrested under the Banishment Act of 1697, he was rescued by an armed crowd of nearly 300. The government was unable to discover and punish his rescuers, and Donnellan remained at liberty until his death in 1706. In Scotland, though not in England, armed gangs of beggars were not uncommon, and they could terrorise rural areas. One such was led by James Macpherson who was hanged at Banff in 1700. It was difficult to enforce laws against smuggling, poaching and illicit distilling, especially in areas remote from centres of authority. Cattle-rustling was a major problem in Highland Scotland as late as the 1720s. Illicit distilling was significant both there and in Ireland. 'Wrecking', looting the cargoes of wrecked ships, and in some cases luring them to their destruction, was a problem in many coastal areas, including Cornwall, Wirral and the Welsh and Irish coasts.

Smuggling increased appreciably in scale and organisation from the 1690s, despite the Smuggling Acts of 1698, 1717, 1721 and 1745. Smugglers began to organise large land-smuggling gangs from the 1720s. In 1720 about 200 members of the Mayfield gang fought revenue officers in Sussex, and hostilities in Sussex in the 1740s were large-scale. By mid-century smuggling

accounted for a major portion of trade with France and the United Provinces and had a major effect on prices and distribution; it was helped by the sympathy of some landowners.

If lawlessness was primarily a problem for individuals, government was more concerned about financial issues, although smuggling represented a fusion of the two. Britain relied upon taxes on property, principally the land-tax, introduced in 1692, and taxes on articles of general consumption, excise duty. Taxes on individuals and households did not play a role in the finances of central government in Britain. From 1697 the land-tax was a fixed tax with a quota of assessment applied to each county, the administration of which was responsible for dividing it between parishes and townships. However, there were serious problems of assessment with assessment practices varying greatly within and between counties, whereas excise duty was easier to assess and collect. In 1747 Henry Rooke, the London agent of the Bishop of Carlisle, warned the bishop that attempts to evade the window-tax were foolish as they might draw attention to the limited amount of land-tax paid by the region: 'The stopping up of windows, which your Lordship mentioned in a former letter, as a thing which people in the North parts were busy in doing; is not well judged . . . as they are favourably dealt with in regard to the Land Tax . . . especially in a time of war, when money must be raised.'[2]

In 1724 most of the existing British customs duties on coffee, tea, chocolate and coconuts were replaced by an excise duty on their domestic consumption. All dealers and retailers had to register with the excise officials, who enjoyed powers of inspection and summary justice, and whose responsibility for the excise on beer and malt ensured a nation-wide presence. The legislation of 1724 led to a major increase in revenue, but Walpole's proposals to extend these arrangements to wine and tobacco in 1733 provoked a furious political row, and the ministry had to abandon the scheme.

After the Seven Years War (1756–63) the government again sought to extend excise duties. Considerable opposition to the cider excise of 1763 led, however, to its repeal in 1766, and the imposition of duties in North America, including those on stamped paper (Stamp Act, 1765) and on glass, paper, lead and tea imported into the colonies (Townshend Acts, 1767), had similar results. By 1770 the Excise had a staff of 4,075 in England and Wales.

The burdens produced by the War of American Independence led to fresh extensions of taxation. In 1777 Charles Mellish, MP wrote from Nottinghamshire to his patron, the 2nd Duke of Newcastle, 'this county is weeping over the tax upon bricks'.[3] In 1784 taxes were imposed on pleasure-horses, hackney-coaches, shooting certificates, bricks, tiles, candles, linens, calicoes, men's hats, gold and silver plate and ladies' ribbons. In 1785 there were new taxes on post-horses, gloves, retail shops, coachmakers' and pawn-brokers' licenses, gun-dogs, sporting guns, new carriages and female servants; 1786 added perfumes and powders, particularly hair-powder, and in 1789, when the unpopular shop tax was repealed, taxes on pleasure-horses and race-horses, carriages and a number of stamp duties were increased. The extension in excises ensured that as a percentage of total revenue they rose from 27 between 1698 and 1701 to 43 between 1786 and 1789, while land-tax fell from 31 to 18 and customs from 32 to 24. Taxes as a percentage of national income rose from 12.9 in 1780 to 15.1 in 1790, by which time income was higher, but the general fiscal policy was conservative. Income tax was not introduced until 1798, when wartime needs called for far more than traditional

Facing page: Charles Montagu, 1st Earl of Halifax (1661–1715) by Sir Godfrey Kneller. A keen supporter of the Glorious Revolution, Montagu became a MP in 1689 and a Lord of the Treasury in 1692. He played a major role in arranging the financing of the Nine Years War and was responsible for the Act establishing the Bank of England in 1694, leading that year to his promotion to Chancellor of the Exchequer. Montagu was also responsible for the recoinage of 1695–99, which partly restored the coinage, for the window-tax and for the issue of the first exchequer bills. First Lord of the Treasury between 1697 and 1699, he was raised to the peerage in 1700 and survived a Tory attempt to impeach him in 1701. Out of office during Anne's reign, Halifax was appointed First Lord of the Treasury again in 1714. President of the Royal Society between 1695 and 1698, he was an active patron of Whig writers and a friend of Newton.

expedients. The Irish Parliament also preferred to tax commerce and did not introduce a land-tax.

Rising taxation was made necessary by the increased cost of government, especially the military, and by the cost of war, much of which was met by borrowing. In 1747, during the War of the Austrian Succession, Charles Wyndham, MP wrote, 'Mr Pelham has opened his budget as we call it in the House of Commons. The services of the current year will not come under the monstrous sum of eleven millions . . . He moved for the raising six millions by subscription, which they say they are sure of having filled immediately.' The government borrowed about 37 per cent of the £83 million it spent in the Seven Years War. In the War of American Independence almost half the cost was covered by borrowing. Annual public expenditure rose from £10.4 million in 1775 to £29.3 million by 1782, £114.6 million was spent between 1776 and 1782 and the national debt rose from £127 million (1775) to £232 million (1783). Owing to debt servicing, peacetime expenditure after each conflict was higher than the pre-war level.

Vast sums were raised, far more easily than elsewhere in Europe. A confidence in the soundness of financial institutions and structures and in the fiscal role and responsibility of parliamentary government enabled the mobilisation of national financial resources in the service of the state. The funded national debt, guaranteed by Parliament and based on the Bank of England which had been founded in 1694, enabled the borrowing of these sums at low rates of interest. Whereas in the early 1690s the government was paying up to 14 per cent for long-term loans, the rate of interest fell to 6–7 per cent between 1702 and 1714, also a period of war, 4 per cent in the late 1720s, at or below 3 per cent in the late 1730s, and, after a wartime rise, 3.5 per cent in 1750. In 1741 Corbyn Morris observed that 'the Public Credit is in some measure the pulse of the Nation'. A pro-government pamphlet of 1755 claimed that 'The high sounding bugbear of eighty millions of debt, when stripped of the rags, with which disaffection and discontent had cloathed it, appeared less formidable, than a debt of fifty millions was formerly; and that it was easier to pay the one at 3 per cent, than the other at 5.' In 1757 the Duke of Newcastle, then First Lord of the Treasury, noted that there appeared to be no difficulty in meeting the new commitment to provide greater military support to Prussia: 'towards that I have already been offered near six millions . . . and all this money will be borrowed (if necessary) something under 3½ per cent; when France gives 11 per cent and cannot fill the subscriptions'.[4]

The general benefit to the economy of low rates of interest on government debt and to the political system of a funded national debt were considerable, though perhaps the funds invested in the national debt might have played a more beneficial economic role if invested elsewhere.

The attitudes and actions of government servants were another problem, interacting with administrative systems that were often weak and archaic. For example, much of the work of the Exchequer was still conducted according to medieval forms, and the efficiency of the Treasury and revenue departments was found wanting during the War of American Independence, leading to reform in the post-war period. In 1758 the Duke of Newcastle noted about money for Hanover, 'His Majesty wanted this money to be sent away in 24 hours. I told him this holiday time nobody was in town, no office open, that caused very severe reflections.'[5]

Corruption was a widespread problem, reflecting the importance of tax revenues as a form of ready wealth, proprietary attitudes towards posts and the general practice of paying officials by allowing them to retain part of the proceeds of their positions; officials saw themselves as office-holders rather than employees. Office was seen as a form of property; it was common for positions to be inherited. The 26-year-old Vicesimus Knox was a good appointment as Headmaster of Tonbridge School in 1778; he was also the son of his predecessor. Coventry Corporation was self-perpetuating and corrupt, a closed corporation in which councillors chose all officials except the town clerk. Leases were granted to councillors at low rents, the funds of charities in their care disappeared and the creation of freemen was manipulated for electoral advantage. In the Armagh district of Ireland the Cust family used the local collectorship of taxes so as to end up as substantial *rentiers* in the area; the unacceptable level of Henry Cust's corruption led to his losing his post in 1761, but he suffered no social or financial penalty and in 1769 was appointed High Sheriff of Armagh.

Corruption was but one aspect of an administrative ethos and practice for which the connotations of the term 'bureaucracy' are inappropriate. Administrative organisations reflected the values and methods of the social system; appointment and promotion often resulted from social rank, patronage and inheritance, rather than from educational qualifications or what might later be seen as objectively assessed merit. Merit in this period meant connection, wealth and rank, and much of the concern about the role of 'corruption' in appointments was a nineteenth-century invention. The universities did not serve to train an administrative elite; instead, particularly in England, they produced numerous clerics and acted as finishing schools for the social elite.

Social assumptions, the role played by patronage, the political importance of administrative posts and the opportunities for gain, both legal and illegal, helped to ensure that senior posts were occupied by men of rank. As a result those who wielded authority and controlled the power for change were often gentlemen amateurs, frequently without vocation or aptitude, rather than professional experts. Their expert assistants were generally too humble in status to be able to push through changes, particularly in a society and administrative ethos where precedent commanded both respect and legal authority.

The dominance of patronage and the vulnerable position of many ministers encouraged them to favour clients and relatives, which further encouraged factionalism, but could also ensure loyal and possibly effective employees. In 1739 Sir James Lowther, MP for Cumberland, wrote of John Hill, MP, a Commissioner of Customs, 'Mr Hill is a great operator for Sir Robert . . . as he finds Sir Robert looks upon me as a hearty friend he would have me to dispose of things in Cumberland both in Customs and Excise. At this rate are things managed in every part of the revenue. It is suffered to go on very often to the prejudice of the public . . . to gratify the friends of great men.' Two years earlier Lowther had informed the Bishop of Carlisle that in order to get his nephew a post in the Customs at Whitehaven, the bishop 'should write directly to Sir Robert Walpole, for it is he alone that disposes of all these places, and expects application for them to be made to himself'.[6] In 1748 the Duke of Newcastle explained to the Duke of Cumberland the choice of 'Mr Elliot, son of Lord Minto for [Sheriff-deputy for] the Shire of Roxburgh . . . Lord Minto is reputed to be zealously attached to His Majesty's government, and to have great influence in the county.'[7] Scotland was a small society with higher patronage levels than in England.

Facing page: Part of Roy's map of
Scotland. The mapping of Britain
improved during the century.
Following the suppression of the
'45, Lieutenant-Colonel David
Watson, Deputy Quartermaster-
General to the forces, assisted by
William Roy, prepared between
1747 and 1755 the map known as
the 'Duke of Cumberland's map' of
the mainland of Scotland, which
was based on a military survey. Roy
(1726–90) also constructed an
encampment near Fort Augustus
and superintended road-making by
the troops in these years. He rose to
be Major-General and was a great
expert on fortifications and
mapping, especially triangulation;
he was also interested in Roman
remains in Britain.

Factionalism was also encouraged by the weakness and sometimes absence
of agreed administrative procedures and the limited authority of government
institutions, which ensured that posts became influential often because of the
individuals who filled them. Similar problems of amateurism and factionalism
affected the armed forces.

The problems of government were not restricted to the maintenance of
law and order, financial difficulties, unreliable officials, factional politics,
unresponsive local communities and the absence of reliable information.
Changes in government and political disorder could create many problems.
These difficulties were not peculiar to the national government; major institutions and landlords faced similar problems, as they strove to reconcile traditional practices and assumptions with the desire to achieve specific goals. The
Glengarry estate in the Scottish Highlands, in which timber was illegally cut
by tenants in 1769, was not the only estate in which it was found difficult to
control the activities of dependants, although it was more remote than most
and its chief particularly unpleasant. Supervision was made difficult for all
institutions by the relatively small size of their staff.

As a result, consent and co-operation played a major role in successful
government, at both the national and the local level. A crucial aspect of this
was the importance of parliamentary support in the establishment and maintenance of the funded national debt. This was both the source of the government's financial strength and the product of the co-operation between Crown
and political society after 1688 that was expressed in the constitutional position of Parliament and the policies of successive ministries. Parliament's business was dominated by local issues, such as turnpikes, canals, enclosures and
bridges. Its views were a reflection of continual pressure from outside
Westminster, through personal contacts, the press and pressure groups.

Despite the problems of government, it would be mistaken to argue that
ministries were opposed to considering change. 'Let sleeping dogs lie',
Walpole's maxim, does not describe the typical late-eighteenth century
administration, for officials and politicians were often willing to act in accordance with the principles of state-directed action. The structure of colonial
administration and commercial regulation received much attention, and there
was considerable administrative reform and government activity, for example
with the navy and, under Pitt the Younger, at the Treasury. Much action was in
response to crises. Just as the administrative and judicial system in Scotland,
especially the Highlands, was remodelled after the '45, so the size of the
national debt at the end of the Seven Years War led to an attempt at financial
retrenchment and reorganisation. Similarly the crisis of the American War led
to a powerful impetus behind post-war reform initiatives which were particularly important in colonial, commercial and financial matters, while the
French Revolutionary War was to lead to major changes, including income
tax, Union with Ireland and a national census.

In addition, work on eighteenth-century administration at the local level,
on JPs, law-enforcement, urban communities and prison administration, has
stressed the significance of planning and policy, showing change as well as
continuity. The local and the national were linked. Thus in 1784 Parliament
passed an act establishing committees of JPs to authorise expenditures, permitted the complete rebuilding of county prisons and authorised JPs to
borrow for this end on the security of the county rates. The Act was followed
by the rebuilding of many prisons, including those at Lancaster, Preston,

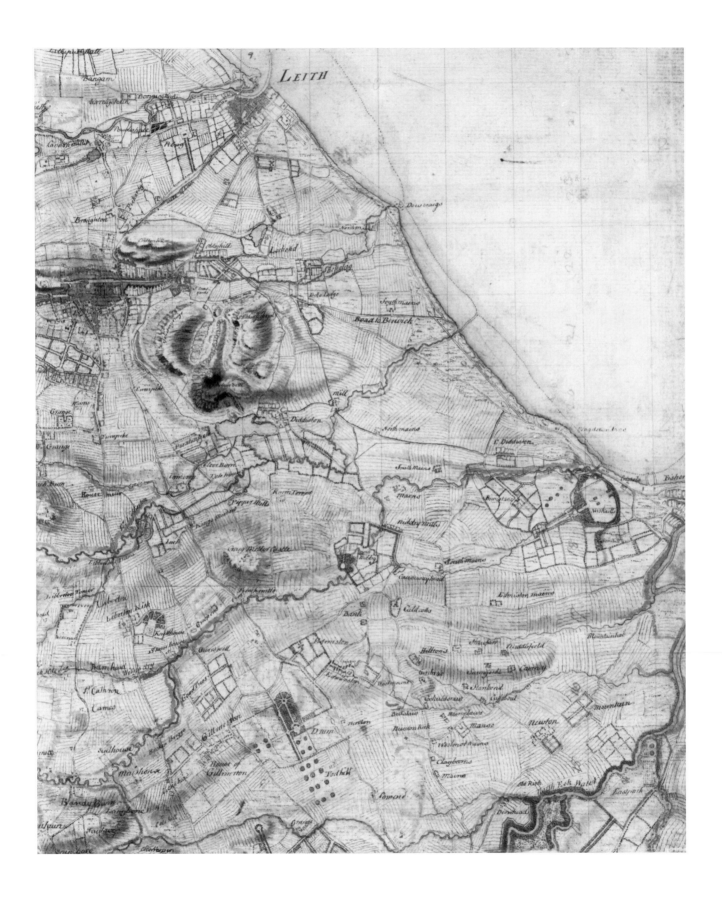

Liverpool and Manchester. But unlike the situation in much of the Continent in the second half of the century, such 'reform' impulses reflected co-operation between centre and localities. 'Enlightened Despotism' in Britain was parliamentary in character. This is important, because a potential challenge to the practice, personnel and ideology of landed power in eighteenth-century Europe came from royal initiatives; indeed, until the French Revolution, they were the sole serious threat. Thus, potentially at least, notions such as Peter the Great's Table of Ranks (1722) were subversive. They made it clear that social and political privilege derived from monarchical approval on a continuing basis. In England there was no comparable attempt to create a 'service nobility'; furthermore, in contrast with Ireland in the 1690s and the Scottish Highlands after 1746, there was no attempt to alter the politico–social complexion of power. As in many other respects, it is a fundamental conservatism that is most striking, certainly in comparison with, say, the Austria of Joseph II.

Yet this conservatism was both sensitive to political expectations and options and able to accommodate, and at times assist, commercial, industrial and imperial growth. There is no reason to suppose that a 'conservative' political system is necessarily incompatible with change. Any emphasis on confrontation, challenge and tension is problematic, because it presupposes a rigidity on the part of the established order, an inability to accommodate change, a necessity of transformation through struggle that reflects modern ideological presuppositions rather than the complex and nuanced reality of the period. As especially with electoral 'management', so more generally both with the role of the landed order in the political system and with the very nature of that system, it is necessary to offer a more sensitive account. It is also important not to read the ideological idioms and clash of the French Revolutionary era back into the previous decades.

10 POLITICS

THE GLORIOUS REVOLUTION

The politics of eighteenth-century Britain involved issues and office, domestic disputes and the conquest of empire, relations between the different parts of the British Isles and with the rest of Europe. They all interacted to produce a situation of considerable complexity that is open to various patterns of discussion and analysis. Any narrative faces the problem of where to place emphasis and how far it is appropriate to suggest causation.

Eighteenth-century Britain really began in 1688. The 'Glorious Revolution' of that year led to constitutional change, set a new political agenda and transformed the relationship between the constituent political parts of the British Isles. It was to be the central point of reference of subsequent discussion of the political system and played a crucial role in the public ideology of the state for over a century.

The Revolution was a consequence of the divisions, tensions and fears of seventeenth-century British politics, especially those of the 1670s and 1680s. In 1688 the last male Stuart ruler of Britain, James II (1685–88), was driven from the throne by his nephew and son-in-law William of Orange, William III (1689–1702). This, the last successful *coup d'état* or revolution in British history, reflected hostility to the policies and Catholic faith of James. In 1688 seven politicians invited William to intervene in order to protect Protestantism and traditional liberties. Motivated rather by a wish to keep Britain out of the camp of his enemy, Louis XIV of France, William had already decided to invade. He was helped by a collapse of will on the part of James, which negated the superiority of his army, and by the abandonment of James's cause by key individuals.

Most people did not want any breach in the hereditary succession, and William had initially pretended that he had no designs on the Crown.

However, as the situation developed favourably, especially when James had been driven into exile, William made it clear that he sought the throne. This was achieved by declaring it vacant and inviting William and his wife, James's elder daughter, Mary, to occupy it as joint monarchs. By claiming that it was only a vacancy that was being filled it was possible to minimise the element of innovation. All Catholics were barred from the succession, a change helped by the extent to which the claims of the infant Prince of Wales were not well established in the public consciousness.

The 'Revolution' neither sought nor produced social or economic changes, and was far from revolutionary in that respect, but it did lead to major changes in government, foreign policy and relations between the parts of the British Isles. The financial settlement of 1689 left William with an ordinary revenue that was too small for his needs, obliging him to turn to Parliament for support, a situation that was exacerbated by the outbreak of war. The Triennial Act (1694) further ensured regular meetings of the Westminster Parliament, and, by limiting their life-span to three years, required regular elections. The Dublin Parliament also became a regular and central feature of Irish politics, sitting every second year from 1692. William's was truly a constricted monarchy. Rights hitherto treated as stemming from royal grant or concession were now regarded by many as the property of people and institutions.

WAR WITH FRANCE

James II received shelter and support from Louis XIV, who in 1689 sent him to Ireland with a French force. War with France in the Nine Years War (1689–97) and the War of the Spanish Succession (1702–13) led to Britain playing a hitherto unprecedented central role in European diplomacy and warfare. British troops were committed to the Continent in large numbers. Little glory was won in the first war. William III was defeated by Marshal Luxembourg at Steenkerk (1692) and Neerwinden (1693), but the commitment of Anglo-Dutch strength denied Louis decisive victory in the Low Countries, and William's capture of Namur in 1695 shook French prestige.

War between Britain and France resumed in 1702 as Britain sought to prevent a French prince from inheriting the Spanish empire, which included much of the New World with its crucial trade. Allied to the Dutch, the Emperor (Austria), Portugal and Savoy–Piedmont, the British sustained the coalition, in large part with financial support. The British were unsuccessful in conquering Spain, but, thanks to John Churchill, 1st Duke of Marlborough (1650–1722), defeated Louis's forces in Germany and the Low Countries.

In 1701 William III appointed Marlborough Captain-General of the British forces in the Netherlands, a post he held until dismissed by the pacific Tory ministry in 1711. Marlborough was skilful in holding the anti-French coalition together, and as a general determined to take the offensive and very able in conducting mobile warfare. His battles were fought on an extended front and thus placed a premium on mobility, planning and the ability of commanders to integrate and influence what might otherwise be a number of separate conflicts. Marlborough was particularly good at this and anticipated Napoleon's skill in this respect, although the Napoleonic battlefield was far larger.

In 1703–04 a combination of France, Bavaria and the Hungarian rebels appeared about to extinguish Austrian power and thus to destroy the basis of

Britain's alliance strategy. The crisis was averted by Marlborough's bold march at the head of an Anglo-German army from Koblenz on the Rhine to the Danube, the most decisive British military move on the Continent until the twentieth century, and his subsequent victory, in co-operation with the Austrian commander, Prince Eugene, at Blenheim (13 August 1704). This was a hard-fought battle, with over 30,000 casualties out of 108,000 combatants. Victory was largely due to Marlborough's tactical flexibility; in particular, his ability to retain control of the battle once fighting had begun and thus to manoeuvre units was crucial. As with many battles, the decisive factors at Blenheim were a mastery of the terrain, the retention and management of reserves and the timing of the decisive stroke. Having pinned down much of the French infantry in defensive engagements, Marlborough broke the French centre with the substantial force he had kept unengaged. Germany was then cleared of the French.

At Ramillies (1706) Marlborough similarly broke the French centre after it had been weakened in order to support action on a flank. This was followed by the conquest of the Spanish Netherlands (Belgium); the French attempt to reverse this in 1708 was thwarted at Oudenaarde. Marlborough was less successful at Malplaquet (1709), as his tactics had become stereotyped, and his hopes of marching on Paris proved misplaced, but Britain had established itself as a major power that was a match for France. This was recognised in the terms of the Peace of Utrecht (1713); Britain obtained Gibraltar, Minorca and commercial concessions from Spain, Nova Scotia and Newfoundland from France.

The French also recognised the Protestant succession in Britain and agreed to expel 'James III', James II's son, the Jacobite Pretender, who had fought for the French in the recent war. This was a crucial stage in the episodic War of the British Succession that had begun in 1688, a war that was to have major consequences for Scotland and Ireland.

THE FATE OF THE BRITISH ISLES

James II's position in Scotland collapsed in December 1688. The Convention of the Estates which met in Edinburgh in the following March was dominated by supporters of William, and on 4 April 1689 the Crown of Scotland was declared forfeit, William and Mary being proclaimed joint sovereigns a week later. Catholics were excluded from the Scottish throne and from public office. The contractual nature of the Revolution Settlement, the extent to which the Crown had been obtained by William and Mary on conditions, was far more apparent in Scotland than in England. James's standard was raised in Scotland in April 1689 by John Graham of Claverhouse, who was backed by the Episcopalians, nearly half of the population, who supported a Scottish Church controlled by bishops, like that of England. Jacobitism in Scotland owed much to opposition to the Presbyterian church settlement there. At the battle of Killiecrankie on 27 July, Claverhouse's Highlanders routed their opponents with the cold steel and rush of a Highland charge, but their leader was killed and the cause collapsed under his mediocre successors. Most of the Highland chiefs swore allegiance to William in late 1691, by which time the cattle trade had been wrecked, although the process of pacification was discredited by the massacre at Glencoe.

James II's supporters had dominated most of Ireland in 1689, though Derry, fearing Catholic massacre, resisted a siege and was relieved by the

English fleet in July 1689. The following month William's forces, mostly Danes and Dutch, landed and occupied Carrickfergus and Belfast. Naval power thus offered William military flexibility and prevented James from controlling all of Ireland. Arriving in Ireland in June 1690, William marched on Dublin, defeating the outnumbered Franco-Jacobite army at the Boyne (1 July). Dublin then fell. The following year the Jacobites were defeated at Aughrim (12 July), and their surviving positions fell. By the Treaty of Limerick (3 October 1691) the Jacobites in Ireland surrendered, many, the 'Wild Geese', going to serve James in France.

The Glorious Revolution led to English domination of the British Isles, albeit domination that was helped by and shared with important sections of the Irish and Scottish population; Irish Anglicans and, more significantly, Scottish Presbyterians. The alternative had been glimpsed in 1689 when James's Parliament in Dublin had rejected much of the authority of the Westminster Parliament. This path had, however, been blocked. Jacobitism, and the strategic threat to England, posed by an autonomous or independent Scotland and Ireland, pushed together those politicians in the three kingdoms who were in favour of the Revolution Settlement.

THE POLITICS OF SCOTLAND

The Union of 1707 between England and Scotland arose essentially from English concern about the newly assertive Scottish Parliament and the possible hazards posed by an autonomous, if not independent, Scotland. Many Scots were angered by the neglect displayed by William III, and by the determination of the succession without consulting Scotland in the 1701 Act of Succession passed by the Westminster Parliament. In 1703 the Scottish Parliament passed the Act of Security, which stated that if Anne died childless, her successor would not be the same as in England unless Scotland was guaranteed the independence of its Crown, its parliamentary freedom and religious settlement, and liberty of trade. This encouraged English support for the Union. There was scant support for the measure in Scotland, which had little choice but to accede to the broad thrust of England's proposals; her independence was limited, the Scottish economy was in a poor state and there was no good Protestant alternative to the house of Hanover, descendants of James VI and I through his daughter. It was this claim that had been established by the Act of Succession. The passage of the Act of Union through the Scottish Parliament in 1706 ultimately depended on corruption and determination not to be shut out of English and colonial markets. In steering a way towards an agreement which would not arouse English ire, but also make sufficient concessions to their countrymen, Scottish Court politicians, particularly the Earl of Mar, managed brilliantly. Modern nationalist historians have failed to acknowledge the achievements of the stubborn Scottish parliamentarians who ensured the continued distinctiveness of Scottish ecclesiastical and judicial arrangements.

Scotland was regarded as important in London primarily as a security threat. The claims of the exiled Stuarts were supported by many Scots in the risings of 1689, 1715 and 1745. The suppression of the last was followed by a major attempt to change the socio-political nature of Highland society. Hereditable jurisdictions were abolished, an attempt was made to use the confiscated estates of the rebels to fund a programme of economic modernisation and the construction of roads, bridges and harbours and the improvement of education were designed to integrate the Highlands into the

Facing page: John, 1st Duke of Marlborough plans the siege of Bouchain with his secretary John Armstrong, artist unknown. John Churchill (1650–1722) was one of the greatest of British generals; he rose under the Stuarts but deserted James II in 1688. William III appointed him Captain-General of the English forces in the Netherlands, a post he held until dismissed by the pacific Tory ministry in 1711. Marlborough was skilful in holding the anti-French coalition together, and as a general was expert in conducting mobile warfare and determined to take the offensive. Bouchain was successfully besieged in 1711, and was Marlborough's last success.

William III, artist unknown. William (1650–1702), king from 1689. Nephew of Charles I, in 1677 William married his cousin Mary, elder daughter of James, Duke of York, later James II. A prominent opponent of Louis XIV, William invaded England in 1688 in order to ensure English support for his cause. William gained the thrones of England and Scotland jointly with Mary in 1689 and reigned alone after she died in 1694. He devoted most of his reign to war with France (1689–97) and was preparing for renewed conflict with Louis when he died following a fall from his horse which had stumbled on a molehill at Hampton Court, leading to the Jacobite toast to `the little gentleman in Velvet'.

rest of the country. Although most of the improving schemes proved to be ill-conceived and in 1784 the estates were returned to the pardoned owners or their heirs, Highland society was by then far less distinctive and independent than earlier, and it was no longer a security threat. Whereas in 1751–55 there were seven marching regiments in Scotland and only four in England, by the early 1770s there was an average of four or five marching battalions in Scotland and ten in England.

The Union of Scotland and England in 1707 led to Scottish representation in the Westminster Parliament – 45 MPs and 16 peers – and this increased the interest of ministers in ensuring that Scottish elections were managed to their satisfaction. The *Protester*, an opposition London newspaper, claimed on 29 September 1753 that the election of the 16 Scottish representative peers was totally controlled by the government: 'a sort of Insect-Lords, generated by court-sunshine in a corrupt soil'. In 1715 and 1745 promises to restore Scottish taxes on the old footing were a key Jacobite pledge.

There were some attempts to bring Scotland more firmly within a unified political and administrative system, the Duke of Newcastle displaying especial interest in mid-century. These failed, partly because of opposition from Scottish politicians, but more because, for most of the century, the ministers in London never maintained sufficient interest to implement a coherent Scottish policy, nor needed to do so. Sir David Dalrymple wrote from Edinburgh to a fellow Scot in 1763, 'It has been often matter of astonishment to me why a minister in England should think a minister *here* necessary; we are so well broke, so thoroughly paced, that we can be managed by a whipcord as well as by a double bridle.' In general, the government preferred to entrust the management of Scottish affairs to local politicians whom they could trust, such as the Earl of Islay, later 3rd Duke of Argyll, from the 1730s until his death in 1761, and Henry Dundas for most of the 1780s and 1790s. Anne and George I, George II and George III did not need or feel it necessary to visit Scotland, Ireland and Wales. Gradually the Scottish ruling class developed a British and imperial outlook. Many Scots served in the British army and overseas administration, and in the army and administration of the East India Company. In 1764 William Pitt the Elder wrote, 'I revere the union as the main foundation of the strength and security of this island.'[1]

THE POLITICS OF IRELAND

In the early eighteenth century there was support for Union with England in Ireland also. The Irish Parliament, a completely Protestant body after 1690, petitioned for it in 1703, while Union had been considered by English ministers in 1697. It seemed, however, to have little to offer to English politicians, and Ireland was treated with scant consideration. The Westminster Parliament's Declaratory Act of 1720 stated its legislative and judicial supremacy over that of Dublin. Legislation in Westminster, the result of protectionist lobbying by English interests, for example the Irish Woollen Export Prohibition Act of 1699, hindered Irish exports, while the granting of Irish lands and pensions to favoured courtiers accentuated the problem of absentee landowners and revenue-holders, with a consequent loss of money to the country. The Irish Parliament had to pay the cost of quartering a large part of the army in Ireland to support the Anglo-Irish establishment and, from the English point of view, to hide the size of the army from English public opinion. It was forbidden to recruit Irish Presbyterians until 1780 and Irish Catholics until 1793. The Irish Parliament did not control the Irish executive, because senior officials were always Englishmen selected by the British government.

There was no Jacobite rising in Ireland at the time of the '15 and the '45, but Ireland did pose serious problems of political management. The preservation of a Parliament in Dublin and its more regular meetings enabled Ireland's Protestant politicians to retain a measure of importance and independence, so that British ministers had difficulties devising strategies for managing the Parliament and governing the country. In the first half of the century reliance was generally placed upon managing the government through local politicians known as 'Undertakers'. A system developed in which bargaining between the Lord Lieutenant and the Lords Justices provided a measure of stability. The Undertakers formed part of a complex and creative

Andrew Fletcher of Saltoun (1655–1716), unknown artist after William Aikman. Andrew Fletcher was a Scottish politician who took part in Monmouth's invasion in 1685 and supported William of Orange in 1688. A republican who rejected English domination, Fletcher opposed the Union of the two kingdoms. He was also an agricultural improver, responsible for the barley-mill at Saltoun which was for over forty years the only one in the country. Aikman (1682–1731), the only son of a Scottish landowner and lawyer, trained in Rome and worked as a portrait painter in Edinburgh from 1712 to 1723, before being persuaded by the Duke of Argyll to move to London, where he worked until his death.

political system in which issues as much as patronage were at stake, but the situation was complicated when instability in English politics affected politics in Dublin, as in the reigns of Anne and George I and after the fall of Walpole. English party attitudes and alignments, for example the Anglican basis of Toryism, were transplanted to Ireland. Nevertheless, despite disputes, Ireland by mid-century was far more stable than it had ever been hitherto under British rule.

The national sentiments expressed by the so-called 'Patriots' in the Dublin Parliament during the money bill dispute of the 1750s encouraged some of the Catholics. Irish Protestants became opposed to Union in the mid-century and in 1759 there were riots in Dublin on the rumour of it alone, but the mirage of a patriot Irish Parliament prepared to extend the hand of friendship to Irishmen of all religious persuasions soon receded. George, 4th Viscount Townshend, Lord Lieutenant between 1767 and 1772, instituted a new system of direct management of the government and resided in Dublin continually, but he failed to assuage mounting resentment against the political and constitutional dependence of Ireland on Britain, and against its economic subordination, and his attempt to increase the size of the military establishment was very unpopular.

Tension increased during the War of American Independence and, in the face of growing unrest and the fear that the Volunteer movement, a citizens' militia formed in Ulster in 1778, would lead to a rebellion, the Tudor legislation which had placed the Dublin Parliament under the control of the Privy Council in London was repealed in 1782, as was the Declaratory Act of 1720; the Dublin Parliament was thereby granted full powers of initiative and legislation. In 1778 Catholics had been permitted to take long leases, and in 1782 they were placed on the same footing as Protestants as far as property rights were concerned. After a further Renunciation Act in 1783, the influence of the Lord Lieutenant was almost the sole means left for keeping the legislative programmes of the two islands in step. The unanimity on political and religious issues engineered in 1782 did not long survive the granting of legislative independence. During the Regency Crisis of 1788–89 caused by the ill-health of George III, the Irish Parliament adopted a position in opposition to that of London, inviting George, Prince of Wales to assume the royal functions without conditions. In ceding to the Dublin Parliament the sort of rights demanded, without success, by the American colonists before their rebellion, the Westminster Parliament thus appeared to have created an unstable relationship. The Prince of Wales supported an independent Ireland, only linked to Britain through himself as king of Ireland, but George III's recovery ended the matter. The instability of the post–1783 constitutional situation did not, however, challenge public order, and it was to be the radicalism and uncertainty resulting from the French Revolution and the outbreak of war with France in 1793 that served in Ireland as a catalyst to activate long-standing politico–religious tensions, not least by providing a radical programme and leadership for an appreciable portion of the Catholic masses.

England might therefore clearly dominate Britain after 1691, but it was not an untroubled relationship, although the degree to which it created serious political problems for the government in London was episodic. A sense of separate identity and national privileges continued to be important for the groups involved in politics in Ireland and Scotland, though not in Wales. This sense of separation was accentuated at the ecclesiastical level, as in 1689 the

Charles, 9th Lord Cathcart by Sir Joshua Reynolds. Cathcart (1721–76) was wounded
at Fontenoy in 1745 and rose to become a Lieutenant-General (1760), Ambassador
at St Petersburg and Lord Commissioner of Police in Scotland. He sat twice for
Reynolds for his portrait and had him arrange that the black patch on his cheek
covering his Fontenoy scar might be visible. Between 1755 and 1763 and 1773 and
1776 Cathcart was Lord High Commissioner in the General Assembly of the
Church of Scotland: the Crown's representative.

Ballincolly Castle. Co of Cork.

64

Scottish Parliament abolished Episcopacy and in 1690 a Presbyterian Church was established there. This distinctiveness was maintained at the Union, as was the different legal system. Ireland maintained its Parliament until the Act of Union of 1800. Wales, however, lacked centralising institutions or social, ecclesiastical and legal arrangements corresponding with its own language.

Protestantism, war with France and the benefits of empire helped to create a British nationhood, which developed alongside the still strong senses of English, Scottish and Irish identity. At the level of the elite, job opportunities, the decline of Gaelic, Welsh and Scots, and the growing appeal of English cultural norms, customs and education, ensured that the sense of separate identity was easily compatible with British nationhood.

THE JACOBITE CHALLENGE

The struggles of 1689–91 thus helped to create a pattern of axes and allegiances that gave shape to much of the politics of the following century. Yet uncertainty over the stability of the regime remained a major issue;

View of Ballincollig Castle, County Cork from Gabriel Béranger's views of Ireland. Dutch-born and of Huguenot descent, Béranger (*c.* 1729–1817) settled in Ireland in 1750 and opened a print shop and artist's warehouse in Dublin. He was employed to sketch antiquities by individuals interested in Irish history, appointed to a government sinecure and made many sketching tours in Ireland. The ruins of Ballincollig Castle reflected the social, political and military transition to an age when the means of organised violence were controlled by the government and directed against foreign foes.

Jacobitism, support for the exiled Stuarts, was seen as an important, albeit episodic, threat until 'Bonnie Prince Charlie', Charles Edward Stuart, the son of 'James III', was defeated at Culloden in 1746. Jacobitism represented an attempt to challenge developed and strengthening patterns of control: of Ireland by England, of Scotland by England, of northern Scotland by the Presbyterians of the Central Lowlands, of northern England by the south; and indeed of the whole of Britain by its most populous, wealthy and 'advanced' region: south-east England.

Jacobitism thus represented amongst other things an attempt to reverse the spatial process of state formation that had characterised recent (as well as earlier) British history. Proximity to centres of power, such as London and the Scottish Central Lowlands, brought a greater awareness of the political reality of 'England' and 'Scotland' than life in many regions that were far from being economically and politically marginal. Such proximity was crucial to processes of state formation and resource mobilisation.

At one level Jacobitism sought to resist this process in Britain; it was the expression of the desire for Scottish, Highland and Irish autonomy. Culloden ensured that the new British state created by the parliamentary union of 1707 would continue to be one whose political tone and agenda were set in London and southern England. This was the basis of British consciousness, a development that did not so much alter the views of the English political elite, for whom Britain was essentially an extension of England, but, rather, that reflected the determination of the Scottish and Irish Protestant elites to link their fate with that of the British state. William III's defeat of Jacobitism in Ireland in 1690–91 ensured that the Catholic challenge to this process was defeated there, and this result was sustained by Culloden. The transfer of wealth and power from the Irish Catholics to the Protestants was already well advanced by 1689; but the war of 1689–91 prevented a reversal of the process. In strategic and geopolitical terms this was of tremendous importance: an autonomous or independent Ireland would probably have looked to the major maritime Catholic powers, France and Spain, rather than Austria, and this challenge to English power within the British Isles would have made it difficult to devote sufficient resources to the maritime and colonial struggle with the Bourbons.

Jacobitism was also, particularly in England and at the court of the exiled Stuarts, an attempt not to dismember Britain or to alter the political relations within the British Isles, but rather to restore the male line of the Stuarts. The degree of their unpopularity is unclear; most of the evidence commonly cited for anti-Stuart feeling in 1745–46 relates to the period after Charles Edward's retreat from Derby and offers little guide to the likely response to a successful invasion. In England neither side appears to have enjoyed the enthusiastic support of the bulk of the population, and certainly not to the extent of action. Any assessment of political culture in this period needs to take note of this quiescence, and to appreciate that the political structure of Britain was based on the successful use of force.

THE NATURE OF BRITISH POLITICS

The state that applied force so successfully, both within and outside the British Isles, is one that has traditionally been described in terms of corrupt politics, weak government and unimportant monarchs. This analysis is now open to reinterpretation.

Corruption is commonly seen as central to the political system of

Hanoverian Britain; traditionally, it has been particularly associated with the elections and electorate of the period. The very phrase 'pocket borough', meaning a seat that was controlled or heavily influenced by a patron, is symptomatic of this analysis. How true was it? How much freedom did electors enjoy? How representative was the Commons of its electorate? Let us first take the traditional view. This would present the corrupt nature of pocket boroughs as integral to the ministerial stability that characterised so much of this period. In this view the government had little to fear from the electorate, for even if the ministry was generally unsuccessful in the larger 'open' constituencies – the counties and the large cities, such as Bristol and London – they could rely on the large number of pocket boroughs. There were many boroughs with small electorates, such as Malmesbury with 13 votes, Gatton with 22 and Whitchurch with 85. In many of the small constituencies there was rarely an election. The Jacobite Earl of Orrery complained in 1721, 'there are so many little venal boroughs that 'tis to be apprehended a majority will hardly be carried by the inclinations of the people only'. William Pitt the Elder, the so-called 'Great Commoner', first entered Parliament when he was elected unopposed for Old Sarum in 1735. This quintessential rotten borough returned two MPs, though it was entirely depopulated. Pitt's grandfather, Thomas 'Diamond' Pitt, who had made a fortune trading to India, had purchased the property that carried the right of election in 1691, and at the general election of 1734 William's elder brother was returned unopposed by the five voters. As he had also been returned unopposed for Okehampton, where he owned much property, Thomas brought his brother in for Old Sarum. William sat for that seat until 1747, then for pocket boroughs under the patronage of the Duke of Newcastle. In December 1756 he was elected for Okehampton and for the pocket borough of his Grenville in-laws at Buckingham, and in 1757 he transferred to Bath, which he had been invited to represent by the corporation, which enjoyed a monopoly of the franchise. Only one of his elections, Seaford in 1747, was contested; and Newcastle was able to swing that election. Three Irish boroughs were entirely uninhabited.

Opposition politicians, such as Viscount Bolingbroke in the 1730s, and opposition publications, argued that thanks to corruption Parliament served the sinister and self-interested ends of government:

> A New Interest House of Commons is begot by the Prime Minister upon the dregs of the people, I mean, such as inhabit those great repositories of ministerial spawn, the boroughs of Wiltshire and Cornwall. This hopeful child, after being brought up to town, lives in an incestuous intercourse with its own father for seven years [the usual length of a Parliament after the Septennial Act of 1716]; at the end of which, the fruit of their amours will be found to be a blessing brood of land-taxes, malt-taxes, salt-taxes, window-taxes etc, excises, votes of credit, standing armies, German subsidies, acts to encumber and prevent matrimony, and for the naturalization of Jews and foreigners.[2]

Irrespective of any urban property, local aristocrats and gentry could be of considerable consequence in controlling or influencing borough representation, the Dukes of Bolton and Chandos in Winchester, the Dukes of Grafton and the Earls of Bristol at Bury St Edmunds, the Earls Gower at Newcastle-under-Lyme, the Norths of Wroxton at Banbury, the Drakes of Shardeloes at Amersham. This was particularly important for towns like Banbury, whose prosperity as market centres greatly depended on local landowners. The town of Ayr was not satisfied with the county's MP, James Mure Campbell, in 1760: 'the Provost and all the Magistracy are much dissatisfied at never hearing anything from Campbell, but what the gazette either does or might inform them of'.[3] Mure Campbell, who indeed had little interest in politics, was not re-elected in 1761, but that was due not to the dissatisfaction of his constituents, but to an aristocratic arrangement about the representation of a number of seats: there was no contest. In 1688 James II had granted Kells a new charter stating that it should be a free borough with a sovereign and burgesses, but the sovereign was always the head of the leading local family, the Taylors. They rose into and in the Irish peerage: Baron Headfort (1760), Viscount Headfort (1762), Earl of Bective (1770), Marquess of Headfort (1800). In 1770 the 1st

Earl completed nearby Headfort House and the family ceased to live in the town itself. Many boroughs, such as Exeter, that in the seventeenth century had chosen townsmen as MPs, chose country gentlemen in the following century. The country elite dominated Parliament. The peers had a considerable influence in the Commons. 'Corruption' acted as a harness between the Lords and the Commons, with MPs often reflecting the views of their patrons in the Lords, and thus prevented conflict between the two chambers. The growth of the peerage particularly from the beginning of the reign of George III (1760–1820), and especially from the 1770s, reflected a trend of promoting MPs to peerages. The cost of county elections and a desire to avoid contests helped to lessen the number of county contests: after 1754 there was no Oxfordshire contest until 1826. There was a similar process in some boroughs.

The central point in the traditional interpretation of the Hanoverian Commons was therefore that it was unrepresentative not only of the population at large, but even of the electorate. As a corollary, it could not be expected to take much of an interest in society other than in order to sustain its position and oppose reform. Indeed Sir Lewis Namier, the great mid-twentieth-century historian of the Commons, emphasised the social and non-political factors that encouraged people to go into the Commons, as well he might, given the numbers who never or rarely spoke in the House. Thus, the Commons stood as a central aspect of an unreformed political system treated by later writers rather as the contemporary Church of England was: apparently ripe for the evangelisation of zeal and commitment (although the Evangelicals respected property and status).

Such a view is increasingly suspect, for a major re-evaluation of the Hanoverian political system is in train. Attention has been cast on electoral independence and the role of issues in politics at both the local and the national level. Indeed corrupt practices can be seen in part as means by which politics continued in a world in which ideology and conviction played a major role. The absence of an electoral contest did not necessarily mean the absence of political activity; people were able to give effective vent to their feelings even in places which seldom if ever went to the poll. The vitality of the unreformed political system can be stressed, even though this vitality was expressed outside the formal type of political structures or party conflicts twentieth-century commentators would look for.

At the local level, the independence of the electorate can emerge clearly, as can the role of issues; the two were sometimes combined in a preference for local men as MPs, against the choice of borough magnates. Thus in 1722 and 1748 Derby successfully resisted the usually dominant interests of the Duke of Devonshire and the Earl of Chesterfield. A Jacobite mob attacked the local Whig magnate, the 2nd Duke of Richmond, at Chichester in 1715. Urban hostility to landowner influence lay behind election riots in Dumfries in 1759. In 1774 the Birmingham interest played a decisive role in the Warwickshire contest. It is clear that electors expected their MPs to forward local interests. Elected for the populous and politically aware seat of Bristol in 1774, Edmund Burke wrote to his constituents that a MP should be guided by 'the general good . . . he owes you, not his industry only, but his judgement; and he betrays you, not serves you, if he sacrifices it to your opinion'. Burke's neglect, however, of 'local prejudices', in the shape of Bristol's negative views on proposals of freer trade for Ireland, helped him to come bottom of the poll at the

Election Jug, 'Clive for Ever'. Having made his fame and fortune fighting in India in the 1750s, particularly as the victor of the battle of Plassey (1757), Robert Clive (1725–74) returned to England and became a major political figure in Shropshire, where he bought an estate. He brought a brother and a cousin into the Commons and sat himself for Shrewsbury. Election jugs were produced as part of the process by which constituents were 'treated'; large amounts of money were spent on providing them with alcohol at election time.

next election. David Hartley published a broadsheet address to the electors after his election for Hull in 1774 that reflected conventional views; after expressing thanks, he assured them

> that it is my determined purpose, to cultivate that confidence and esteem to the utmost of my power, by such a mutual intercourse with you, as may convince you, that I intend to keep up that connection, which in the very idea of representation, ought to subsist between the Electors and the Elected . . . the general and commercial interests of this important borough . . . shall be the constant object of my most vigilant attention.[4]

Many seats had distinct identifiable local interests, although others had too many to lead to coherent interest-based politics.

PARLIAMENT

MPs were expected to forward local legislation at Westminster, this being one of the most important links between localities and national institutions; and this was a period when local legislation was relatively far more important than today. Private and local Acts took up much parliamentary time and reflected the great importance of legislation to individuals and localities. The number of private bills passed by the Commons rose from 68 in 1760 to 210 in 1800. Parliament, therefore, played a crucial role in serving the interests of the localities as understood by and mediated by the local elites. Thus in 1758 the Earl of Clanricarde wrote to Sir John Ruthout, MP, 'a most unreasonable opposition being given in the House of Commons to a turnpike bill . . . I shall take it as a very particular favour if you will attend and influence your friends that day. The road is from Gosport to London . . . I have ordered a printed state of the case to be left.'[5]

Parliament's role was representative, yet undemocratic, arguably intrinsically

English and just what made it work. In his *The Role of Transportation in the Industrial Revolution: A Comparison of England and France* (Montreal, 1991), Rick Szostak argues that the political institutions and culture of England were more conducive to the local initiatives and control required for the creation of new transportation links – canals and turnpikes – whereas in France control lay more in the hands of a small bureaucracy that was less responsive to local needs. The situation in England was eased by the possibility of establishing trusts by Private Acts of Parliament, while in France the insistence on central government control precluded necessary private investment and led to a concentration on a small number of prestige projects. This view of Parliament, as a very sensitive legislative tool, does not sit well, however, with some of the political narrative of the century, in which Parliament appears to be obstructive to the cause of good government, keener to oppose than to propose.

Parliament was also useful at the national level, and was indeed crucially a national institution. First, Parliament played a crucial role in legitimating the constitution, especially as a result of the settlement of the Hanoverian succession by the Act of Settlement of 1701. This was important; at a time of dynastic conflict, it was valuable that a forum of legitimation existed, although the process was not accepted by those whom it did not affirm. At one level, this could and can be presented as a form of corruption. In purely dynastic terms the Jacobites had the best claim and the Glorious Revolution was a usurpation or, as Lord Glenamara, formerly Ted Short, Labour Secretary of State for Education, put it in the House of Lords in 1986, a squalid *coup d'état*. Parliament was therefore invaluable to both William III and the Hanoverians, as it provided a means of legitimating this coup. Both the Glorious Revolution and the Hanoverian Succession were legitimated by Parliament. When James II died in 1701 and Louis XIV recognised his son as James III, Parliament passed an Act imposing an Oath of Abjuration on all officials, which expressly denied the right of the Pretender to the throne. The Pope condemned the Oath. Furthermore, Parliament had an important comprehensiveness: between 1689 and 1750 a significant proportion of the Commons, albeit a clear minority, was sympathetic to Jacobitism, but, even so, retained a commitment to the parliamentary system.

Secondly, the Commons was important because of the role of Parliament in enabling the government to harness national resources for conflict. The eighteenth century was an age of conflict, far more so, indeed, than the century from Waterloo to the First World War: in the latter period Britain only once fought a European power, and the Crimean War involved no threat to British security or independence. Perhaps, therefore, Whig historians writing in the nineteenth century paid insufficient attention to the importance of military strength and success. This emphasis was unrealistic given the Nine Years War (1688–97), the War of the Spanish Succession (1702–13), the War of the Austrian Succession (1743–48), the Seven Years War (1756–63), the War of American Independence (1775–83), and the French Revolutionary and Napoleonic Wars (1793–1815). These were not wars on the margins of empire, nor were they the essentially contained conflicts of the 1620s, 1650s, 1660s and 1670s with Spain, France and the Dutch. In the eighteenth-century wars the independence of Britain was at stake. The French planned attempted invasions of the British Isles in 1692, 1696, 1708, 1744, 1745–46, 1759, 1779, 1796, 1798 and 1805. They sought to exploit opposition in Ireland and Scotland. Between 1778 and 1783 the French played a major role in dividing the English-speaking world, a crisis of empire that was more serious than any until the loss of Britain's Asian empire in the 1940s. Britain was demographically weaker than France and for most of the eighteenth century not noticeably stronger economically.

Parliament has been seen as enabling Britain to overcome these difficulties by raising taxation and guaranteeing low-interest national debt. Warfare was incredibly expensive, in large part because of the cost of the largest navy in the world, as well as the burden of subsidising allies on the Continent. The French government was in a weaker financial position: rates of interest were generally higher than in Britain, government finances were intertwined with those of the private financiers, there was no consolidated revenue fund, the Treasury's authority and knowledge were limited, and the public had limited confidence in a system that was all too private.

In Britain Parliament provided an opportunity for commercial groups to exert influence and to seek to define public support for commerce, greater than that offered by the French Council of Commerce of the 1700s or the Bureau of Commerce of the 1780s. Commercial pressure groups played a major role in the House of Commons. These could be either narrow, as in the case of the Liverpool and Lancaster MPs who sought to defend the Slave Trade, or formidably broad, as with the extensive pressure in the Commons for war with Spain in 1739. More indirect, but also considerable, was the pressure exerted by those engaged in one way or another in the trade with India and the Far East, partly, but only partly, institutionalised in the East India Company, which was very important to public finances. Commercial pressure did not lead to social tension: an appreciable number of the businessmen in the Commons came from elite families; there was little class barrier here between upper and middle class. Indeed 'rotten' boroughs provided an important route for the political expression of the aspirations of such groups. An important aspect of the success of the Commons was its admission of the new emergent mercantile and industrial interests of the century, as well as professional men, both in membership of the Commons and in the House's consideration of commercial interests.

The conclusion might therefore seem clear. Parliament was the crucial nexus of political, social and economic relationships; thanks to Parliament, it was possible to obtain public support for the government's fiscal needs, both through borrowing and through taxation. An income tax was introduced in 1798 when wartime needs called for far more than traditional expedients.

This is the current Whiggish, teleological account of Britain's rise to greatness; parliamentary authority was the crucial source of national strength and imperial expansion. It is, however, an analysis that is questionable for a number of reasons; first, it was by no means the case that Parliament accepted what the government felt to be necessary. Sir Robert Walpole's proposals to extend new excise regulations to wine and tobacco in 1733 provoked a furious political row, and the ministry had to abandon the scheme. The absence of a reliable party unity on which government could rest left ministers feeling vulnerable to attack. Despite devoting so much of their time to electoral patronage and parliamentary management, ministers such as Walpole and the Duke of Newcastle knew that it was difficult to maintain the impression of governmental control of the Commons. In 1744–46, Lord Carteret was weakened by his inability to secure the management of the Commons; in October 1756 the approach of the parliamentary session destroyed the Newcastle ministry and in the subsequent political crisis the creation of a viable leadership in the Commons was the key issue. The large proportion of borrowing to taxation can be presented in part as a measure of Parliament's successful resistance to the latter.

Secondly, even if Parliament did support government proposals, that did not necessarily imply that popular consent was gained; the Cider Excise of 1763, a tax upon cider and perry made in Britain, encountered considerable opposition and was repealed in 1766. After the Seven Years War the government sought to ease the burden of its debts and to reaffirm parliamentary authority in American affairs by imposing a number of duties, including those on stamped paper (Stamp Act, 1765) and on glass, paper, lead and tea imported into the American colonies (Townshend Act, 1767). These played a major role in exacerbating Anglo-American relations. Indeed, the danger of a parliamentary system, whether democratic, quasi-democratic or neither, was clearly reflected in this episode, because those who cannot prevail in the assembly or feel unrepresented in it will not necessarily accept its injunctions.

Thirdly, even if consent could be obtained, it is far from clear that Britain's success should be ascribed primarily to parliamentary public finance. The great French historian Fernand Braudel suggested that the volume of borrowing might have had very different results had Britain been defeated in her quest to become a world power.

The comparative perspective can be helpful here. The Hanoverian age was not a great one for representative institutions, although there was widespread interest in constitutionalism. The role of the British Parliament appeared especially important to Continental visitors, for only in Sweden, Poland and the United Provinces (the Netherlands) were there comparable institutions, and none was so successful: the Swedish Age of Liberty came to an end in 1772, while the Dutch Estates General and the Polish Diet were proverbial for delay and disagreement. Their systems of government were also discredited, the Dutch by the political breakdown and civil conflict of 1786–87, the Polish by the failures leading to the three partitions of the country (1772, 1793, 1795). The British system, in contrast, could be presented as excellent, an excellence that reflected the balanced nature of the constitution and that was demonstrated by the successes of Britain in imperial triumphs abroad and in avoiding autocracy at home.

Thus Parliament enabled Britain to compete successfully with the growing military strength of the other European powers – a different constitutional cum governmental route to military power – and at the same time was crucial to the global power of the British state: there was no collapse of naval finances during the Seven Years War comparable to that which affected France.

Yet this analysis is all too simplistic, and bears little reference to the hopes and fears of contemporaries. The modern tendency to concentrate on 'structural' factors, the inherent strength and character of Britain and France, are of considerable importance, but they lend a misleading appearance of inevitability to the outcome of the conflict. To treat the wars as a single unit entails offering a somewhat schematic interpretation that diminishes the role of circumstances and individuals; in order to understand the military and political nature of the conflicts it is necessary to rediscover the play of contingency, to recover narrative.

It is easy to point to crises, such as the congruence of Jacobite advance and

Column of Liberty at Gibside. The Gibside estate includes a 132-foot Column of British Liberty erected in 1750–57, a monument to Whiggery. The Roman Doric column is higher than Nelson's Column; begun by Daniel Garrett, it was completed by James Paine. The 12-foot high, originally gilt statue of Liberty at the top, dressed in classical drapery, was carved by Christopher Richardson in 1756–57 and holds the staff of maintenance and cap of liberty. Garrett had already built a smaller column, dedicated to the Peace of Aix-la-Chapelle in 1748 and bearing a copy of the Apollo Belvedere, for Sir Hugh Smithson at Stanwick Hill.

French invasion preparations during the '45, the disastrous early stages of the Seven Years War in 1756–57, the Bourbon invasion attempt of 1779 or the repeated failures at the hands of Revolutionary and Napoleonic France, especially between 1795 and 1800. It is then possible to ask how far Parliament helped in the response. On occasion this is not a directly pertinent question; Parliament sat for less than half the year and, in particular, was in recess during the summer, the campaigning season. Thus, Parliament was not in session during the 1779 invasion panic, or when the Revolutionary French overran the Austrian Netherlands (Belgium) in November 1792, or when George II and Carteret mishandled the victory at Dettingen in 1743.

For much of the course of the War of American Independence, Parliament provided firm support for the government, helped by Lord North's victories in the elections of 1774 and 1780. There were serious domestic problems, particularly in Ireland, and in England the Association Movement and the Gordon Riots, but Parliament was firm. Yet after the surrender of one of the British armies at Yorktown (1781) this support collapsed. There was increasing pressure for a change of ministry or at least policy. One MP wrote on 30 November 1781: 'There was a strong opposition to the Address in both houses on the ground of their pledging themselves by it to American war . . . It seems to be pretty generally allowed that the prosecution of it internally is no longer possible.' The country gentlemen who usually supported the government in the House of Commons were no longer willing to continue supporting the cost of an unsuccessful war. On 7 February 1782 the ministry's majority fell to only twenty-two on a motion of censure. On 22 February an address against continuing the American war was only narrowly blocked, and on 27 February the government was defeated on the issue. The motion encapsulated the opposition view on policy towards America:

> that the further prosecution of offensive warfare on the continent of North America, for the purpose of reducing the revolted colonies to obedience by force, will be the means of weakening the efforts of this country against her European enemies, tends under the present circumstances dangerously to increase the mutual enmity, so fatal to the interests both of Great Britain and America, and, by preventing a happy reconciliation with that country, to frustrate the earnest desire graciously expressed by His Majesty to restore the blessings of public tranquillity.

Lord North announced the government's resignation to the Commons on 20 March 1782. Britain, of course, was at war at this point. Her forces still held New York, Charleston and Savannah; the naval war with France was starting to turn in her favour. Thus the role of Parliament can be presented in two lights: it can be seen as forcing a change of policy on an unwilling government, especially on George III, or as dangerously and publicly undercutting a ministry seeking to adapt to adverse circumstances. The latter claim can also be made about Shelburne's subsequent failure to win parliamentary support for the peace terms, and is more plausible in the latter instance.

Similar comments can be made about the 1740s and 1750s. In 1745 when Charles Edward Stuart invaded Britain, Pitt the Elder saw the parliamentary session as an opportunity to put pressure on George II, in order to force his way into office; on 23 October 1745 he moved a motion designed to embarrass the ministry, an address to George to recall all British troops still opposing France in the Austrian Netherlands. All the infantry had, in fact, already been recalled to confront the probable Jacobite invasion of England, and cavalry were difficult to transport, but Pitt's motion offered an opportunity to press the ministers on a sensitive subject and to demonstrate the problems he could create. The First Lord of the Treasury, Henry Pelham, defeated the motion in the Commons by a majority of only eight, an extremely low figure by the standards of an age when the absence of marked party discipline lent an air of instability to ministries that could not command substantial majorities.

Pitt's tactics led to a government attempt to win him over, but his demands were impossible if Britain's alliances were to be maintained. The Earl of Chesterfield complained that Pitt's speeches needlessly exposed views 'both to the Dutch, and to the French'. On 19 December 1745 Pitt attacked the use of foreign troops, at the very time when the Hessians, whose use Pitt castigated, were widely seen as necessary for planned operations against the Jacobites. Pitt again attacked Britain's foreign and military policy in 1756, for example unsuccessfully opposing an address to George II to send for Hanoverian troops to prevent a threatened French invasion of England. Pitt's policy helped to lead to the resignation of the Duke of Newcastle's ministry that year.

Again, the role of Commons' opposition can be seen in two lights: Pitt can be seen as a cynical opportunist, needlessly threatening political and governmental stability at a time of national crisis; alternatively, it can be argued that the existing government could not cope, that war accentuated a central feature of the political system, namely that successful parliamentary management required competent leadership and acceptable policies, as well as patronage, and that, especially in periods of real and apparent crisis, such policies had to take note of the wider political world. The constitutional theory of Parliament in the eighteenth century, and right up to John Stuart Mill in the following century, was that it formed the representatives of the people, keeping a check on the tendency of the executive to assume arbitrary and unjustified power, and even in extreme cases providing a mechanism for getting rid of unsatisfactory governments without violence, for example in 1742 and 1782. This thesis depended on Mill's argument that public opposition to and criticism of government is a strengthening rather than a weakening force, provided it is conducted in a 'patriotic' rather than a 'factious' manner. On the whole, free societies are more effectively governed than despotisms, at least in modern Europe.

The main enemies in such a constitutional theory were and are, first, patronage in the hands of central government, leading to corruption, and, secondly, party discipline. The preponderance of pocket boroughs in the eighteenth century need not undermine the theory, provided the boroughmongers remained 'independent', which in many ways was easier for them than for modern politicians, dependent for their continued presence in Parliament on the goodwill of their party.

Parliament's political role in the eighteenth century has to be considered in the context of contemporary controversy over policies and personnel. It is difficult to be certain about its importance, because the very nature of a political crisis was that it involved a number of factors. The extent to which government policy and the response to it, which indeed could play a role in shaping policy, were affected by the existence of Parliament and the consequent need for government to consider how best to win parliamentary support or reply to parliamentary criticisms, were unclear to contemporaries.

Much clearly depended on the particular issue and occasion. As Parliament was the public forum in which the ministry formally presented and defended its policy and was criticised in a fashion that obliged it to reply, it was Parliament where the public debate over policy can be seen as most intense and effective. There was an obligation to respond that was lacking in the world of print, and an immediate linkage between the taking of decisions and the debates, the debates themselves being occasioned by the discussion of these very decisions. Thus, Parliament had a role that it otherwise lacked in a direct constitutional sense.

To note the problems created for government by Parliament is to emphasise that its existence caused serious difficulties, as well as the advantages that are generally stressed in schematic accounts. It is unclear how much weight should be placed on these problems; much clearly depends on an obviously subjective response to the issues of stability, continuity and order. What can be emphasised is that at a time when the modern role of Parliament is being questioned, and may be fundamentally revised as a consequence of devolution within Britain, and both federalism and constitutional–legal changes within Europe, it is possible to look back and note that even in an earlier 'glorious' era doubts can be raised. Yet it is also worth stressing that the alternatives were bleak. Enlightened Despotism was not only autocratic in Protestant as well as Catholic states; it could also be inept and unsuccessful, as the Emperor Joseph II, ruler of the Austrian Habsburg dominions, showed in the 1780s. France was scarcely much of an advertisement for a more 'constitutional', yet still powerful monarchy. Impatience with representative assemblies led to William IV of Orange's seizure of power in Holland and Zealand in 1747 and to Gustavus III doing the same in Sweden in 1772. Both led to serious problems and were unsuccessful in the long term.

The Westminster Parliament was the sole successful representative assembly of the period. By 1800 Poland had been partitioned and the United Provinces, Swiss Confederation and Venice conquered; republican experiments in France had proved short-lived. Only in the United States did distance from powerful enemies permit the development of a decentralised representative system. In Britain the Westminster Parliament extended to incorporate those of Edinburgh (1706–07) and Dublin (1800–01), although this was not a single process. As already indicated, this should not be seen in a triumphalist fashion, but it can be viewed as an increasingly distinctive feature of Britain in this period. Although consensus is difficult to gauge, the relationship between centre and locality, state and population, sovereign and subjects, was more consensual, apparently and obviously, formally and informally, than in most of the rest of Europe: tension was integral to this relationship, but it brought important advantages and was fundamental to British political culture.

THE MONARCHY

It is also possible to reinterpret the position of the monarchy. Although it scarcely fits with our general image of them, William III, Anne and George I, George II, and George III were among the most successful monarchs in British history, conspicuously so in contrast with the position since the late fourteenth century. This may seem a surprising assertion. These were not the most popular of monarchs, and were sometimes bitterly unpopular: William III in 1698–1700, George I in 1721, George II in 1744 or George III in 1763.

Facing page: Henry Fox by John Eccardt. Fox (1705–74) was a leading mid-century politician. A Member of Parliament from 1735 until created Lord Holland in 1763, his posts included Lord of the Treasury (1743–55), Secretary at War (1746–55), Secretary of State (1755–56), Paymaster General (1757–65) and leader of the House of Commons (1762–63). Fox sought to succeed Henry Pelham in 1754 and competed with Pitt. A manager rather than an orator, Fox inspired no one; thinking of politics in terms of office rather than policy, he was not a leader for years of war and crisis. Fox lacked the killer instinct generally necessary to rise to the top in politics, but knew how to look after his own interests. Born in Germany, Eccardt was a leading mid-century portrait painter patronised by Horace Walpole.

They were not the most competent of monarchs. The British monarchy lost a large portion of its subjects when George III lost the Thirteen Colonies, while, more generally, the power of the monarchy has generally been seen as very limited following the 'Revolution Settlement', the constitutional changes of 1689–1701 that resulted from the 'Glorious Revolution' of 1688.

Yet these kings were also successful. First, they were so in a dynastic sense. The succession was established and maintained in the Hanoverian line and there was no repetition in Britain either of the republican episode of 1649–60 or of the monarchical coup of 1688: republicanism was successful only in North America. This was a particularly important achievement, because the Glorious Revolution of 1688–89 created in Jacobitism a fundamental schism of loyalty in Britain. It was even more important because the succession was uncertain: William III was childless and Anne had no surviving children.

Two rival princes competed at Culloden in 1746: the heir to the Jacobite cause, Charles Edward Stuart ('Bonnie Prince Charlie'), and George II's second and favourite son, William, Duke of Cumberland, Captain-General from 1745 to 1757. Thus, in the crisis of the Hanoverian state and monarchy, the royal family played a major role. Cumberland took the leading role in 1745–46 and was an active general more akin among the royal generals of the 1740s to Frederick the Great, his first cousin, than to Louis XV. In this he emulated William III, who devoted much of his reign to active leadership in war against France, although often without success.

After Culloden the Hanoverian monarchy was stronger, its legitimacy unchallenged. When 'James III' died in 1766 the Pope refused to recognise the claims to the throne of Charles Edward Stuart. The crisis in North America did not lead to comparable problems in Britain, although from the early 1790s the example of France helped to encourage radicalism within Britain (radicalism had begun earlier, but increased markedly in the 1790s). Yet this again was a challenge that the British monarchy and state surmounted. Just as parliamentary unions – with Scotland in 1707 and Ireland in 1801 – reflected the crises of those periods but also produced a more unitary state, so, in some measure, the monarchy likewise benefited from challenges. The challenge of the French Revolution helped to produce a rallying of the social elite and of much opinion, around country, Crown and Church in the 1790s. The monarchy, although not the person of the monarch, served as a potent symbol of national identity and continuity, especially after the execution of Louis XVI of France in January 1793. This led to a powerful reiteration of monarchical ideology in Britain, now part of the process by which the British were differentiated from the French.

On 30 January 1793, Samuel Horsley, Bishop of St David's and a supporter of William Pitt the Younger and his government, gave the annual Martyrdom Day sermon in Westminster Abbey before the House of Lords. This marked the anniversary of the execution in 1649 of Charles I, the individual elevated most closely to sainthood by the Church of England. In the first half of the century 30 January had often been a focus for discontent, for riots and a Jacobite challenge to the dynasty. Now it served to affirm, not the Stuart house but the institution of monarchy itself, and thus attracted former Stuart sympathisers. In 1793 Horsley delivered a powerful attack on political speculation and revolutionary theory. He dismissed the notion of an original compact arising from the abandonment of a state of nature, and instead stressed royal authority. According to Horsley, the existing constitution was

the product and safeguard of a 'legal contract' between Crown and people, while the obedience of the latter was a religious duty. Horsley's forceful per-oration linked the two executions: 'This foul murder, and these barbarities, have filled the measure of the guilt and infamy of France. O my Country! Read the horror of thy own deed in this recent heightened imitation! Lament and weep, that this black French treason should have found its example, in the crime of thy unnatural sons!' The congregation rose to its feet in approval. If the fate of religion and monarchy in Britain seemed clearly challenged by developments in France, that did not mean that all rallied to the cause of kings, but rather that the monarchy was a vital part of the entire political and social system, and that it played a greater role in political ideology than it had done between 1689 and 1746. In the earlier period, an emphasis on monarchy had been compromised by serious differences over the legitimacy of the dynasty as well as the contentious nature of constitutional arrangements after 1688. No such problems hindered a stress on monarchy on the part of

Queen Anne and the Knights of the Garter, by Peter Angelis. Anne (1665–1714), Queen from 1702, was the younger daughter of James II and the last of the Stuarts to reign. A committed supporter of the Church of England, she suffered from ill-health. Married to Prince George of Denmark, Anne had numerous children, none of whom survived her. She has recently been re-evaluated as a more important and adept political figure than she had been regarded hitherto. Angelis was born in Dunkirk and worked in London before going to Rome.

conservative elements from the 1790s: however much the failings and foibles of individual members of the royal family, not least George III's ill-health, were to pose difficulties, the role of the monarchy was one that conservatives could support.

This was an important part of the success of the Hanoverian monarchy. It was helped by the course of the Revolutionary and Napoleonic wars. The royal family did not win personal glory in these conflicts; nor indeed did they take as prominent a role as William III had done in Ireland and the Low Countries in the 1690s or as Cumberland had done in Scotland and the Low Countries between 1744 and 1748. The 1799 landing in Holland under George III's son Frederick, Duke of York (now best remembered in the nursery rhyme for marching troops up and down hills) ended in failure, although York played a significant role in improving the army thereafter. His brother Ernest, who served against the French with Hanoverian forces in 1793–94, 1806 and 1813–14, did so without particular success, although he acquired a justified reputation for bravery.

Nevertheless, there were no disasters and humiliations akin to those that affected most of the European dynasties. French troops did not seize London as they did Berlin, Lisbon, Madrid, Moscow, Naples, Turin and Vienna. The royal family was not obliged to accept a royal marriage with Napoleon as the Habsburg Francis I had to do. There was no forcible abdication to make way for one of Napoleon's relatives, as happened in Spain. A Napoleonic marshal did not gain the throne, as did Bernadotte in Sweden. Survival was not obtained by humiliating subservience as in the case of Bavaria, Prussia and Saxony. In 1742, 1744 or 1782 the British monarchy had appeared one of the weakest in Europe, its rulers unable to sustain in office ministers who enjoyed royal confidence – Walpole, Carteret, North and Shelburne; yet by 1810 it was the strongest in Europe after Napoleon's monarchical dictatorship, which lacked comparable legitimacy. Other European rulers, such as Louis XVIII, the rulers of Naples, Portugal and Sardinia and the Prince of Orange, took shelter in Britain or behind the cover of British forces, particularly the Royal Navy. British ministers had to consider what would happen if Napoleon invaded – would they have an army in Dover or concentrate forces south of London? – but it never happened.

In addition, Britain became *the* world empire in this period. In 1714 Britain was already one of the leading colonial powers, with extensive territories in North America, valuable sugar islands in the West Indies and important bases in West Africa, India and the Mediterranean. Yet Britain was not yet the leading colonial power. If she had gained Gibraltar, Minorca, Newfoundland, Nova Scotia and recognition of her claim to Rupert's Land to the south of Hudson's Bay at the Peace of Utrecht (1713) which had ended the War of the Spanish Succession, Britain's colonial territories were far less extensive, populous and wealthy than those of Spain, while France was still a major colonial rival and the Dutch still an important colonial force. The British attempt to seize Quebec from the French in 1711 had been unsuccessful, and there was little sign that the British would be able to gain colonies from other European powers, as opposed to seizing territory from often weaker non-European peoples, as in North America.

By 1837 the situation was totally transformed. Spain had lost her empire in Latin America, and France had lost most of her eighteenth-century empire: Canada, Mauritius, St Lucia and the Seychelles conquered by Britain;

Louisiana sold to the United States. Britain had lost her Thirteen Colonies and the 'Old North-West' beyond the Appalachians; and had failed in her expeditions to Argentina in 1806-07; but she was the strongest state in the world, the leading power on the oceans and had the best system of public finance. Australia and New Zealand were British colonies, the colony of South Australia being founded in 1836. Canada was under British control. The British dominated much of India, particularly Bengal and the south, and also ruled Ceylon and parts of Burma. Cape Town had been acquired from the Dutch during the Napoleonic wars, while other gains at the Congress of Vienna (1815) included Trinidad, Tobago, St Lucia, Malta, Guyana and the Ionian Islands. In the two decades after the Napoleonic war British policy and power played a major role in securing the independence of Greece and of Latin America.

If Britain was so successful during this period, it might fairly be asked how much was due to the monarchs. There is an apparent paradox in the unpopularity of William III and the Hanoverian monarchy, at least under George I, George II and George IV, and the success of the British state. In many ways, the connections between the growing capacity/status of the British state and the monarchy were indirect, but dynastic stability was a precondition of the Hanoverian political settlement. When the reasons for the success of Britain in these years are discussed they are generally considered to be economic growth, financial resources, naval capability and such like. The kings do not feature, and indeed in so far as Britain's triumph owed much to military success this was scarcely surprising. The martial qualities of the Hanoverians did not become more pronounced. George II was the last British monarch to take part in a battle, at Dettingen in 1743. In 1793 Sir William Beechey painted a massive *George III Reviewing the Troops*, a work destroyed in the fire at Windsor Castle on 19 November 1992. This depicted an equestrian group of George, the Prince of Wales and the Duke of York, who became a Field Marshal in 1795 and Commander-in-Chief in 1798, reviewing the 10th hussars and the 3rd dragoons. It was at one with the military poses struck by the Prince in this period, and that of his second cousin, William V of Orange, who declared in December 1792, when the French were apparently about to invade the United Provinces (modern Netherlands), that 'he would resist to the utmost, and die upon the spot'. In fact, William survived the French invasion of 1795; dying heroically was more fashionable in both Neo-classical and Romantic iconography than it was in practice for the monarchs of the period. George IV's military pretensions verged on the ridiculous: later in life he used to tell people that he had been at Waterloo, and would seek confirmation from the Duke of Wellington, winning the tactful reply, 'So you have told me, Sir.'

George III's third son, the Duke of Clarence, later William IV, was made a Rear-Admiral in 1790, a Vice-Admiral in 1794, an Admiral in 1799 and in 1811 Admiral of the Fleet, and thus Commander-in-Chief. These were years of British naval triumph and hegemony, but Clarence was not responsible for them. Whereas he had seen active service during the War of American Independence and commanded ships in peacetime between 1786 and 1790, thereafter he did not serve afloat other than for brief ceremonial purposes. This was scarcely a career to match that of Horatio Nelson, who served with William in the West Indies in the 1780s and was a friend. When Nelson was married, William gave away the bride, and Nelson praised his abilities as an officer; but there are no signs that he had the capability to be an effective

George II, Studio of Charles Jervas. George (1683–1760), king from 1727, maintained only poor relations with his father but continued his support for the Whig ministry of Sir Robert Walpole and, thereafter, maintained his backing for the Whigs. Very keen on the army and the Electorate of Hanover, George was the last British king to lead his troops in battle, at Dettingen in 1743. A stubborn and somewhat fussy man who was overshadowed by his wife, Caroline of Ansbach, George was abler than is often appreciated. He himself claimed to be a 'king in toils', but may have been disingenuous in claiming to be so.

Admiral, and he was never given a chance.

A lack of impressive military service is not the same as a neglect of military matters. The kings took their duties seriously, especially George I and George II, who both promoted the principle of long service as the main way to advancement and did their best to counter the purchase of commissions. George II used his formidable memory for names to good effect in keeping oversight of the leading members of the officer class. He personally signed military commissions.

Even the unmartial George III took a keen interest. He exerted influence on military policy, especially after his son Frederick became Commander-in-Chief. George was portrayed in military uniform, for example by Zoffany in *c.* 1771, and this was clearly part of his 'self-image'. He reviewed the fleet at Portsmouth in 1773 and off Plymouth in 1789; in 1780 he took a close interest in the suppression of the Gordon Riots, and pressed for firm action, 'for I am convinced till the magistrates have ordered some military execution on the rioters this town will not be restored to order'. George also took a close interest in naval affairs during the invasion scare of 1779. He corresponded with the First Lord of the Admiralty, the Earl of Sandwich, and displayed interest in and knowledge of the fleet. All monarchs devoted great attention to military appointments.

Nevertheless, it cannot be said that the monarchs after William III were great military administrators. None matched the aptitude or energy of Cumberland, and even his military career was brought to an ignominious close in 1757 when he failed to prevent a French invasion of Hanover and signed the humiliating and politically embarrassing Convention of Klosterseven to save his army from destruction. George III and George IV were no Napoleons, and the contrast between them exemplified different forms of monarchy. Napoleon personified meritocratic monarchy, but one of the major aspects of the success of the British state and of British monarchy was that there was no need for either George to be a great war-leader. A system of hereditary monarchy deals with the basic question of legitimacy by providing a succession within a family, and by the eighteenth century the rules of succession were very clear. It is appropriate for a society structured around privilege and hereditary succession and with a markedly inegalitarian distribution of wealth and opportunity. Such a society, however, confronts the problems of the continual need for energetic and talented leadership and administrators. To a certain extent, talent will be found within its ranks, but it does not necessarily correspond to the hierarchies of society. It is notable how many of the talented leaders and ministers of Hanoverian Britain did not come from the pinnacle of society. A surprising number, though sons of peers, were not eldest sons, for example Henry Pelham, Henry Fox, Charles James Fox and William Pitt the Younger. William Pitt the Elder was a second son. Many others did not come from the highest social bracket, for example Walpole, Jenkinson, Nelson and Wolfe.

Similarly at the level of royalty, any system that requires a continuous level of talent poses problems. It is difficult to supply this in a hereditary system, while any alternative faces problems of legitimacy and stability. On the European scale George IV might not have been an impressive rival to Napoleon, but Charles IV of Spain (1788–1808) was far worse. The Emperor Francis I (1792–1835) was more industrious than George, but he was also stubborn and fell out with the leading royal general, Archduke Charles. Like

George, Frederick William II of Prussia (1786–97) was a follower of the politics of the boudoir, but he was also interested in mystical religion and his tergiversations made consistent policy-making difficult. The same was true of Paul I of Russia (1796–1801), while his successor Alexander I (1801–25) was a less than impressive general. The difficulties of the dynastic system were also revealed within the Napoleonic family. Not Louis, King of Holland (1806–10), nor Joseph, King of Naples (1806–08) and of Spain (1808–12), nor Jerome, King of Westphalia, had the ability or determination of their meteoric brother.

The British system can be seen as a successful compromise that reflected the strengths and weaknesses of hereditary monarchy: this was how it was presented by contemporaries. Such an approach may seem complacent, indeed Whiggish, and it risks smoothing over detailed crises in favour of a more schematic approach. Nevertheless, the 'limited' or 'parliamentary' monarchy of the period was flexible, neither the constitution nor the political arrangements and culture so rigid that they were unable to adapt to the differing interests and abilities of individual monarchs, to changes in their responses to the political world and to alterations in their position; for no monarch should be seen as an invariable feature of the political landscape, especially not monarchs who reigned for as long as George II (1727–60) and George III (1760–1820). The role of the Church and clergy in legitimising the Hanoverian monarchy – all those higher clergy straining their sinews to inculcate obedience to their new masters – was also important.

So indeed were the personalities of the rulers. George I and George II were particularly modest men. George I's diffidence, honesty and dullness and George II's amiable lack of imagination produced a complacency with very practical consequences: they were pragmatists who did not have an agenda for Britain (unlike, for example, James II). The kings' place in politics was not of their choosing, but rather a consequence of 1688–89, the Act of Settlement (1701) and the Union of 1707. They were sensible enough to adapt and survive. Nevertheless, by driving the Tories into the political wilderness, the Georges weakened their own position, including their position among the lower clergy: their attitude was very different from that of Charles II at the Restoration.

Much of the credit for Britain's constitutional monarchy rests with those who defined the royal position between 1689 and 1707, but, precisely because there was no rigid constitution, the attitude and role of individual monarchs were also crucial. Survival was all the early Hanoverians sought: George I and George II did not have pretensions to mimic the grandiose palaces of the Continental monarchies, and the same applies to their lifestyles and incomes. Both appeared in a relatively modest way in London society: at the parks, theatre and opera and so on. This was not a case of the vast parades of some Continental monarchs. They were also accommodating, quite prepared to be prodded into levees, ceremonies and public appearances that were alien to them. George III displayed a similar modesty in his lifestyle, although he did have a political agenda for Britain that involved greater use of royal prerogative and an attack on political factionalism.

Clearly there were moments when the absence of consensus extended from issues of place and policy to the very constitution. Such crises did not have to centre on the position of the monarch: as already suggested, the radicalism and republicanism of the early 1790s onwards was less challenging because it

George I by Sir Godfrey Kneller.
George (1660–1727), king from
1714, owed the throne to the lack of
surviving heirs of William III,
Mary, and Anne, to his descent
from James I via the German
marriage of his daughter, and to the
exclusion of the male Stuart line
and other Catholic claimants after
the Glorious Revolution. An active
supporter of the interests of his
native Electorate of Hanover and
of the Whigs, who were clearly
committed to the Hanoverian
succession, George was not very
popular. He was a Lutheran, and
not a master of the English
language.

Frederick, Prince of Wales (1707–51), by Philip Mercier. Eldest son of George II and created Prince of Wales in 1729, Frederick, following the Hanoverian dynastic tradition, had very poor relations with his father and actively supported the opposition to Walpole and, after a reconciliation in 1742, reverted to opposition in 1747. Politically volatile, Frederick was an important and discerning patron of the arts who, for example, enriched the Royal Collection of silverware with many fine pieces and patronised the leading sporting painter, John Wootton.

threatened the entire system. In the early 1780s, however, George III was so outraged by the necessity to part with Lord North in 1782 and to accept the Rockinghamites in 1782 and the Fox–North ministry in 1783 that he talked of abdication. He was far from alone in seeing this as a crisis. John, 2nd Earl of Buckinghamshire, a former diplomat, took time off from admiring the scantily-clad bathing beauties at Weymouth to meditate on the crisis:

> this unhappily disgraced country surrounded by every species of embarrassment, and without even a distant prospect of establishing an Administration so firm and so respectable as to restore to England any proportion of her defeated dignity. The state is now circumstanced as a human body in the last stage of a decline. Whig as I am and sufficiently vain of my descent from Maynard and Hampden, it sometimes occurs to me that something might be obtained by strengthening the hands of the Crown.[6]

A clear sense of crisis, current or imminent, emerges from much of the political correspondence of the early 1780s, and it can be seen in the letters of politicians with very different ideas. The hostility of George III and the Fox–North ministry created a particularly serious political situation, and its resolution in 1784 in the form of a ministry under William Pitt the Younger winning electoral and parliamentary support, was far from inevitable. Yet, once Crown-elite consensus had been restored, at least in so far as was measured by the crucial criterion – the ability of George III to co-operate with a ministry enjoying the support of Parliament – Britain was politically stable. This stability was a reflection of that ability; one that required a willingness to adjust, if not compromise, by both parties.

A similar pattern can be seen in the reign of George's grandfather, George II, a figure of great political importance. Although the fall of Walpole in 1742 is generally cited as a defeat for the Crown, it also testified to the importance of the royal family. Walpole had done badly in the general election of 1741, due less to any groundswell of popular opposition than to the defection of a number of important electoral patrons, most seriously George II's eldest son, Frederick, Prince of Wales, who, as Duke of Cornwall, controlled many boroughs in a county that was heavily over-represented in Parliament. The refusal of Frederick to accept any political settlement with his father unless Walpole fell played a crucial role in the minister's decision, following his loss of the ability to deliver parliamentary majorities, to resign. Frederick was very much in the hands of superior political intelligences and personalities, but the attitude of the immediate successor to the throne was in this case a decided advantage to the opposition.

Although defeated politically on a number of occasions, George II was certainly no cipher. Contemporaries were with reason convinced that he played a central role in ministerial politics, as in 1742 when a prominent Tory, and sometime Jacobite, was kept out of the Admiralty Board: 'A List was drawn up; amongst them Sir John Hynde Cotton was put down; upon the scheme, as was before said, of placing the administration upon the broad bottom. This list was presented to the King. He struck out Sir J. H. Cotton with his own hand. This alarmed all people to a high degree. The seeds of a vehement and formidable opposition were sown anew.'[7] The court was a crucial political sphere, although it declined under Anne. There were, however, reasons for this decline. Leading politicians could not hope for the physical proximity to the monarch that was possible under a king. That drawback was eliminated after 1714, though George I's somewhat reclusive character and linguistic limitations posed problems. As long as the monarch was and remained the ultimate political authority, his court necessarily remained the political centre, since it provided access to him. The indications are that the court revived, though not in cultural terms, under the Georges. However, Whig historiography in the following century sidelined the Georgian court: instead Parliament was seen as the Crown's dominant partner after the Glorious Revolution and the court was presented as dropping out of the political picture. George II's Closet was not Henry VIII's Privy Chamber, but the insignificance of the Hanoverian court has been greatly overplayed. There is a great deal of evidence of competition for royal favour.

Furthermore, the parliamentary opposition can often be presented in terms of a rival court. If Parliament as an institution did not have the confidence to thwart or bring down the king's ministers, opposition factions within it did –

but they were arguably dependent on the heir to the throne. The political crises of 1717–20 sound very modern if presented in terms of parliamentary politics, but viewed as rivalry between two royal courts, they carry less contemporary resonance. Without Leicester House, where the courts of George II and George III as heirs and of Frederick, Prince of Wales were based, to give opposition respectability, parliamentary opposition had little chance: the support of the heir hoped to overcome early Georgian repugnance both to 'storming the closet' – unacceptable politicians forcing their way into office (storming the closet referred to gaining access to the private quarters in which the monarch discussed confidential matters) – and also to systematically opposing the king's government. The Prince of Wales was as crucial in Walpole's closet-storming of 1720 as the next Prince of Wales was in his fall in 1742. Leicester House's move into open opposition between 1755 and 1757 was a crucial element in the crisis that took Pitt to power. Though that crisis can be explained in terms both of parliamentary followings and events outside Parliament, one dimension of it could as plausibly be presented as a feud between Cumberland and Leicester House. Ministers had scant influence on such crucial quarrels within the royal family.

The crisis of 1746 was serious, but also showed the importance of the crown. George II was totally responsible for creating an abnormal situation, resulting from his attitude to the Pelhams (the Duke of Newcastle and his brother Henry Pelham, the First Lord of the Treasury) after they had refused to work with George's favourite, Carteret, now Earl Granville. By withholding his confidence from his ministers, George II undermined their position in Parliament. Hence the desperate resignation of the Pelhams at a time of war and rebellion, which left George little room for manoeuvre. George's self-imposed limitations contributed to the same end. He did not want to turn to the Tories to support the ministry; and wanted to employ favourites such as Granville and the Earl of Bath, yet also regarded as essential the Old Corps Whigs, led by the Pelhams, who detested them. Having got himself into a difficult position, George II lacked the nerve to play his ace and dissolve Parliament. The '45 was as good as over: Charles Edward had retreated to Scotland and the French had not landed. With a parliamentary majority, George II could perhaps have cleared out the Old Corps as George III did in the 1760s and prefigured the displacement of the Fox–North ministry in 1783–84. The year 1746 was an extraordinary crisis, but it cannot be regarded as typical of the eighteenth-century constitution.

The thwarting of royal ministerial choice usually reflected abnormal divisions within the court – or rather between two courts. When that happened the monarch could lose his majority in Parliament. There was nothing uniquely British about royal ministers needing a majority in whatever Estates controlled supply, which it was their ministers' first duty to secure. What would have made Britain unique was the habitual inability of court ministers to deliver such a majority. Unless there were two courts, the king's and his heir's, this was not the case. When it was, it can usually be attributed to old-style dynastic feuding rather than modern-style parliamentary politics.

To contemporaries, George I was a distant figure. Unlike William III, who was familiar with English politics and politicians from earlier visits, marriage into the British royal family and extensive intervention in English domestic politics, George knew relatively little of England, and his first experience of it was as an older man than was the case with William (or James I). George's failure to learn English and his obvious preference for Hanover further contributed to this sense of alien rule, while as an individual he was a figure of suspicion as a result of the incarceration of his adulterous wife and the disappearance of her lover, and as a consequence of rumours about his own personal life. Scurrilous ballads made much of the theme of the royal cuckold. *Sir James King's Key to Sir George Horn's Padlock* dwelled on the theme, while an *Address to Britannia* included the lines, 'Pray let no Cuckold be still ruler over thee / Nor any German bastard begot in Privity.' Another manuscript verse in circulation satirised George and his alleged mistresses, condemning their influence on him and satirising their competition for his attention by comparing them with the goddesses vying for the attention of Paris. As later with radical pornography in the 1790s and 1800s, humiliation was a powerful political weapon. To demystify the monarch and subject him to ridicule and abuse was part of a determined attempt to weaken his position. Royal popularity was of course difficult to gauge. The Swiss visitor César de Saussure recorded the London mob cheering George I in 1725 and mourning him in 1727, and celebrating George II's accession. It is unclear whether this was simply the fickle mob using any opportunity for an 'event', or a purely London phenomenon; or evidence that the unpopularity of George I and George II has been overstated. They were the Whigs' monarchs, although it is unclear how much personal popularity this brought them.

It could be argued that the scurrilous ballads and verse that circulated provided an opportunity for popular expression about the monarchs, perhaps especially George I and George IV, that helped secure their position. Such expression was tolerated, in marked contrast to the more repressive situation in Continental Europe. It also provided the monarchy with an identity that was not Hanoverian. It was far better for George I to be lampooned for human weaknesses than to be perceived as alien; although the latter critique was also advanced. His son was also to be criticised for sexual waywardness; Amalie Sophie Marianne von Wallmoden, whom George II made Countess of Yarmouth, became an influential political figure because of her access to the king. She was alleged to have recommended at least three peerage creations in return for bribes. George II's favour for her was not ignored by the populace. In December 1736 William Pulteney reported:

> One Mrs Mopp, a famous she Bone-setter and mountebank, coming to Town in a coach with six horses on the Kentish Road, was met by a Rabble of People, who seeing her very oddly and tawdrily dress'd, took her for a Foreigner, and concluded she must be a certain great Person's Mistress. Upon this they followed the Coach, bawling out, 'No Hannover Whore, no Hannover Whore'. The Lady within the Coach was much offended, let down the Glass, and screamed louder than any of them, she was no Hannover Whore, she was an English one, upon which they all cry'd out, 'God bless your Ladyship', quitted the pursuit, and wished her a good Journey.[8]

Apart from his personal life, George I's obvious preference for Hanover caused considerable complaint, among Whigs as well as Tories. Lady Anne Paulet was ready to believe a report that the king would not return to Britain for the winter of 1716–17 'for I fancy he is so much easier where he is that he will like to be from us as long as he can'.[9] This was exacerbated by a sense that the preference for Hanover entailed an abandonment of British national interests, as resources were expended for the aggrandisement of the

Electorate and as the entire direction of British foreign policy was set accordingly. A reasonable critique of foreign policy was advanced on this basis, but, nevertheless, George I and George II were comparatively restrained in their Hanoverianism. The establishment in 1714 and 1727 was far more like the theory of the dual monarchy of nineteenth-century Austria–Hungary than the wholesale Hanoverian takeover that some feared. In spite of periodic rows about Hanoverian interests, the kings did not swamp Britain with German ministers or systems; if anything, they adopted admirably to British institutions. They conformed to the Church of England in spite of their strong Lutheranism. Even their dynastic disputes were fitted into a parliamentary framework with court and Leicester House parties at Westminster.

Concern over Hanover contributed powerfully to the 'Whig Split', a deep division among the Whigs between 1717 and 1720 that led a large section under Robert Walpole to seek co-operation with the Tories in order to achieve the overthrow of the Whig government. This can be seen in a number of lights; the split can be presented as a major defeat for George I; in 1714 all the Whigs had welcomed him to the throne and had indeed been prepared to fight to achieve the Hanoverian Succession. The following year, the Whigs united in defence of the king (and themselves) when challenged by a major Jacobite rising. Yet in 1717 George's policies helped to divide the government and to lead loyal Whigs to look for Tory support; they were opposed both to the direction of British foreign policy, which they presented as dictated by Hanoverian interests, and to George's handling of the struggle for influence between the leading Whigs.

On the other hand, George I was scarcely to blame for Whig divisions. Furthermore, his choleric quarrel with his son and heir, which interacted with and seriously exacerbated the political disputes, was an aspect of a classic feature of dynastic politics: the tension between ruler and heir and between those who looked to one or the other. If George I, George II and George III clashed with their heirs, so also did other dynasties. Peter the Great had his son Alexis murdered, while Catherine the Great and her son, the future Paul I, were rivals. Frederick William I had very poor relations with his son, the future Frederick the Great, as did Maria Theresa with her son and heir, Joseph II. Victor Amadeus II of Sardinia was imprisoned by his heir, Charles Emmanuel III, when he tried to retract his abdication, while Philip V of Spain had very poor relations with the future Ferdinand VI.

To note common problems is not, however, the same as to deny responsibility or blame. If the Hanoverians faced both tensions in their family and divisions among their ministers, then part of the art of royal politics was the ability to tackle such problems. The assertion of royal will, without the creation or exacerbation of serious political divisions, was crucial, whatever the formal constitutional powers of the sovereign. In 1717 George I proved unable to do so, and thus helped to precipitate a serious crisis.

A central problem was that of the degree to which the ruler would allow a minister or group of ministers in effect to deploy royal power or influence. In 1717 George lost the support of Walpole and Townshend because he was too closely associated with their rivals, Stanhope and Sunderland. The last wrote in 1717, 'upon the whole, I don't doubt, but the King's steadiness will carry it'.[10] Once thus associated, it was, however, difficult to avoid the consequences of criticism and opposition from those opposed to the minister, and, more particularly, to escape damage if the minister was weakened. Thus,

George I had eventually to accommodate himself to the rise of Walpole: 'The King is resolved that Walpole shall not govern, but it is hard to be prevented.'[11] For ministers it was essential to win the public support of the monarch in order to underline their own influence and stability. Thus in 1724 the Duke of Newcastle, one of Walpole's allies, wrote to Robert's brother:

> the King has not a thought with relation to his affairs either at home or abroad, that is not entirely agreeable to the sentiments of your friends . . . he has certainly done more towards declaring his inclinations than the most sanguine man among us could ever hope for . . . it was our misfortune last summer that His Majesty was apt to think he did every thing that we could in reason expect from him, when in reality there was nothing essential done that could convince the world with whom he placed his credit and confidence.[12]

This state of anxiety, if not tension, over royal–ministerial relations was common to all eighteenth-century monarchical states, and is a reminder against assuming that the British monarchy was particularly weak or peculiarly prone to foibles. If British rulers were constrained or at least affected by the need to find ministers who could manage Parliament, this usual formula begs a few questions. In normal circumstances, by a mixture of patronage and moral support from the monarch and loyalty from most MPs, the king's choice *ipso facto* commanded a parliamentary majority. The crucial issue, as the Georges all saw, was the appointment of ministers, but generally it was only necessary for the monarch to find ministries acceptable to himself; acceptance by Parliament would follow in normal circumstances. The different views of Charles James Fox have generated much confusion about contemporary views of the eighteenth-century constitution. His modernity in the eyes of late nineteenth-century historians, such as G. O. Trevelyan, commended his merits as a Hanoverian commentator. But his preference for parliamentary majorities rather than royal choice as the basis of ministries was more eccentric in the 1780s than it seemed after 1867, although it was not so far removed from the Tories in 1714 who thought that George I would have to work with a Tory parliamentary majority.

The relationship between monarch and ministers can also be viewed in two other lights. First, in the absence of unified parties with clear leadership on the modern pattern, it was possible for the ruler to seek to create a ministry around the most acceptable politician who might be able to manage Parliament, and, conversely, to keep at a distance those whom he disliked. Secondly, even if the monarch had to accept ministers who were not his first choice, as in 1720, 1742, 1744, 1746 and 1757, it was possible to use a ministry that could manage Parliament in order to win support for royal interests. George I and George II were reasonably successful in this, but, thereafter, the situation changed. George III found that ministries he did not want – the Rockingham and Fox–North governments – sought to push through unacceptable policies.

There were three reasons for this shift, a shift that arguably marked a weakening in royal influence. First, whereas ministries had been bound to George I and George II (and to a considerable extent to William III) by a fear of Jacobitism, this was no longer so from the late 1740s on. Indeed, the room for manoeuvre enjoyed by the elderly George II in the political crisis of 1754–57 was lessened by the impossibility of uniting Whigs on an anti-Jacobite/Tory platform.

Secondly, George I and George II had concentrated their attention on foreign policy, and in particular on the details of German affairs. It was difficult to arouse public and sustained political interest in these questions, although the issue of subsidies for Hanover and the conduct of Hanoverian troops caused outrage in 1742–44. From the accession of George III, the Hanoverian issue receded as a source of contention, for, with the exception of a short-lived crisis in 1785, George was not publicly associated with Hanover, most clearly because he never went there. In contrast, George III was more associated with domestic issues that were both very contentious in their own right and in which the role of the monarch was especially sensitive. This was true of the matter of ministerial choice in the 1760s and early 1780s and of policy towards the North American colonies from 1765 until 1783.

Thirdly, and linked to the last, was the ability of some politicians to create a coherent political connection or party that focused much of its ideology and energy on hostility to what was seen as royal views; and even extended to a much more dangerous antipathy to monarchy as it was generally understood in eighteenth-century Britain. Thus the theme of the king as a pernicious political force taking a malevolent role in British affairs was strongly revived in the 1760s after two reigns in which the negative image of the monarchs arose largely from their Hanoverian concerns. John Brewer, in his *Party Ideology and Popular Politics at the Accession of George III* (Cambridge, 1976), argued that under George III constitutional conventions were a matter of fundamental disagreement, in effect between those who looked to the past and those who anticipated the future: a Whiggish interpretation. Apart from Fox and possibly the Rockinghams, however, there was little dissent from the belief that monarchs should appoint ministers. Fox was a maverick and hypocrite who wanted to change the constitution and whose attitudes were widely rejected – hence the erosion of Fox and North's majority against Pitt in early 1784 and the verdict of the subsequent election. There was a whiff of republicanism about Fox and his friends which put them well outside the general run of politicians angling for power, although he hoped to profit from the accession of the Prince of Wales.

Politically, George III was the most interesting (and longest-ruling) of the Hanoverians. He came young to the throne and had little earlier political experience: one of the most pernicious consequences of the bad relations between the Hanoverians and their heirs was that the latter had no real apprenticeship, and what they did have was as a totem of opposition activity: scarcely the most helpful training for the commitments of the throne. George III was not the brightest of monarchs, and he was certainly not the most sparkling. He had, however, several qualities that are worthy of note, while, in addition, he matured in office, becoming both a practised politician and a man more capable of defining achievable goals. George's conscientious nature shines through his copious correspondence. It was not novel: both his predecessors were conscientious and hard-working monarchs, and the same was true of each ruler since Charles II. As Prince of Wales, George II's son Frederick had given few such signs and indeed in his artistic interests, political opportunism and self-indulgence he had prefigured George IV, but as Frederick did not become king he left the task of re-creating the monarchical habits associated with Charles II to his grandsons, George III's numerous progeny.

If George III was scarcely unique in being industrious, his energies were directed in different courses from those of his predecessors. In addition, he came to play a role in a political world that had grown accustomed during the last fourteen years of the reign of his elderly grandfather, George II, to a monarch of lesser energy who accepted the direction of most domestic affairs by his leading ministers.

George III, in contrast to his predecessor, devoted considerable energy to domestic politics and the internal workings of his ministries. Whereas George I and George II had been principally concerned with the army and foreign affairs, George III, although interested, particularly in the latter, had different priorities. His stress on domestic policy was an aspect of his concern for a proper conduct of British government and society, a concern that also illuminated his committed Anglicanism, his determination to ensure the proper government of the Church of England, his interest in public morality and, not least, his desire that the royal family should set an example of appropriate behaviour. George's cultural preferences, particularly his interest in the work of Handel, were related to his moral concerns. Handel said of George: 'while that boy lives, my music will never want a protector'.

To further his goals, George III thought it necessary that he personally should take a central political role. This was not only his constitutional role as one of the three elements in the constitution, but also his moral duty. The two fused in the potent idea of George as a 'Patriot King', a notion that stemmed from Viscount Bolingbroke's earlier discussion of such a concept in his *Idea of a Patriot King* (1749), which called for a monarch powerful enough to override parties. These were the ideas so beloved of Frederick, and which were inculcated in George as a youth. George was influenced by the concept of patriarchal government implicit in Bolingbroke's book. Thus, in maintaining his right to choose ministers and his ability to block legislation, George was ensuring that he could discharge his function, which, to use a concept that he understood, was service to the state. The king was to act as a political redeemer, a notion that reflected a powerful optimistic element in the political iconography of kingship, and that had earlier focused on William III.

For George these roles were hindered primarily by the self-interest of others, more particularly by the willingness of politicians to group together for factional ends, most particularly the pursuit of office. As much as any Continental ruler who did not have to face a powerful representative institution, George was determined to reject the objectives and politics of faction, to thwart the efforts of unacceptable politicians to force their way into office. The determination of his grandfather, George II, to pick his own ministers had played a major role in the instability of 1742–46 and 1754–57, but in the case of George III there was an additional problem: like other rulers, George found it most difficult to create acceptable relationships with senior political figures at his accession, when he had to persuade politicians who had enjoyed a good working relationship with his predecessor, and those who had looked for a dramatic change, to adjust to the wishes of a new monarch. This was largely responsible for the ministerial instability of the 1760s, and the anxieties, tensions and hostile images of that period helped to colour subsequent views of the king.

George's opponents argued that he acted in an unconstitutional fashion, and Whig historians naturally believed them. It was, however, the assertion of royal will that was crucial. The real problem in the eyes of the politicians, whatever they alleged, was not George's unconstitutional tendencies, but the opposite – that for the first time since William III a monarch was determined to deploy to the full the powers that could be seen as his and were universally accepted to be so. Except, perhaps, with George Grenville in May 1765, when George III climbed down in the face of the opposition of his first minister, with particular respect to Stuart Mackenzie and control of Scottish patronage, George III was prepared for confrontation, although he frequently complained that it would ruin his health and endanger his mental stability. He displayed a cool nerve, total conviction of rectitude and bloody-minded determination to have his way. Opponents were enraged, spiteful and helpless. The myth of despotism was their only recourse.

George III found that he was expected by many politicians to obey a set of unwritten conventions that dictated his choice of ministers. The 4th Duke of Devonshire, a member of the inner Cabinet, argued that George should retain his grandfather George II's ministers:

> the Duke of Newcastle had united with him the principal nobility, the moneyed men and that interest which had brought about the [Glorious] Revolution, had set this Family [the Hanoverian dynasty] on the throne, and supported them in it, and were not only the most considerable party but the true solid strength that might be depended on for the support of government . . . they were infallibly the people that the king must trust to for the effectual support of his government.[13]

George had different views. Having made his favourite, Lord Bute, first minister in 1762 and seen him fail to retain his position in the face of bitter criticism, George complained to the French ambassador in 1763 about

> the spirit of fermentation and the excessive licence which prevails in England. It was essential to neglect nothing that could check that spirit and to employ firmness as much as moderation. He was very determined not to be the toy of factions . . . and his fixed plan was to establish his authority without breaking the law.[14]

Thus the ambiguity of a number of constitutional points, such as the collective responsibility of the Cabinet and the degree to which the monarch had to choose his ministers from those who had the confidence of Parliament, exacerbated a political struggle that was essentially a commonplace of monarchical regimes, the efforts of a new ruler to take control of the government. It was not until 1770 that George found, in the person of Lord North, a satisfactory minister who could manage Parliament.

George's earlier attempts to do so helped to spawn a critical political literature that condemned his alleged despotic attitudes and policies, a literature that influenced the American response to his government's plan to increase its American revenues. Failure in the subsequent war led to the fall of North, and in 1783–84 George, in the eyes of his opponents, breached several fundamental political conventions in his attempt to create and sustain a new acceptable (to him) ministry, but the subsequent political and popular impact was far less damaging than that created by George's support for Bute: the loss of America had been a cathartic experience and the particular circumstances of 1783–84 made it harder to present Fox–North as a 'patriot opposition'. Instead, the notion of a 'patriot king' above party seemed to be fulfilled, and the royal-backed Pitt ministry achieved considerable success in the general election of 1784.

George III's conservative and often moralistic conviction of his crucial constitutional role and preference for stability were, thanks to the signs of support for royal policy in early 1784, married to a greater awareness of the possible popular resonance of the Crown. Thus George could feel in the 1780s that the monarch could reach out, beyond antipathy and factional self-interest on the part of politicians, to a wider responsible and responsive royalist public opinion.

So, in the mid-1780s George III was able to create a political world that accorded with his aspirations at his accession: royal proclamations could be used to galvanise public opinion on a range of issues. This contrasted greatly with the situation from 1763 until the end of the decade: his apparent unpopularity and his failure to create a stable effective ministry. The early 1770s had brought an improvement, although it was one that was to be swallowed up by the American crisis.

George's obduracy created greater problems for his ministers when in the 1790s he opposed the extension of full political rights to Catholics in Ireland or Britain. This helped to precipitate Pitt's resignation in 1801 and the fall of the Grenville ministry in 1807. In some respects, George reflected the stronger emphasis on a monarchical, as opposed to a 'balanced', constitution that characterised the 1790s. George's attitude also made religious issues even more central in the politics of the early nineteenth century than they might otherwise have been. This was not only true in the political sense: he took theology seriously. His firmness, not to say rigidity, contrasted with the more flexible attitude of his non-Anglican predecessors, George II, George I, William III and, arguably, Charles II; it also helped to focus the defence of order, hierarchy and continuity in a period of revolutionary and radical threats much more on religion than would otherwise have been the case. The insistence upon religious uniformity as a qualification for full civil rights was undermined, however, by, and in turn undermined, the Union with Ireland of 1801, by focusing attention on the large Catholic population, and had the Thirteen Colonies remained part of the Empire this might also have been a source of renewed strife.

George was motivated not only by his religious convictions, but also by the argument that the position of the Church of England rested on fundamental parliamentary legislation. Any repeal would also thus challenge the constitutional safeguards that were similarly founded and secured. It is not, therefore, surprising that Edmund Burke's emphasis in his *Reflections on the Revolution in France* (1790) on continuity and the value of the Glorious Revolution found favour with George III. His duty was involved in resisting both radicalism at home and French atheism abroad.

Yet, whereas George III's resistance to Catholic Emancipation had been successful, George IV had, despite bitter hostility, to accept it in 1829. This reflected different political circumstances, but also a shift in the position of the monarchy, as well, arguably, as the contrasting character of the two monarchs. Long-term trends lessened the role of the monarchy, despite George III's growing popularity from the 1783–84 crisis on. The growth of business and the increased scope of government lessened the ability of one man, whether monarch or minister, to master the situation. This helped to encourage the development of the Cabinet. The ministries of Pitt the Younger (1783–1801, 1804–06) and Lord Liverpool (1812–27) were especially important in this process. The discussions and decisions of the inner core of ministers, the Cabinet council, became more formal. Collective responsibility and loyalty to the leading minister increased, and this strengthened the Cabinet's ties with that minister and increased his power with reference to the monarch:

cabinet unanimity was a potential weapon against the Crown. When it could be obtained, most obviously with the mass resignations of 1746, such unanimity was effective, but, conversely, a lack of cabinet unity could strengthen the king's position with respect to the Cabinet, as with the clash between George III and Pitt over Catholic Emancipation in 1801. The abolition of the slave trade in 1806–07 by the Ministry of the Talents could be seen as a defeat for George III. George IV muttered against his ministries and ministers, but he was not strong enough to overthrow them. Liverpool was strongly supported by his Cabinet. Royal influence and patronage declined with the abolition of sinecures, the diminishing influence of court favourites and the growing accountability of Parliament.

Personal factors were very important to this process: the breakdown of George III's health in 1788 and the consequent Regency Crisis of 1788–89, the subsequent slackening of his grasp, and his later illnesses; the lack of interest displayed by George IV; the impact of Pitt's long stay in office. As a consequence, even with strains evident over policy and patronage after 1794, greater Cabinet cohesion and influence and consistent united Cabinet control of policy-making was more a feature from the 1790s on than of the 1780s. The monarchy, or perhaps the *image* of the monarchy, was reconstructed in important ways in the later years of George III's reign. The peculiar patriotism of war and the king's virtual disengagement from day-to-day politics combined fruitfully to facilitate the celebration less of the reality and more of the symbol of monarchy. The Jubilee celebrations of 1809 were a case in point. In this sense, the precondition of the creation of a popular monarchy was the perceived decline in the Crown's political authority; although the somewhat paranoid Charles James Fox, who had never freed himself from ideas of royal conspiracies, felt able to tell his nephew Holland in 1804 'There is not a power in Europe, no, not even Bonaparte's, that is so unlimited', as monarchical authority in Britain.[15] Nevertheless such authority was very much that of the government, rather than simply the monarch, and within the government the executive role of the monarch, particularly in the initiation of policy, declined. This was an uneven, hesitant process, but it can be seen as beginning under George III.

POLITICAL ISSUES

A discussion of Parliament and the monarchy can lead to an excessive focus on the national dimension of politics. It is important also to give due weight to the localities, both urban and rural, to their political agendas, to the autonomy of local politics and the diversity of the local dimension of national politics. Too little is still known about the local and regional dimensions of politics, but it is clear that religion played a major role, especially tension between the Church of England and Dissent in England and Wales and between Presbyterianism and Episcopalianism in Scotland.

An emphasis on religion is a reminder of the need to stress the role and nature of issues, the content as well as the structure of politics. This does not involve denying the importance of the pursuit of office and the nature of patronage, but rather explaining that power was sought not only for its own sake, but also in order to advance or support particular policies and interests. Ideology and issues were far from static. This interacted with the greater importance of extra-parliamentary political activism in the second half of the century. This was both an aspect of the traditional multi-faceted political world, and a reflection of new or developing features, including the greatly expanded role of the press and the rising importance of national and local lobby and interest groups. These were related to, though not limited by, urbanisation, professionalisation and the broadening strata of the middling orders in society. Care was taken to keep these groups informed of political developments and to win their support. Thus in January 1761 the major London brewer Samuel Whitbread took an oath before the Lord Mayor stating his opposition to the new tax on strong beer and had it printed in the press, the item by Whitbread in *Lloyd's Evening Post* of 4 February explaining that 'Many false and malicious reports' condemned him for supporting the tax and that he felt it necessary to clear his name.

Meetings, petitions and newspapers were all aspects of an interactive political world, one in which widespread interest and commitment were necessary and present. The press developed in London, the English provinces, Scotland and Ireland; John Magee's *Dublin Evening Post* claimed a circulation of 3,000 in 1781.

Extra-parliamentary politics should not be thought of primarily in terms of popular mass action and radicalism; much popular action can be defined as 'conservative'. This conservatism can be found in explicitly political action, most obviously hostility to the French Revolution and its British supporters in the 1790s, and also in what has been seen as the 'moral economy' of the populace, their determination to preserve customary rights and charges. Support for government policies could be just as significant and valid an expression of public opinion as opposition to them, as in the divisions over policy towards the American colonists in the 1770s.

Similarly, most extra-parliamentary politics was peaceful, although riots were also a feature. Some of these were politically motivated, but others were a response to food supplies and prices, labour relations, religious disputes and issues of sexual morality. National politics in the first half of the century had centred on the clash between the Whig and Tory parties; the Whigs were keen defenders of the Revolution Settlement, the Tories enthusiastic supporters of the Church of England. Some, but by no means all, Tories were Jacobites, but suspicion of the loyalty of most Tories led George I and George II to rely heavily on the Whigs. The Tories were excluded from most senior posts in government, the armed forces, the judiciary and the Church. Under Sir Robert Walpole, First Lord of the Treasury and leader of the ministry between 1721 and 1742, the Whigs largely discarded their more radical strain and ran an effective but oligarchical political system with only limited interest in change. Walpole played an important role in stabilising the post-Revolution parliamentary system. He kept Britain at peace, thus denying the Jacobites foreign support. He was certainly corrupt, but he caused offence principally to those who took a close interest in politics, rather than to the wider political nation, whose position was eased by his generally successful determination to reduce taxation, especially on land. Walpole's political abilities were much valued by George I and George II and led the latter to retract his decision to replace him as first minister when he came to the throne in 1727. Four years earlier, Viscount Townshend wrote to Walpole after the election of the London sheriffs, 'I never saw His Majesty more pleased in my life than he was with that good news, and your successful management in so difficult and essential a point has gained you much credit.[16] Walpole's system broke down, however, in his last years.

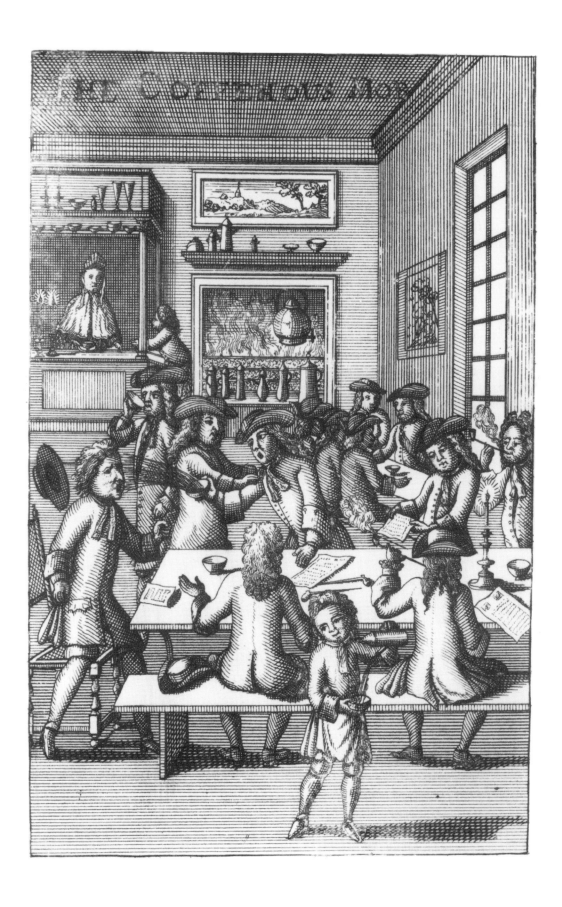

MID-CENTURY POLITICS

The collapse of Anglo-Spanish relations over vigorous Spanish policing of what the Spanish claimed was illegal British trade with their Caribbean and South American possessions, symbolised by the display to a committee of the House of Commons of the allegedly severed ear of a merchant captain, Robert Jenkins, led to a war (1739–48) that Walpole sought to avoid. Lack of success in the conflict, the hostility of Frederick, Prince of Wales, and a general sense that the government led by the now elderly Walpole would not last without major change, gravely weakened the ministry, so that it did badly in the general election of 1741. Walpole's inability to continue to command majorities in the Commons led to his fall in February 1742.

Divisions within the Whig ministry that replaced Walpole, especially between his former supporters, led by the Pelhams, and former Whig opponents, led by Carteret and Bath, helped to cause ministerial instability between 1742 and 1746, but from 1746 the Pelhams were in control until Henry Pelham's unexpected death in 1754. This led to another period of ministerial instability until a ministry centred on the Duke of Newcastle and William Pitt the Elder was formed in 1757. This ministry lasted until 1761, and was responsible for British strategy in the Seven Years War (1756–63). The war ended with the Thirteen Colonies on the eastern seaboard of North America, and the British possessions in India, secure, with Canada, Florida, and many Caribbean islands acquired, and with Britain as the leading maritime power in the world, thus fulfilling what the Scot James Thomson had seen as the national destiny in his ode 'Rule Britannia' (1740):

> 'Rule Britannia, rule the waves:
> Britons never will be slaves.'

This was the achievement of a number of able military leaders, including Wolfe, Clive, Hawke and Boscawen. Robert Clive's victory at Plassey, over the vastly more numerous forces of the Indian Prince, Surajah Dowla, in 1757, laid the basis for the virtual control of Bengal, Bihar and Orissa by the East India Company. The French were subjugated in India in 1760–61, and Britain emerged as the most powerful European state in the Indian subcontinent. The French attempt to invade Britain on behalf of the Jacobites was crushed by the British naval victories of Lagos and Quiberon Bay (1759). That year, British troops also beat the French at Minden in Germany, while, after a hazardous ascent of the cliffs near Quebec, the city was captured, General James Wolfe dying at the moment of glorious victory on the Plains of Abraham. The bells of victory rang out across Britain; the ringers at York Minster were paid four times between 21 August and 22 October for celebrating triumphs, beginning with Minden and ending with Quebec. The victories were also a tribute to the national unity that had followed the defeat of Jacobitism: Scots played a major role in the conflict, and from the 1750s the governing and middle class of the Scots central belt were particularly interested in making 'Britain' work as a concept, certainly more so than their southern counterparts. In 1762 British forces campaigned round the globe; they helped the Portuguese resist a Spanish invasion, fought the French in Germany and captured Martinique from the French and Havana and Manila from the Spaniards, an extraordinary testimony to the global reach of British power, particularly naval power, and the strength of the British state.

The British position was strengthened further in the decade after the Seven

Facing page: The Coffeehouse Mob from *Vulgus Britannicus* (1710), a satire on the Whigs and the mob, by Edward Ward (1667–1731), a London humourist, shows newspaper-reading in a coffee-house. Four years earlier, Ward had been roughly treated by the mob when placed in the pillory as a result of his attacks on the government in *Hudibras Redivivus*: 'as thick as eggs at Ward in pillory', wrote Alexander Pope.

The London Magazine, 1740.
Magazines were a major
development of the 1730s, most
prominently the *Gentleman's
Magazine*, a London monthly
launched in 1731. The *London
Magazine* was founded as a rival the
following year by a group of
London booksellers. The two
journals were similar; longer and
more varied than newspapers, they
greatly expanded the culture of
print and were also politically
important, as they published
parliamentary debates, although this
led to parliamentary action in 1747
which led to the ending of
parliamentary reporting in the
Gentleman's Magazine and the end of
the attribution of speeches to
individual members in the *London
Magazine*.

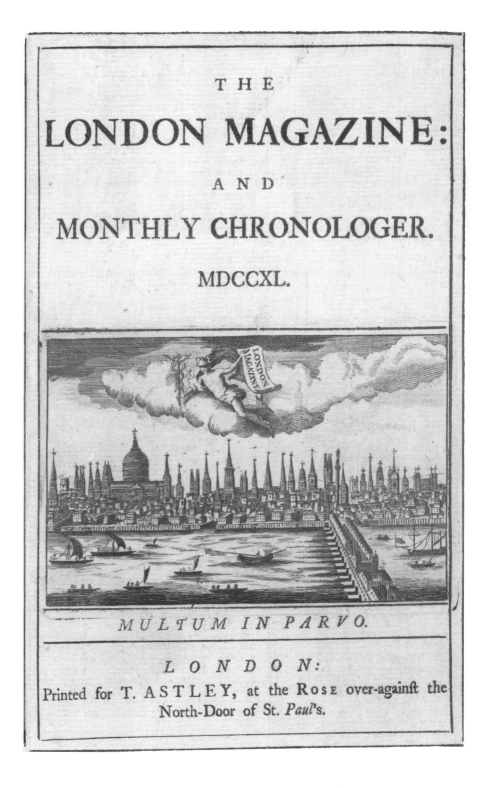

Years War: the victory of Buxar (1764) consolidated the British position in Bengal; the Northern Circars were added in the late 1760s, Benares and Ghazipur in 1775; in 1770–71 the Spanish challenge to the British position in the Falkland Islands led to a confrontation in which Spain and France backed down. However, growing problems in Britain's North American colonies challenged this imperial might.

THE POLITICS OF THE 1760s

National triumph at the beginning of the 1760s could not prevent political problems stemming first from George III's inability to work with the ministry, and, secondly, from a volatile political atmosphere in London. The first led to the fall of Pitt (1761) and Newcastle (1762). George's determination to dispense with political parties completed the disintegration of the Whig–Tory divide. An item in the *Bristol Chronicle* of 28 March 1761 celebrated the uncontested nature of the Bristol election:

Admiral Vernon by Thomas Gainsborough. Vernon (1684–1757) was most famous for his capture of Porto Bello from Spain in 1739. The first victory in the War of Jenkins's Ear, this made him a national hero and appeared to justify claims that the war would be a speedy success. A bitter critic of Walpole's government, who opposed the Salt Tax in 1732 and the Excise Bill in 1733, Vernon rose to be an Admiral and was given command of the squadron assembled in 1745 to block any French invasions.

Sir Peter Warren (*c.* 1703–52), by Roubiliac. Warren had a distinguished naval career which revealed the increasing range of British power. In the 1720s he served off Africa, in the Baltic and in the Caribbean, and was mostly in Caribbean and North American waters from 1735 until 1745, when he was in command of the squadron that forced its way into the harbour of Louisbourg. Second in command at the first battle off Cape Finisterre (1747), Warren became MP for Westminster. He made a fortune from prizes captured by his warships and was regarded as one of the wealthiest commoners in the kingdom. He married a New Yorker in 1731 and bought a farm on Manhattan Island as well as estates in his native Ireland.

See! Blues with Yellows mix their Dye
. . . The High and Low agree!
. . . No Whig nor Tory boast . . .
Party is no more!

This political idyll was to be short-lived.

Dissatisfaction in London with the political situation and economic discontent were exploited by a squinting anti-hero, John Wilkes, an entrepreneur of faction and libertine MP, who fell foul of George and the government as a result of bitter attacks in his newspaper the *North Briton*. An article in number 45 implied that George III had lied to Parliament, and the government took a number of contentious steps, issuing a general warrant for the arrest of all those involved in the publication and seeking to arrest Wilkes in spite of his parliamentary privilege (1763). Wilkes was eventually expelled from the House of Commons (1764) and this was exploited by opposition politicians keen to throw doubt on the legality of ministerial actions. Wilkes was elected for Middlesex in 1768 and 1769 only to be declared ineligible to be elected by the Commons, a thwarting of the views of the electors that aroused anger. Wilkes was the focus of more widespread popular opposition to the government which led in 1768 to a series of riots in London. The government point of view was expressed by Richard Phelps, an Under-Secretary of State: '. . . the libels which have, for so many months, swarmed in this capital, in defiance of all order, and government, and to the great reproach of this country, especially in the eyes of foreigners . . . that licentious spirit of faction, which, if suffered to proceed, must soon have endangered that liberty, whose cause it affected to support'.[17]

THE LOSS OF AMERICA

The discontent and divisions of the 1760s over the determination of George III to pick ministers of his own choice and over Wilkes paled into insignificance, however, beside the collapse of the imperial relationship with America. The determination to make colonies, not represented in Parliament, pay a portion of their defence burden was crucial, though so also was the increasing democratisation in American society, a millenarian rejection of British authority, concern about British policy in Canada, and the borrowing of British conspiracy theories about the supposed autocratic intentions of George III. The Seven Years War had left the British government with an unprecedentedly high level of national debt, and it looked to America to meet a portion of the burden. The Americans, however, no longer felt threatened by French bases in Canada and were therefore no longer willing to see British troops as saviours. The Stamp Act of 1765 led to a crisis as Americans

A View of the Siege of Louisbourg by Thomas Davies, 1758. The 3,920 French defenders supported by a squadron of 10 ships were heavily outnumbered by a British force of 13,140 supported by a fleet of 39 ships. The British landed on Cape Breton on 8 June and Louisbourg surrendered on 26 July with the loss of the French troops and squadron; 410 French and 200 British were killed. The capture of Louisbourg and the destruction of the French squadron were crucial preludes to the operations against Quebec in 1759 and against Montreal in 1760.

rejected Parliament's financial demands and, thereafter, relations were riven by a fundamental division over constitutional issues. There was growing hostility towards parliamentary claims to authority over American affairs, culminating in the Boston Tea Party of 16 December 1773, which represented a defiance of the principles and practice of the British empire as a trading zone. This forced the government to confront the growing problems of law and order and the maintenance of authority. They believed these arose from the actions of a small number in America, rather than from widespread disaffection, and thus mistakenly hoped that tough action against Massachusetts, the so-called Coercive or Intolerable Acts of early 1774, would lead to the restoration of order.

Fighting broke out near Boston in 1775 as a result of the determination of the government of Lord North to employ force, and the willingness of sufficient Americans to do likewise. An ill-advised attempt to seize illegal arms dumps led to clashes at Lexington and Concord, and the British were soon blockaded by land in Boston. Their attempt to drive off the Americans led to very heavy losses at the battle of Bunker Hill. The Americans declared independence (1776) and the British were driven from the bulk of the Thirteen Colonies, but held Canada (1775–spring 1776), before counterattacking to regain New York (1776). The British seizure of Philadelphia was matched by defeat at Saratoga (1777), and after the French entered the war on the revolutionary side (1778), the British lacked the resources necessary for America and were pushed on to the defensive in a world war. Spain joined France in 1779 and at the end of 1780 the Dutch were added to the list of Britain's enemies in what was truly a global conflict.

Though the Franco-Spanish attempt to invade England failed (1779), and the British held on to Gibraltar, India and Jamaica (though not Minorca), defeat at Yorktown (1781) was followed by a collapse of the will to fight on and by the acceptance of American independence. This split the unity of the English-speaking world. America, inhabited by an independent people of extraordinary vitality, was to be the most dynamic of the independent states in the western hemisphere, the first and foremost of the decolonised countries, the people that were best placed to take advantage of the potent combination of a European legacy, independence, and the opportunities for expansion and growth that were to play an increasingly important role in the New World created from 1776.

THE POLITICS OF THE 1780s

As so often in British history, defeat led to the fall of the government. Lord North's resignation in 1782 was followed by a period of marked ministerial and constitutional instability. George III was forced to accept ministers whom he disliked, threatened abdication, and in 1783–84 breached several fundamental political conventions in engineering the fall of the Fox–North ministry and supporting that of the 24-year-old William Pitt the Younger, the austere but sometimes drunk second son of Pitt the Elder, although it lacked a Commons majority. Pitt's victory in the 1784 general election was also therefore a triumph for George and it began a period of largely stable government that lasted until Pitt's resignation in 1801. Like Walpole and North, Pitt understood the importance of sound finances, and, although he was interested in electoral reform, he did not push this divisive issue after it had been defeated in 1785. The War of American Independence more than doubled the national

Facing page: Sir Jeffrey Amherst (1717–97) by Sir Joshua Reynolds, (National Gallery of Canada, Ottawa). The conqueror of Canada, Amherst served on the staff of General Ligonier and later the Duke of Cumberland in major battles of the 1740s. Promoted Major-General thanks to Pitt in 1758, he was given command of the expedition that captured Louisbourg. Commander-in-Chief in North America in 1759, he captured Ticonderoga and Crown Point and, in 1760, Montreal. He was made Governor-General of British North America, but failed to put down the Pontiac rising of native Americans in 1763. He was Governor of Virginia in 1768, and Commander-in-Chief of the Army 1772–82, 1783–95, and advised on policy in the War of American Independence. He was created Lord Amherst in 1776 and Field-Marshal in 1796.

debt, but Pitt's prudent financial management and reforms and a dramatic growth in trade, not least with America, stabilised the situation. As so often in a monarchical state, continuity was, however, threatened by the succession, for George III's eldest son, George, later George IV, was not only opposed to the frugality, virtue and duty of his father, but also to Pitt, preferring instead the latter's chief opponent, Charles James Fox, who, unlike the Prince, had talent, but, like him, lacked self-control. When in late 1788 an attack of porphyria led to the conviction that George III was mad, the resulting Regency Crisis nearly produced the fall of the government, but, fortunately for Pitt, the king recovered in early 1789.

Defeat at the hands of America had led to reform, especially in the Royal Navy, and this was to help Britain in the more serious challenge that lay ahead. She recovered from the loss of the Thirteen Colonies, Florida and various Caribbean islands (in the Treaty of Versailles, 1783), to establish the first British foothold in Malaysia (Penang, 1786) and the first European colony in Australia (1788), and to thwart Spanish attempts to prevent her from trading and establishing settlements on the western coast of modern Canada (Nootka Sound crisis, 1790).

Facing page: The Death of the Earl of Chatham by Benjamin West, 1778, 28⅛ x 36¼ in. By courtesy of the Kimbell Art Museum, Fort Worth, Texas. On 7 April 1778 Chatham made his last parliamentary appearance. The Duke of Richmond argued that Britain had to recognise American independence in order to free herself for the imminent war with France. Chatham, obviously ill, wrapped in flannel and supported on crutches, replied that Britain could wage both struggles simultaneously and claimed that the abandonment of the colonies would be a national humiliation and would lead to national ruin. After Richmond had replied, Chatham rose to speak, but collapsed. He was carried from the chamber and died two days later. There was a definitely heroic note to his collapse in the Lords and it struck many contemporaries in that light. The heroic image was propagated visually, especially in paintings by John Copley and Benjamin West. West, an American supporter of George III, succeeded Reynolds as President of the Royal Academy.

John, 4th Earl of Sandwich in Turkish Dress by Joseph Highmore, 1740. First Lord of the Admiralty from 1748 to 1751 and again from 1771 to 1782, during the War of American Independence, and Secretary of State from 1763 to 1765, Sandwich (1718–92) had earlier in 1738–39 toured the Mediterranean by sea, visiting Sicily, Greece, Turkey, Rhodes, Cyprus, Egypt and Malta.

Foudroyant and Pégase *entering Portsmouth harbour* by Dominic Serres, c. 1782. The *Foudroyant* had been captured from the French in the Mediterranean in 1758. An 80-gunner, it in turn captured the 74–gun *Pégase* from the French in the Bay of Biscay in 1782. The career of the painter, as well as his subject, illustrates British naval power. A Frenchman, he was captured by a British frigate in the Seven Years War, settled in England and became a leading painter of naval pieces. One of the founding members of the Royal Academy in 1768, Serres exhibited 105 works there, many of them scenes of imperial triumph, such as *The Siege at Fort Royal, Martinique* (1769). He was appointed Marine Painter to George III.

The 1780s thus closed with Britain in a far stronger state than had seemed possible in the early years of the decade. Earl Cornwallis was delighted in 1788 to see his 'country rise from the late humiliating situation'.[18] As yet there was no hint of the travails of the following decade: defeat by France, social tension and rebellion in Ireland. The origins of the last two can of course be traced earlier, but essentially the politics, domestic and international, of the 1790s reflected a different agenda that arose from the maelstrom of that revolutionary decade. The British state was to surmount the crisis only with considerable difficulty. Its success was far from inevitable, but two crucial elements were already present: the strength of the economy and public finances, and Britain's position as the leading maritime power in the world.

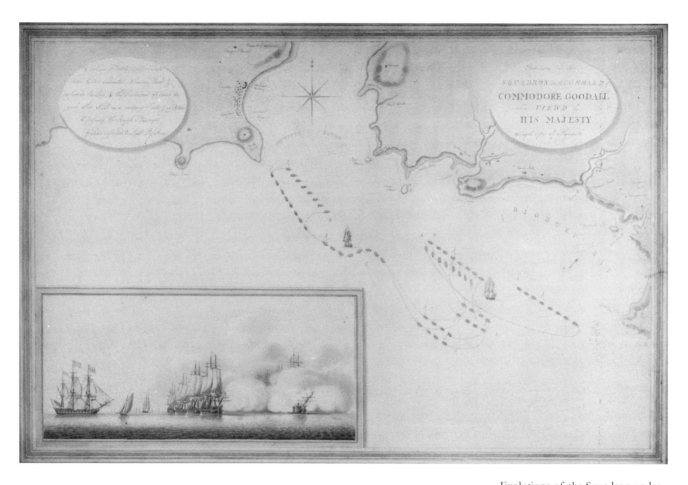

Evolutions of the Squadron under
the Command of Commodore
Goodall, 1789. Samuel Goodall (d.
1801) first served in the Seven
Years War, capturing a French
privateer off Norway in 1760 and
taking part in the capture of
Havana (1762). After serving in the
Mediterranean in 1769–70, he took
part in the War of American
Independence at the battles of
Ushant (1778) and the Saints (1782)
and the relief of Gibraltar (1781).
Commander-in-Chief in
Newfoundland in 1792, he was sent
to the Mediterranean in 1793.
George III attended the naval
manoeuvres of 1789.

NOTES

Place of publication London unless otherwise cited.

CHAPTER 1

1 Paper from Society for Bettering the Condition of the Poor, 1 January 1805, London, British Library, Department of Manuscripts, Additional Manuscripts (hereafter BL Add.) 35645 f. 143.
2 Owen to Edward Weston, 9 April 1757, Iden Green, Weston–Underwood papers.
3 Richard to Edward Tucker, 3 December 1755, Oxford, Bodleian Library, MS. Don b 23 f. 9.
4 Southwell to Townshend, 12 July 1769, New Haven, Connecticut, Beinecke Library, Townshend MSS. Box 12.

CHAPTER 2

1 Halifax, Calderdale Archives, SH7/JL/25.

CHAPTER 3

1 Halifax, Calderdale Archives, SH7/JL/65.
2 Bristol, Public Library, Southwell Papers, vol. 3.
3 Gloucester County Record Office (hereafter CRO) D214F1/65; BL Add. 28065 f. 33.
4 *Collected Novels and memoirs of William Godwin V. Fleetwood* (1805, 2nd ed; 1832), p. 173.
5 Northumberland, CRO ZRI 27/8.
6 A. Young, *A Six Weeks Tour Through the Southern Counties of England and Wales* (1772), pp. 323–4.

CHAPTER 4

1 Winnington to Hanbury Williams, 28 July 1744; Wyndham to Hanbury Williams, 9 July 1745; Fox to Digby, 30 November 1750; Harris to Hanbury Williams, 6 July, 16 October, 1750, Farmington, Lewis Walpole Library, Hanbury Williams papers, vol. 68, fos. 110, 43, 52, 85, 146, 151.
2 Gage to Hotham, no date, 19 August, 1749, Hull, University Library, Hotham papers DDHo 4/3.
3 J. C. Hodgson, *Six North Country Diaries* (1910), p. 64. I am grateful to Bill Gibson for this reference.
4 Brownlow was MP for Lincolnshire, his wife Eleanor his first cousin. Brownlow had no children by either of his marriages.
5 Thomas Burnet (1694–1753), third son of Gilbert Burnet, Bishop of Salisbury, was a notorious rake.
6 The Hague.
7 Chesterfield to James, Lord Waldegrave, 12 October 1728, Chewton House, Chewton Mendip, papers of the 1st Earl Waldegrave.
8 Waldegrave to ?, no date [1725]; Robinson to Waldegrave, 26 January 1732; Essex to Waldegrave, 18 April, 4 July 1734, Chewton; Sutton to George Tilson, Under-Secretary of State in the Northern Department, 17 May 1729; Kinnoull to

Charles Delafaye, Under-Secretary in the Southern Department, 19 August 1730, London, Public Record Office, State Papers (hereafter PRO SP), 81/123, 97/26.
9 Farmington, Connecticut, Lewis Walpole Library, Hanbury Williams papers vol. 69 fos. 80–1.
10 Friedrich Wilhelm von der Schulenburg to Friedrich Wilhelm von Görtz, 12 February 1717, Darmstadt, Gräflich Görtzisches Archiv, F23, 153/6 f. 14.
11 *Reading Mercury*, 27 May, 3 June 1771; *Newcastle Courant*, 12 January 1788; *Westminster Journal*, 15, 22 May 1773; Trevor to Stephen Poyntz, 21 December 1729, BL Althorp MSS. E3.
12 *Reading Mercury*, 20 January 1777; *Berrow's Worcester Journal*, 13 September 1770.
13 Charles to Mary Russell, 9 June 1742, BL Add. 69381.
14 Journal du voyage de M. le Cte. de Gisors, Paris, Archives des Affaires Étrangères, Mémoires et Documents Angleterre 1 fos. 25–6.
15 John to Richard Tucker, 2 November 1745, Bodleian Library, MS Don c 7 f. 157.
16 John Terrett to John Parsons, 10 April 1783, Gloucester CRO D. 214 F1/45.
17 Russell to Pitt the Elder, undated, Bowood, Shelburne papers, Box 17.

CHAPTER 5

1 Lady to Lord Burlington, 26 April 1735, BL Althorp papers B4.
2 Wharton to Earl Cowper, 9 August 1721, Hertford CRO Panshanger MSS D/EP F57 f. 79.
3 Browne to his father, 3 June 1765, 6 August 1757, BL RP 3284.

CHAPTER 6

1 G. Eland (ed.), *Shardeloes Papers* (1974), p. 50.
2 Brand to Wharton, 12 March 1790, Durham University Library, Wharton papers.
3 Wesley to Matthew Ridley, 26 October 1745, Northumberland CRO ZRI 27/5.
4 Richard Browne to his father, 24 August 1765, BL RP 3284.

CHAPTER 7

1 Exeter, Devon CRO 64/12/29/1/26.

CHAPTER 8

1 Lyttelton to Elizabeth Montagu, 21 July 1762, BL RP 2377i.

CHAPTER 9

1 Zamboni to Kaunitz, 6 March 1752, Vienna, Haus-, Hof- und Staatsarchiv, England, Varia 10 f. 104.
2 12 May 1747, Carlisle, Cumbria CRO D/Sen/Fleming/17.

3 5 May 1777, Nottingham, University Library, NeC 2815.

4 Wyndham to Duke of Somerset, 8 December 1747, Exeter, Devon CRO 1392 M/L 18 47/7; Anon., *Reflections upon the Present State of Affairs* (London, 1755), p. 27; C. Morris, *A Letter from a By-Stander* (London, 1741), p. 9; Newcastle to Andrew Mitchell, 8 December 1757, BL Add. 6832 f. 31.

5 Newcastle to Lord Chancellor Hardwicke, 3 January 1758, BL Add. 35417 f. 171.

6 Lowther to John Spedding, 8 December 1739; Lowther to Bishop Fleming, 30 October 1737, Carlisle, Cumbria RO D/Lons/W, D/Sen/Fleming/14.

7 Newcastle to Cumberland, 18 March 1748, Windsor Castle, Royal Archives, Cumberland Papers 32/339.

CHAPTER 10

1 Dalrymple to Sir Gilbert Elliot, 26 February 1763, Edinburgh, National Library of Scotland, MS. 11016 f. 56; W. S. Taylor and J. H. Pringle (eds), *Correspondence of William Pitt, Earl of Chatham* (4 vols, 1838) II, p. 302.

2 Anon., *A New-Year's Gift for the New-Interest Freeholders* (London, 1754), p. 5.

3 James Stuart Mackenzie to Earl of Bute, 19 April 1760, Mount Stuart 4/8.

4 Reading, Berkshire CRO D/EHy 0 8/3.

5 Clanricarde to Rushout, 2 March 1758, Worcester, CRO 705:66 BA 4221/26.

6 Hull, University Library, DDHo/4/22, Buckinghamshire to Sir Charles Hotham, 12 July 1783.

7 BL Add. 379334 f. 32, anon. to anon. (1742).

8 Public Record Office, State Papers 35/24/75, 35/6/66; Pickering and Chatto list 40, September 1984, item 109; Mme B. van Muyden (ed.), *A foreign view of England ...* (1902), pp. 60, 229, 233; Pulteney to Swift, 2 December 1736, BL Add. 4806 f. 178; J. Brooke (ed.), Horace Walpole, *Memoirs of King George II* (3 vols, New Haven, 1985), I, pp. 118–19.

9 Hertford CRO, Panshanger papers D/EP F204 f. 16, Lady Paulet to Lady Cowper, 4 August 1716.

10 BL Add. 32686 f. 108, Sunderland to Duke of Newcastle, 1 October 1717.

11 BL Add. 32686 f. 193, Carteret to Newcastle, 27 August 1721.

12 Newcastle to Horatio Walpole, 21 May 1724, BL Add. 9152 f. 3.

13 P. D. Brown and K. W. Schweizer (eds.), *The Devonshire Diary. William Cavendish, Fourth Duke of Devonshire, Memoranda on State of Affairs, 1759–1762*, Camden Society, Fourth Series, vol. 27 (1982), pp. 54, 60.

14 Paris, Archives des Affaires Étrangères, Correspondance Politique, Angleterre 450 f. 337.

15 L. G. Mitchell, *Charles James Fox* (Oxford, 1992), p. 194.

16 Townshend to Walpole, 16 July 1723, PRO 43/4 f. 88.

17 Phelps to Earl of Buckinghamshire, 2 December 1763, PRO 91/72 f. 200.

18 G. Cornwallis-West, *The Life and Letters of Admiral Cornwallis* (1927), p. 143.

INDEX